Applied PC Interfacing, Graphics and Interrupts

APPLIED PC INTERFACING, GRAPHICS AND INTERRUPTS

William Buchanan
Napier University

ADDISON-WESLEY

HARLOW, ENGLAND • READING, MASSACHUSETTS • MENLO PARK, CALIFORNIA • NEW YORK
DON MILLS, ONTARIO • AMSTERDAM • BONN • SYDNEY • SINGAPORE
TOKYO • MADRID • SAN JUAN • MILAN • MEXICO CITY • SEOUL • TAIPEI

Addison Wesley Longman Limited
Edinburgh Gate
Harlow
Essex CM20 2JE
England

and Associated Companies throughout the World.

Published in the United States of America by Addison Wesley Longman Inc., New York.

Cover designed by Designers & Partners Ltd, Oxford
and printed by The Riverside Printing Co. (Reading) Ltd
Cover design incorporates 'Variation VI' by Wassily Kandinsky
Typeset by the author
Printed and bound by T.J. Press, Padstow, Cornwall

First printed 1996

ISBN 0-201-87728-7

British Library Cataloguing-in-Publication Data
A catalogue record for this book is available from the British Library.

Library of Congress Cataloging-in-Publication Data is available.

This book is dedicated to my mother for all her help
over the years and for the appreciation of the love she
has for her grandchildren, Billy, Jamie and David.

Preface

The number of devices which connect to PCs seems to increase by the year. This is mainly due to the increasing processing power of PCs and also the availability of large amounts of electronic memory. A typical modern PC now contains devices such as a hi-resolution graphics display, a hard-disk, a floppy-disk, a sound card, a modem, a CD-ROM drive, serial and parallel ports, and so on.

The objective of this text is to provide an understanding of how devices are programmed using software and also how they integrate to create a system. This should help in the writing of interface software and should also provide an understanding of system specifications. Tutorial and project work relates to practical programming examples. Projects include the development of a traffic light controller, a real-time serial communications system, an air-conditioning system, a mouse-driven menu system and a graphics package for displaying electronic circuits.

The book is primarily aimed at Engineering and Computer Science students. It can also be used by professionals in industry as it discusses key interfacing areas, especially related to interrupts, graphics and serial communications. Discussion of the electrical aspects of the interface devices, such as voltages and currents has been kept to a minimum as this would spoil the flow of the text.

The main areas covered are digital interfacing, counter/timer interfacing, analogue interfacing, serial communications, direct memory addressing, direct video text interfacing, graphics, mouse interfacing, keyboard interfacing, disk interfacing, interrupts and file access. Chapters on digital input/output, counter/timing and analogue interfacing require extra hardware to connect to the PC, but most other chapters use standard PC hardware, such as serial communication, mouse interfacing, keyboard interfacing, graphics, and so on. To reduce the need for external hardware a software emulator is included to emulate calls to digital input/output devices.

The text uses C as the main software language as it allows low-level, direct access to the hardware. In earlier chapters Turbo Pascal and Assembly Language are used to show how different software languages can be used to implement equivalent C programs.

Many books currently on the market only discuss how PC hardware interconnects and how Assembly Language communicates with them. This can be confusing, or even off-putting, as most industry programs are written using high-level languages. Assembly Language is normally only used when high-speed operations are required, it also gives little scope for keyboard input and output, disk operations and also for graphics.

Over the years I have been involved in consultancy work with several companies. Much of this work has involved interfacing PCs to remote instrumentation. Typically these instruments process their data and transmitted it in a digital form using RS-232 communications. This interface can cause many problems, including the use of different connectors, different frame formats, different connections, differing handshaking, and so on. It is for this reason I have included a whole chapter on the theory of serial communications and how software can be written to control it. The usage of serial communications will increase as many electronic systems now have an RS-232 connector fitted as standard. It provides an excellent method to send and receive data from remote systems. I have met many people who use RS-232, and have even written programs which use it, but they have little understand about its operation. It provides one of the best interfacing examples as it is available on all PCs and requires only two PCs and an interconnecting cable.

Another area which I feel is lacking in many books is the coverage of hardware and software interrupts. This book discusses these and shows how a practical system uses then to connect external hardware. It also shows how a program accesses functions to communicate with standard devices, such as reading from the keyboard or outputting text to the screen. Accessing memory directly is also discussed and the text shows how to access up to 1 MB of physical memory using a C program.

Background theory on video displays and memory is provided in the appendices as well as an introduction to C.

A copy of all the programs contained in the text, some tutorial soluations and updates to the emulator programs, is available on the World Wide Web (WWW) page:

```
http://www.eece.napier.ac.uk/~bill_b/ibook.html
```

Additional information on the author is available on the WWW page:

```
http://www.eece.napier.ac.uk/~bill_b/bill_b.html
```

A disk containing all the programs is available by sending a stamped addressed envelope and a 3.5 or 5 inch floppy disk to the following address:

```
W.J. Buchanan,
Senior Lecturer,
Department of Electrical, Electronic and Computer
   Engineering,
Napier University,
219 Colinton Road,
Edinburgh EH14 1DJ,
UK.
```

Helpful tips, requests for advice and comments can be sent via the e-mail address:

```
w.buchanan@central.napier.ac.uk
```

Lecturers and tutors can also request a free disk with solutions to selected tutorial programs.

CONTENTS

1
Introduction

1.1 Introduction

Personal computers (PCs) have revolutionized many areas of life. The number of devices which interface to them increases as their computing power and memory capacity increases. A standard PC contains a video interface adaptor, serial and parallel ports, a hard disk drive, a floppy disk drive and a keyboard. A modern PC may also contain a fax, a modem, a compact disc player, a network card, an audio card, a joystick port, video accelerator, and so on. Figure 1.1 shows some typical interface devices.

Interface devices either input and/or output data to the PC. A keyboard provides an input of data to the PC, whereas it is output to a video adaptor. Most devices, though, are input/output (I/O) as they can take data from the PC and also give data. Examples of I/O devices are disk drives, modems, fax, and so on.

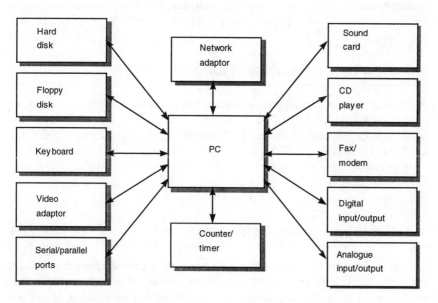

Figure 1.1   Sample interface devices.

The software required to control interface devices was, at one time, developed in low-level languages, such as assembly language; this was mainly due to speed limitations. Now, ultra-fast PC systems allow the development of interface software using high-level languages such as C and Pascal. These languages have many advantages over low-level languages because they:

- Are easy to modify and maintain;
- Are less prone to errors;
- Are easier to test;
- Give an improved user interface;
- Give relatively fast development times.

High-level languages have now replaced much of the low-level programming. Only in areas of very high-speed applications, such as bit-mapped video transfer or in some real-time applications, is it still used.

1.2 Hardware and software

An electronic system consists of hardware and software. Hardware is 'the touchable bits' that is, the components, the screws and nuts, the case, the electrical wires, and so on. Software is the programs that run on programmable hardware and can change its operation depending on the inputs to the system. The program itself cannot exist without some form of programmable hardware, such as a microprocessor or controller. In most applications, dedicated hardware is faster than hardware that is running software. Hardware systems running a software program, though, tend to be easier to modify and require less development time.

1.3 Bits, bytes, words and long words

A computer operates on binary digits named bits. These can either store a '1' or a '0' (ON/ OFF). A group of four bits makes a nibble and a group of eight bits makes a byte. Eight bits provide 256 combinations of ON/OFF, from 00000000 to 11111111. A word is a 16-bit field and a long word a 32-bit field.

Memories store data either in a permanent form (non-volatile) or non-permanent form (volatile). These are arranged as bytes and each byte has a different memory address, as illustrated in Figure 1.2.

1.4 Basic computer architecture

The main elements of a basic computer system are a central processing unit (or microprocessor), memory, and I/O interfacing circuitry. These connect by means of three main buses: the address bus, the control bus and the data bus. A bus is a collection of common electrical connections grouped by a single name.

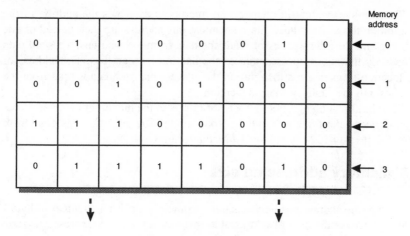

Figure 1.2   Memory storage (each address holds eight bits).

Figure 1.3 shows a basic system. External devices such as a keyboard, display, disk drives can connect directly onto the data, address and control buses or through the I/O interface circuitry.

Electronic memory consists of RAM (random access memory) and ROM (read only memory). ROM stores permanent binary information, whereas RAM is a non-permanent memory and loses its contents on a loss of power. Applications of this type of memory include running programs and storing temporary information.

The microprocessor is the main controller of the computer. It only understands binary information and operates on a series of binary commands known as machine code. It fetches binary instructions from memory, decodes these instructions into a series of simple actions and carries out the actions in a sequence of steps. A system clock synchronizes these steps.

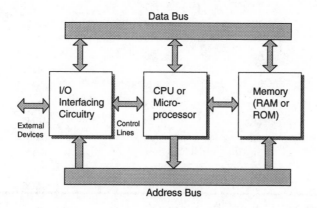

Figure 1.3   Block diagram of a simple computer system.

To access a location in memory the microprocessor puts the address of the location on the address bus. The contents at this address are then placed on the data bus and the microprocessor reads the data from the data bus. To store data in memory the microprocessor places the data on the data bus. The address of the location in memory is then put on the address bus and data is read from the data bus into the memory address location.

The classification of a microprocessor relates to the maximum number of bits it can process at a time, that is their word length. The evolution has gone from 4-bit, 8-bit, 16-bit, 32-bit and to 64-bit architectures.

1.5 Memory addressing size

The size of the address bus indicates the maximum addressable number of bytes. Table 1.1 shows the size of addressable memory for a given address bus size. For example:

- A 1-bit address bus can address up to two locations (that is 0 and 1).

- A 2-bit address bus can address 2^2 or 4 locations (that is 00, 01, 10 and 11).

- A 20-bit address bus can address up to 2^{20} addresses (1 MB).

- A 24-bit address bus can address up to 16 MB.

- A 32-bit address bus can address up to 4 GB.

Table 1.1 Addressable memory (in bytes) related to address bus size.

Address bus size	Addressable memory (bytes)	Address bus size	Addressable memory (bytes)
1	2	15	32K
2	4	16	64K
3	8	17	128K
4	16	18	256K
5	32	19	512K
6	64	20	1M†
7	128	21	2M
8	256	22	4M
9	512	23	8M
10	1K*	24	16M
11	2K	25	32M
12	4K	26	64M
13	8K	32	4G‡
14	16K	64	16GG

* 1K represents 1024

† 1M represents 1 048 576 (1024 K)

‡ 1G represents 1 073 741 824 (1024 M)

1.6 Intel microprocessors

Intel marketed the first microprocessor, named the 4004. This device caused a revolution in the electronics industry because previous electronic systems had a fixed functionality. With this processor the functionality could be programmed by software. It could handle four bits of data at a time (a nibble), contained 2000 transistors, had 46 instructions and allowed 4 KB of program code and 1 KB of data. The PC has since evolved using Intel microprocessors (Intel is a contraction of *Int*egrated *El*ectronics).

The second generation of Intel microprocessors began in 1974. These could handle 8 bits (a byte) of data at a time and were named the 8008, 8080 and the 8085. They were much more powerful than the previous 4-bit devices and were used in many early microcomputers and applications such as electronic instruments and printers. The 8008 has a 14-bit address bus and can thus address up to 16 kB of memory (the 8080 has a 16-bit address bus giving it a 64 kB limit).

The third generation of microprocessors began with the launch of the 16-bit processors. Intel released the 8086 microprocessor which was mainly an extension to the original 8080 processor and thus retained a degree of software compatibility. IBM's designers realized the power of the 8086 and used it in the original IBM PC and IBM XT (eXtended Technology). It has a 16-bit data bus and a 20-bit address bus. The maximum addressable capacity is thus 1 MB.

A stripped-down 8-bit external data bus version called the 8088 is also available. This stripped down processor allowed designers to produce less complex (and cheaper) computer systems. The 8086 could handle either 8 or 16 bits of data at a time (although in a messy way). An improved architecture version, called the 80286, was launched in 1982, and was used in the IBM AT (Advanced Technology).

In 1985, Intel introduced its first 32-bit microprocessor, the 80386DX. This device was compatible with the previous 8088/8086/80286 (80X86) processors and gave excellent performance handling 8, 16 or 32 bits at a time. It has full 32-bit data and address buses and can thus address up to 4 GB of physical memory. A stripped-down 16-bit external data bus and 24-bit address bus version called the 80386SX was released in 1988. This processor can thus only access up to 16 MB of physical memory.

In 1989, Intel introduced the 80486DX which is basically an improved 80386DX with a memory cache and math co-processor integrated onto the chip. It had an improved internal structure making it around 50% faster than a comparable 80386. The 80486SX was also introduced, which is merely a 80486DX with the link to the math co-processor broken. Clock doubler/ trebler 80486 processors were also released. In these devices the processor runs at a higher speed than the system clock. Typically, systems with clock doubler processors are around 75% faster than the comparable non-doubled processors. Typical clock doubler processors are DX2-66 and DX2-50 which run from 33 MHz and 25 MHz clocks, respectively. Intel have also produced a new range of

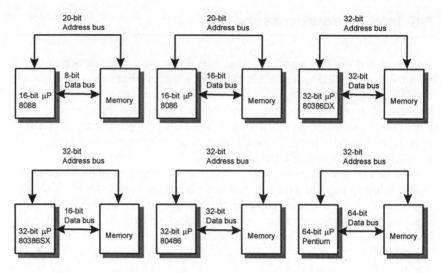

Figure 1.4 Intel microprocessors and their external interfacing.

microprocessor which run at three or four times the system clock speed and are referred to as DX4 processors. These include the Intel DX4-100 (25MHz clock) and Intel DX4-75 (25MHz clock).

The Pentium (or P-5) is a 32-bit 'superscalar' processor. It can execute more than one instruction at a time and has a full 64-bit (8-byte) data bus and a 32-bit address bus. In terms of performance, it operates almost twice as fast as the equivalent 80486. It also has improved floating-point operations (roughly three times faster) and is fully compatible with previous 80x86 processors. Figure 1.4 shows how Intel processors interface to external equipment.

1.7 Inside the PC

A typical PC consists of a microprocessor, memory, mass storage device, monitor, keyboard and peripherals. Figure 1.5 shows an illustration of a PC motherboard. The memory consists of either random access memory (RAM) or read only memory (ROM). Modern PCs memories normally have at least 4 MB of RAM and 256KB of ROM memory (called BIOS memory). Expansion to memory is normally achieved through plug-in single in-line memory modules (SIMMs) contained in banks of dynamic RAM (DRAM). This type of memory is relatively slow and consumes relatively high amounts of power. For this purpose, the base memory is usually made up of static RAM (SRAM) ICs which are fast and consume small amounts of power compared with DRAM.

The system uses system expansion slots to connect other devices such as a hard disk, video controller, CD-ROM, disk drives, and so on. It is also possible for these applications to be built into the motherboard. For example many systems have a hard-disk controller built into them.

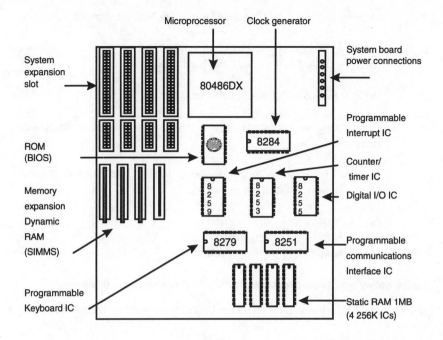

Figure 1.5 Layout of PC main system board.

Access to devices such as the keyboard and monitor is though a ROM named BIOS (basic input/ output system). The BIOS contains small programs which communicates with serial and parallel ports, hard-disk and floppy disk drives and so on.

PC memory is organised into three basic sections. The section that resides in lowest memory consists of up to 640 KB of RAM memory. The memory space between the 640 KB and the 1 MB boundary consists of several pages of special-purpose memory. This memory consists primarily of BIOS memory, display memory, and pages reserved for memory mapping. Together these sections make up to 1 MB of memory. This 1 MB of memory is accessed through a 20-bit address bus (compatibility with original PC). The third section of memory above the 1MB base memory is the expanded memory.

1.8 Exercises

1.1   What do the following contractions represent ?

(a)	PC	(b)	RAM	(c)	ROM
(d)	SRAM	(e)	DRAM	(f)	IC
(g)	I/O	(h)	BIOS		

1.2 Determine if the following are classified as hardware or software:

(a) a C program   (b) a keyboard
(c) a DRAM IC   (d) a hard-disk drive

1.3 What is the main difference between RAM and ROM ?

1.4 How many bits does a nibble, a byte, a word and a long word represent ?

1.5 In what classification group do the following Intel microprocessors belong (that is, 4-bit, 8-bit and so on) ?

(a) 4004   (b) 8080   (c) 8086
(d) 8088   (e) 80386 SX   (f) 80386 DX
(g) 80486 DX   (h) Pentium

The following questions are multiple choice. Please select from a – d.

1.6 An 8-bit address bus can address up to how much memory:

(a) 128 B   (b) 256 B
(c) 1024 B   (d) 16 KB

1.7 A 16-bit address bus can address up to how much memory:

(a) 16 KB   (b) 32 KB
(c) 64 KB   (d) 128 KB

1.8 The original IBM PCs had how many address lines:

(a) 16   (b) 20
(c) 24   (d) 32

1.9 The Intel 80386 is classified as:

(a) an 8-bit microprocessor
(b) a 16-bit microprocessor
(c) a 24-bit microprocessor
(d) a 32-bit microprocessor

1.10 A computer which can address up to 16 MB has how many address lines:

(a) 8   (b) 16
(c) 24   (d) 32

1.11   The 80386DX and the 80386SX differ in which respect:

    (a)   the 80386DX has a math co-processor on board
    (b)   the 80386DX runs at a faster clock speed
    (c)   the 80386SX has a reduced instruction set
    (d)   the 80386SX has a stripped down external data and address bus

1.12   How much memory can an 80386DX address:

    (a)   1 MB   (b)   8 MB
    (c)   16 MB   (d)   4 GB

1.13   How much memory can a 80386SX address:

    (a)   1 MB   (b)   8 MB
    (c)   16 MB   (d)   4 GB

1.14   The 80486DX and the 80486SX differ in which respect:

    (a)   the 80486DX has a math co-processor on board
    (b)   the 80486DX runs at a faster clock speed
    (c)   the 80486SX has a reduced instruction set
    (d)   the 80486SX has a stripped-down external data and address bus

1.15   How does the 80486 differ from the 80386:

    (a)   it is a totally different design
    (b)   it is an improved 80386 with a memory cache on board
    (c)   it is an improved 80386 with a disk cache on board
    (d)   it has a larger data and address bus

1.16   The Intel Pentium is classified as:

    (a)   16-bit microprocessor
    (b)   32-bit microprocessor
    (c)   64-bit microprocessor
    (d)   128-bit microprocessor

1.17   How many bytes can the Pentium operate on at a time:

    (a)   4   (b)   6
    (c)   8   (d)   16

2
Computer Input/ Output Cards

2.1 Input/output (I/O) interface cards

The type of interface card used greatly affects the performance of a PC system. Early models of PCs relied on expansion options to improve their specification. These expansion options were cards that plugged into an expansion bus, as shown in Figure 2.1. A total of eight slots were usually available and these added memory, video, fixed and floppy disk controllers, printer output, modem ports, serial communications and so on.

There are six main types of interface cards available for the PC. The number of data bits they handle at a time determines their classification. They are:

- PC (8-bit)
- ISA (16-bit)
- EISA (32-bit)
- MCA (32-bit)
- VL-Local Bus (32-bit)
- PCI bus (64-bit)

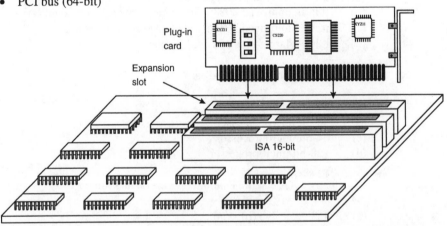

Figure 2.1 Connecting I/O cards.

2.1.1 PC bus

The PC bus uses the architecture of the Intel 8088 processor which has an external 8-bit data bus and 20-bit address bus. A PC bus connector has a 62-pin printed circuit card edge connector and a long narrow or half length plug-in card. Since it uses a 20-bit address bus it can address a maximum of 1 MB of memory. The transfer rate is fixed at 8 MHz, thus a maximum 8 000 000 bytes can be transferred every second. Figure 2.2 shows a PC card.

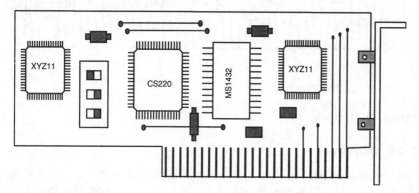

Figure 2.2   PC card.

2.1.2 ISA bus

IBM developed the ISA (Industry Standard Architecture) for their 80286-based AT (Advanced Technology) computer. It had the advantage of being able to deal with 16 bits of data at a time. An extra edge connector gives compatibility with the PC bus. This gives an extra 8 data bits and 4 address lines. Thus, the ISA bus has a 16-bit data and a 24-bit address bus. This gives a maximum of 16MB of addressable memory and like the PC bus it uses a fixed clock rate of 8 MHz. The maximum data rate is thus 2 bytes (16 bits) per clock cycle, giving a maximum throughput of 16MB/sec. In machines that run faster than 8 MHz the ISA bus runs slower than the rest of the computer.

A great advantage of PC bus cards is that they can be plugged into an ISA bus connector. ISA cards are very popular as they give good performance for most interface applications. The components used are extremely cheap and it is well proven reliable technology. Typical applications include serial and parallel communications, networking cards and sound cards. Figure 2.3 illustrates an ISA card and Appendix G gives the pin connections for the bus. It can be seen from Appendix G that there are four main sets of connections, the A, B, C and D sections. The standard PC bus connection contains the A and B sections. The A section includes the address lines A0-A19 and 8 data lines, D0-D7. The B section contains interrupt lines, IRQ0-IRQ7, power supplies and various other control signals. The extra ISA lines are added with the C and D section, these include the address lines, A17-A23, data lines D8-D15 and interrupt lines IRQ10-IRQ14.

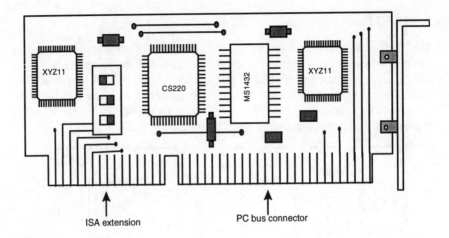

Figure 2.3 ISA card.

2.1.3 MCA bus

IBM developed the Microchannel Interface Architecture (MCA) bus for their PS/2 computers. This bus is completely incompatible with ISA bus. It can operate as a 16-bit or 32-bit data bus. The main technical difference between the MCA and PC/ISA (and EISA) is that the MCA has an asynchronous bus whereas PC/ISA/EISA use a synchronous bus. An asynchronous bus works at a fixed clock rate whereas a synchronous bus data transfer is not dependent on a fixed clock. Asynchronous buses take their timings from the devices involved in the data transfer (that is, the processor or system clock). The original MCA specification resulted in a maximum transfer rate of 160 MB/sec. Very few manufacturers have adopted MCA technology and even IBM has since dropped it in favour of ISA/EISA.

2.1.4 EISA bus

Several manufacturers developed the EISA (Extended Industry Standard Architecture) bus in direct competition to the MCA bus. It provides compatibility with PC/ISA but not MCA. The EISA connector looks like an ISA connector (see Figure 2.4). It is possible to plug an ISA card into an EISA connector, but a special key allows the EISA card to be inserted deeper into the EISA bus connector. It then makes connections with a 32-bit data and address bus. An EISA card has twice the number of connections over an ISA card and there are extra slots that allow it to be inserted deeper into the connector. The ISA card only connects with the upper connectors because it has only a single key slot.

EISA uses an asynchronous transfer at a clock speed of 8 MHz. It has a full 32-bit data and address bus and can address up to 4 GB of memory. In theory the maximum transfer rate is 4 bytes for every clock cycle. Since the clock runs at 8 MHz, the maximum data rate is 32 MB/sec.

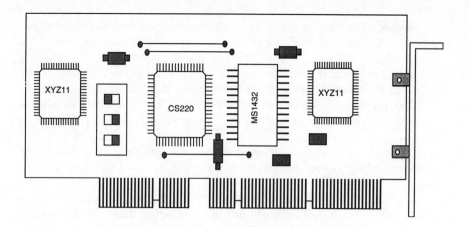

Figure 2.4 EISA card.

2.1.5 VESA VL-Local Bus

The main problem with the PC, ISA and EISA buses is that the transfer rate is normally much slower than the system clock. This is wasteful in processor time and generally reduces system performance. For example, if the system clock is running at 50 MHz and the EISA interface operates at 8 MHz then for 84% of the data transfer time the processor is doing nothing. An improvement is to transfer data at the speed of the system clock. For this reason the Video Electronics Standards Association (VESA) created the VL-local bus to create fast processor-to-video card transfers. It uses a standard ISA connector with an extra connection to tap into the system bus (Figure 2.5).

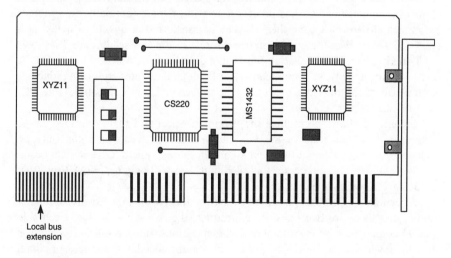

Local bus
extension

Figure 2.5 Local bus interface card.

Memory transfers, graphics and disk transfers are the heaviest for data transfer rates, whereas applications such as modems, Ethernet and sound cards do not require fast transfer rates. The VL-local bus addresses this by allowing the processor, memory, graphics and disk controller access to a 33 MHz/ 32-bit local bus. Other applications still use the normal ISA bus, as shown in Figure 2.6. The graphics adaptor and disk controller connect to the local bus whereas other slower peripherals connect to the slower 8 MHz/ 16-bit bit ISA bus. A maximum of three devices can connect to the local bus (normally graphics and disk controllers). Note that the speed of the data transfer is dependent on the clock rate of the system and that the maximum clock speed for the VL-Local bus is 33 MHz.

Appendix G lists the pin connections for the 32-bit VL-local bus and it shows that, in addition to the standard ISA connector, there are two sides of connections, the A and the B side. Each side has 58 connections giving a total of 116 connections. It has a full 32-bit data and address bus. The 32 data lines are labelled DAT00-DAT31 and 32 address lines are labelled from ADR00-ADR31. Note that while the data and address lines are contained within the extra VL-local bus extension, some of the standard ISA lines are used, such as the IRQ lines.

2.1.6 PCI Bus

Intel have developed a new standard interface, named the PCI (Peripheral Component Interconnection) local bus, for the Pentium processor. This technology allows fast memory, disk and video access. A standard set of interface ICs known as the 82430 PCI chipset is available to interface to the bus.

As with the VL-Local bus, the PCI bus transfers data using the system clock, but has the advantage over the VL-local Bus in that it can operate over a 32-bit or 64-bit data path. The high transfer rates used in PCI architecture machines limits the number of PCI bus interfaces to two or three (normally the graphics adaptor and hard-disk controller). If data is transferred at 64 bits (8 bytes) at a rate of 33 MHz then the maximum transfer rate is 264 MB/sec. Figure 2.7 shows PCI architecture. Notice that an I/O bridge gives access to ISA, EISA or MCA cards. Unfortunately, to accommodate for the high data rates and for a reduction in the size of the interface card, the PCI connector is not compatible with PC, ISA or EISA.

Figure 2.8 shows a graph of the maximum speeds of main interface cards. The maximum data rate of the PCI bus is 264 MB/sec, which can only be achievable using 64-bit software on a Pentium-based system. On a system based on the 80486/80386 processor this maximum data will only be 132MB/sec (that is, using a 32-bit data bus).

Appendix G lists the pin connections for the 64-bit PCI Local bus and it shows that there are two lines of connections, the A and the B side. Each side has 94 connections giving a total of 188 connections. It has a full 32-bit address bus and 64-bit address bus. The PCI bus runs at the speed of the processor which for the Pentium processor is at least 60 MHz (as compared to the VL-local bus which gives a maximum transfer rate of 33 MHz).

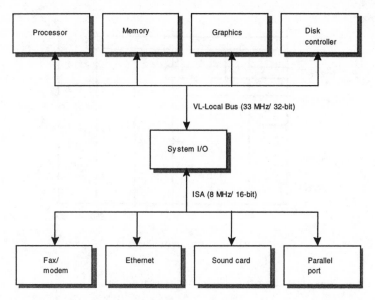

Figure 2.6 VESA VL-local bus architecture.

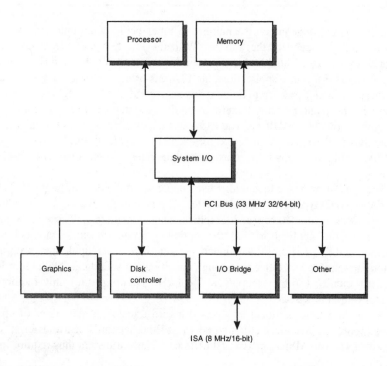

Figure 2.7 PCI bus architecture.

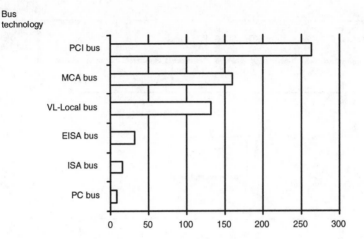

Bus
technology

Maximum data rate (MB/sec)

Figure 2.8   Maximum data rate for different bus technologies.

2.2 Comparison of different types

Data throughput depends on the number of bytes being communicated for each
transfer and the speed of the transfer. With the PC, ISA and EISA buses this
transfer rate is fixed at 8 MHz, whereas the PCI and VL local buses use the
system clock. For many applications the ISA bus offers the best technology as it
has been around for a long time, it gives a good data throughput and it is
relatively cheap and reliable. It has a 16-bit data bus and can thus transfer data at
a maximum rate of 16 MB/sec. The EISA bus can transfer 4 bytes for each clock
cycle, thus if 4 bytes are transferred for each clock cycle, it will be twice as fast
as ISA. Table 2.1 shows the maximum data rates for the different interface
cards.

The type of interface technology used depends on the data throughput. Table
2.2 shows some typical transfer data rates. The heaviest usage on the system are
microprocessor to memory and graphics adaptor transfers. These data rates
depend on the application and the operating system used. Graphical user
interface (GUI) programs have much greater data throughput than programs
running in text mode. Notice that a high specification sound card with recording
standard quality (16-bit samples at 44.1 kHz sampling rate) only requires a
transfer rate of 88 kB/sec.

A standard Ethernet local area network card transfers at data rates of up 10
Mbps (approx. 1 MB/sec), although new fast Ethernet cards can transfer at data
rates of up to 100 Mbps (approx. 10 MB/sec). These transfers thus require local
bus type interfaces.

16   *Computer Input/Output Cards*

Table 2.1 Maximum data rates for different I/O cards.

I/O card	Maximum data rate	
PC	8 MB/sec	
ISA	16 MB/sec	
EISA	32 MB/sec	
VL-Local bus	132 MB/sec	(33MHz system clock using 32-bit transfers)
PCI	264 MB/sec	(33MHz system clock using 64-bit transfers)
MCA	20 MB/sec	(160MB/sec burst)

Table 2.2 Typical transfer rates.

Device	Transfer rate	Application
Hard disk	4 MB/sec	Typical transfer
Sound card	88 KB/sec	16-bit, 44.1 KHz sampling
LAN	1 MB/sec	10MBit/sec Ethernet
RAM	66 MB/sec	Microprocessor to RAM
Serial Communications	1 KB/sec	9600 bits/sec
Super VGA	15 MB/sec	1024×768 pixels with 256 colours

The PCI Local bus has become a standard on most new PC systems and has replaced the VL-local bus for graphics adaptors. It has the advantage over the VL-local bus in that it can transfer at much higher rates. Unfortunately, most available software packages cannot use the full power of the PCI bus because they do not use the full 64-bit data bus.

2.3 Exercises

The following questions are multiple choice. Select from a – d.

2.1   The I/O cards used in the PC are:

    (a)   PC, ISA, EISA, MCA, VL-Local bus, PCI bus
    (b)   PC, ISA, ANSI, MCA, VL-Local bus, PCI bus
    (c)   PC, ESA, EISA, MCA, VL-Local bus, PCI bus
    (d)   PC, ISA, EISA, MCA, VL-Local bus, PCM bus

2.2   How many bytes can be communicated, at a time, with a PC card:

    (a)   1   (b)   2
    (c)   4   (d)   8

2.3   What clock speed does the ISA card use:

    (a)   4.77 MHz   (b)   8 MHz
    (c)   16 MHz   (d)   the system clock speed

2.4   What is the maximum data rate of an ISA card:

        (a)   8 MB/sec   (b)   16 MB/sec
        (c)   32 MB/sec   (d)   64 MB/sec

2.5   What clock speed does the EISA card use:

        (a)   4.77 MHz   (b)   8 MHz
        (c)   16 MHz   (d)   the system clock speed

2.6   What is the maximum data rate of an EISA card:

        (a)   8 MB/sec   (b)   16 MB/sec
        (c)   32 MB/sec   (d)   64 MB/sec

2.7   How does MCA technology differ from ISA/EISA:

        (a)   MCA uses a cache system
        (b)   MCA uses a common address and data bus
        (c)   MCA uses a serial interface
        (d)   MCA technology uses an asynchronous bus

2.8   What clock speed does the VL-local bus card use:

        (a)   4.77 MHz   (b)   8 MHz
        (c)   16 MHz   (d)   the system clock speed

2.9   How many data lines does the VL-local bus have:

        (a)   16   (b)   24
        (c)   32   (d)   64

2.10   How many address lines does the VL-local bus have:

        (a)   16   (b)   24
        (c)   32   (d)   64

2.11   How many data lines does the PCI local bus have:

        (a)   16   (b)   24
        (c)   32   (d)   64

2.12   How many address lines does the PCI local bus have:

        (a)   16   (b)   24

(c)   32   (d)   64

2.13   Which of the following is the most intensive in data transfer:

(a)   processor to memory transfer   (b) sound card
(c)   local area network card   (d) modem transfer

2.14   Which of the following peripherals are likely to be connected to a local bus:

(a)   video and sound card
(b)   hard disk drive and video card
(c)   video and fax card
(d)   hard disk and local area network card

2.15   PCs of the future are likely to be based around which interface technology:

(a)   VL-local bus   (b)   P-5 bus
(c)   PCI bus   (d)   MCA bus

3
Interfacing Methods

3.1 Introduction

There are two main methods of communicating with an interface card. Either they are mapped into the physical memory and given a real address on the address bus (memory mapped I/O) or they are mapped into a special area of input/output memory (isolated I/O). Figure 3.1 shows the two methods. Devices mapped into memory are accessed by reading or writing to the physical address. Isolated I/O provides ports which are gateways between the interface device and the processor. They are isolated from the system using a buffering system and are accessed by four machine code instructions. The IN instruction inputs a byte, or a word, and the OUT instruction outputs a byte, or a word. C and Pascal compilers interpret the equivalent high-level functions and produce machine code which uses these instructions.

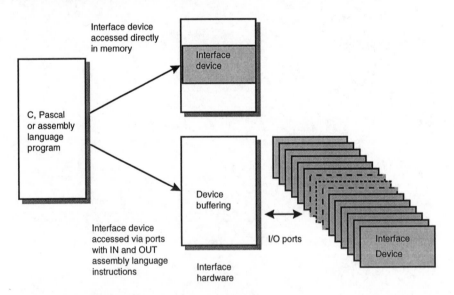

Figure 3.1   Memory mapping or isolated interfacing.

3.2 Interfacing with memory

The 80x86 processor interfaces with memory through a bus controller, as shown in Figure 3.2. This device interprets the microprocessor signals and generates the required memory signals. Two main output lines differentiate between a read or a write operation ($R/\overline{W}$) and between direct and isolated memory access ($M/\overline{IO}$). The $R/\overline{W}$ line is low when data is being written to memory and high when data is being read. When $M/\overline{IO}$ is high, direct memory access is selected and when low, the isolated memory is selected.

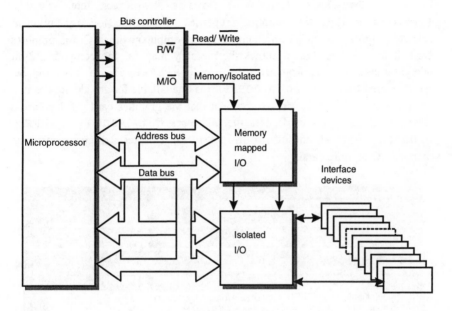

Figure 3.2 Access memory mapped and isolated I/O.

3.3 Memory mapped I/O

Interface devices can map directly onto the system address and data bus. In a PC-compatible system the address bus is 20 bits wide, from address 00000h to FFFFFh (1 MB). If the PC is being used in an enhanced mode (such as with Microsoft Windows) it can access the area of memory above the 1MB. If it uses 16-bit software (such as Microsoft Windows 3.1) then it can address up to 16 MB of physical memory, from 000000h to FFFFFFh. If it uses 32-bit software (such as Microsoft Windows 95) then the software can address up to 4 GBs of physical memory, from 00000000h to FFFFFFFFh. Table 3.1 and Figure 3.4 show a typical memory allocation.

Microsoft Windows 95 can display the memory mapped usage by selecting

Table 3.1   Memory allocation for a PC.

Address	Device
00000h-00FFFh	Interrupt vectors
00400h-0047Fh	ROM BIOS RAM
00600h-9FFFFh	Program memory
A0000h-AFFFFh	EGA/VGA graphics
B0000h-BFFFFh	EGA/VGA graphics
C0000h-C7FFFh	EGA/VGA graphics

Control Panel → System → Device Manager, then selecting Properties. From the computer properties window the Memory option is selected. Figure 3.3 shows an example for a computer with a Cirrus graphics card. It can be seen that it shows the memory map for the complete 32-bit address range, that is, from 00000000h to FFFFFFFFh. In this case the memory area from 000000h to 009FFFh is unavailable for any devices as it is used to run programs. It can also be seen that the graphics card (in this case a Cirrus Logic graphics card) uses the addresses from 0A0000h-0AFFFFh, 0B0000h-0BFFFFh and 0C0000h-0C7FFFh. Chapter 8 discusses memory mapped I/O in more detail.

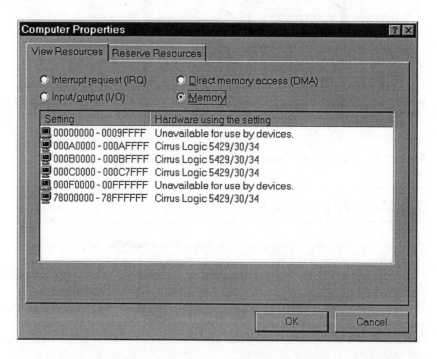

Figure 3.3   Example PC memory usage.

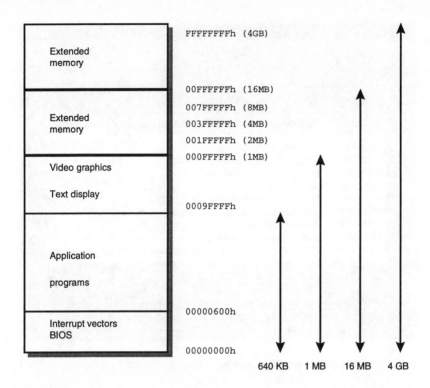

Figure 3.4   Typical PC memory map.

3.4 Isolated I/O

Devices are not normally connected directly onto the address and data bus of the computer because they may use part of the memory that a program uses or they could cause a hardware fault. On modern PCs only the graphics adaptor is mapped directly into memory, the rest communicate through a specially reserved area of memory, known as isolated I/O memory.

Isolated I/O uses 16-bit addressing from 0000h to FFFFh, thus up to 64 KB of memory can be mapped. Microsoft Windows 95 can display the isolated I/O memory map by selecting Control Panel → System → Device Manager, then selecting Properties. From the computer properties window the Input/output (I/O) option is selected. Figure 3.5 shows an example for a computer in the range from 0000h to 0064h and Figure 3.6 shows from 0378h to 03ffh.

It can be seen from Figure 3.5 that the keyboard maps into address 0060h and 0064h, the speaker maps to address 0061h and the system timer between 0040h and 0043h. Table 3.2 shows the typical uses of the isolated memory area.

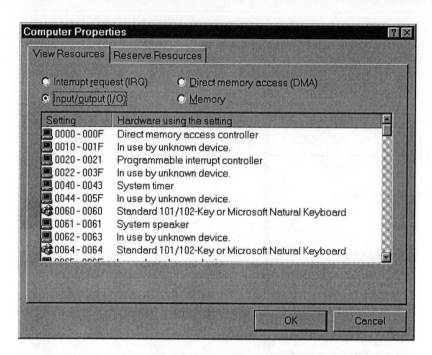

Figure 3.5   Example I/O memory map from 0000h to 0064h.

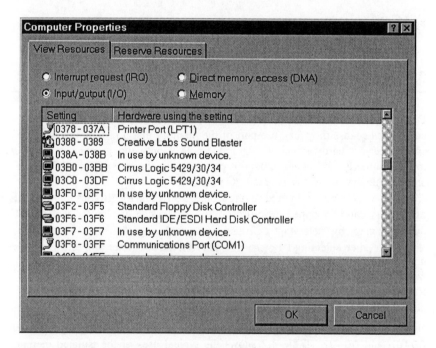

Figure 3.6   Example I/O memory map from 0378h to 03FFh.

Table 3.2 Typical isolated I/O memory map.

Address	Device
000h–01Fh	DMA controller
020h–03Fh	Programmable interrupt controller
040h–05Fh	Counter/Timer
060h–07Fh	Digital I/O
080h–09Fh	DMA controller
0A0h–0BFh	NMI reset
0C0h–0DFh	DMA controller
0E0h–0FFh	Math coprocessor
100h–1F0h	Available
170h–178h	Hard-disk (Secondary IDE drive or CD-ROM drive)
1F0h–1F8h	Hard-disk (Primary IDE drive)
200h–20Fh	Game I/O adapter
210h–217h	Expansion unit
278h–27Fh	Second parallel port (LPT2:)
2F8h–2FFh	Second serial port (COM2:)
300h–31Fh	Prototype card
378h–37Fh	Primary parallel port (LPT1:)
380h–38Ch	SDLC interface
3A0h–3AFh	Primary binary synchronous port
3B0h–3BFh	Graphics adapter
3C0h–3DFh	Graphics adapter
3F0h–3F7h	Floppy disk controller
3F8h–3FFh	Primary serial port (COM1:)

3.4.1 Inputting a byte

The assembly language command to input a byte is:

```
IN AL,DX
```

> where DX is the Data Register which contains the address of the input port. The 8-bit value loaded from this address is put into the register AL.

For Turbo/Borland C the equivalent function is inportb(). Its general syntax is as follows:

```
value=inportb(PORTADDRESS);
```

> where PORTADDRESS is the address of the input port and value is loaded with the 8-bit value from this address. This function is prototyped in the header file dos.h.

For Turbo Pascal the equivalent is accessed via the port[] array. Its general syntax is as follows:

```
value:=port[PORTADDRESS];
```

where PORTADDRESS is the address of the input port and `value` the 8-bit value at this address. To gain access to this function the statement uses `dos` requires to be placed near the top of the program.

3.4.2 Inputting a word

The assembly language command to input a word is:

```
IN AX,DX
```

where DX is the Data Register which contains the address of the input port. The 16-value loaded from this address is put into the register AX.

For Turbo/Borland C the equivalent function is `inport()`. Its general syntax is as follows:

```
value=inport(PORTADDRESS);
```

where PORTADDRESS is the address of the input port and `value` is loaded with the 16-bit value at this address. This function is prototyped in the header file `dos.h`.

For Turbo Pascal the equivalent is accessed via the `portw[]` array. Its general syntax is as follows:

```
value:=portw[PORTADDRESS];
```

where PORTADDRESS is the address of the input port and `value` is the 16-bit value at this address. To gain access to this function the statement uses `dos` requires to be placed near the top of the program.

3.4.3 Outputting a byte

The assembly language command to output a byte is:

```
OUT DX,AL
```

where DX is the Data Register which contains the address of the output port. The 8-bit value sent to this address is stored in register AL.

For Turbo/Borland C the equivalent function is `outportb()`. Its general syntax is as follows:

```
outportb(PORTADDRESS,value);
```

where PORTADDRESS is the address of the output port and value is the 8-bit value to be sent to this address. This function is prototyped in the header file dos.h.

For Turbo Pascal the equivalent is accessed via the port [] array. Its general syntax is as follows:

```
port[PORTADDRESS]:=value;
```

where PORTADDRESS is the address of the output port and value is the 8-bit value to be sent to that address. To gain access to this function the statement uses dos requires to be placed near the top of the program.

3.4.4 Outputting a word

The assembly language command to input a byte is:

```
OUT DX,AX
```

where DX is the Data Register which contains the address of the output port. The 16-bit value sent to this address is stored in register AX.

For Turbo/Borland C the equivalent function is outport (). Its general syntax is as follows:

```
outport(PORTADDRESS,value);
```

where PORTADDRESS is the address of the output port and value is the 16-bit value to be sent to that address. This function is prototyped in the header file dos.h.

For Turbo Pascal the equivalent is accessed via the port [] array. Its general syntax is as follows:

```
portw[PORTADDRESS]:=value;
```

where PORTADDRESS is the address of the output port and value is the 16-bit value to be sent to that address. To gain access to this function the statement uses dos requires to be placed near the top of the program.

3.5 Tutorial

3.1   At which isolated memory address are the following located:
      (a)   Primary serial communications port (COM1:);
      (b)   Secondary serial communications port (COM2:);
      (c)   Primary parallel printer port (LPT1:);
      (d)   Secondary parallel printer port (LPT2:);
      (e)   Programmable interrupt controller.

3.2   Which isolated I/O addresses does the keyboard use?

3.3   Which isolated I/O addresses does the speaker use?

3.4   Which header file is required for the Borland C functions `inportb()` and `outportb()`?

3.5   Which uses file is required for the Turbo Pascal array `port[]`?

4
Digital I/O Using the PPI

4.1 Introduction

Digital input/ output (DIO) involves the inputting and outputting of binary levels, that is, a '0' or a '1'. Many systems interface to equipment through a digital technique as this allows for a reliable and accurate method of control and/or sensing. An input device such as a mechanical switch can provide a digital signal; for example an open switch could correspond to a logic '1' and when closed a logic '0'. As an output a computer could provide an ON or OFF signal which corresponds to logic level '1' or '0'. For example if a logic '1' is outputted then this may turn an electric motor on.

Other output devices require computers to output a digital value which corresponds to a given level, such as a speed control device for a motor. In this case the computer outputs a binary code which is then converted into the required output level. Input devices which generate certain levels are also converted into a digital form so that the computer can read the value. For example, the output from a temperature sensor is fed into a device which converts the temperature into a binary code.

Figure 4.1 shows an example set-up. The inputs are taken from a speed sensor and a switch, the outputs are fed to the motor to turn it ON or OFF and to a speed control device. All inputs and outputs from the computer are digital levels (that is, a '0' or a '1'). The actual speed of the motor is returned to the computer as a binary code and the required speed is sent to the speed controller as a binary code.

PC systems can be fitted with an 8255 PPI (programmable peripheral interface) integrated circuit (IC) to give DIO capability. Each IC provides 24 lines of digital parallel input and/or output. These ICs can be fitted onto an interface card. Normally, these contain two 8255 ICs mounted on a standard PC card, as illustrated in Figure 4.2. The address at which these ICs map into the isolated memory is normally set by in-line switches or jumpers. Connection to external equipment is typically achieved either with a 37-way D-type connector or two 50-way IDC connectors.

Chapter 19 shows the pin connections for the 8255A IC. It has 40 pins and uses an 8-bit bi-directional data bus to communicate with the 24 input/output lines.

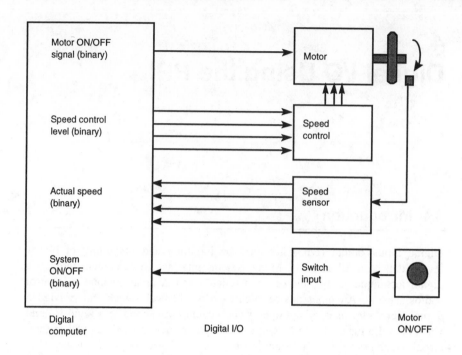

Figure 4.1 Example application using digital I/O.

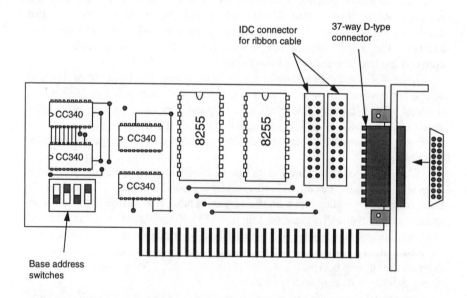

Figure 4.2 DIO board.

4.2 Programming the PPI

Each 8255 has 24 input/output lines. These are grouped into three groups of 8 bits and are named Port A, Port B and Port C. A single 8-bit register, known as the control register, programs the functionality of these ports. Port C can be split into two halves to give Port C (upper) and Port C (lower). The ports and the control register map into the input/ output memory with an assigned base address. The arrangement of the port addresses with respect to the base address is given in Table 4.1.

Table 4.1 PPI Addresses.

Port address	Function
BASE_ADDRESS	Port A
BASE_ADDRESS+1	Port B
BASE_ADDRESS+2	Port C
BASE_ADDRESS+3	Control register

Figure 4.3 shows the functional layout of the 8255. The control register programs each of the ports to be an input or an output and also their mode of operation. There are four main parts which are programmed: Port A, Port B, Port C (upper) and Port C (lower).

Figure 4.4 shows the definition of the Control Register bits. The msb (most significant bit) D7 either makes the device active or inactive. If it is set to a 0 it is inactive, else it will be active. The input/output status of Port A is set by D4. If it is a 0 then Port A is an output, else it will be an input. The status of Port B is set by D1, Port C (lower) by D0 and Port C (upper) by D3.

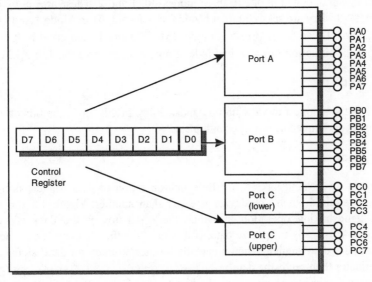

Figure 4.3 Layout of PPI.

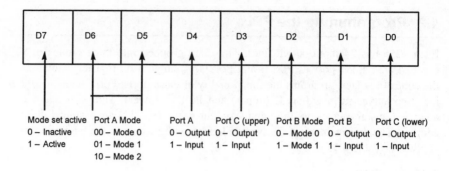

Figure 4.4 PPI Control Register Bit Definitions.

Table 4.2 Example bit patterns for control register.

Bit pattern	Mode of operation
01101000	Device is inactive as D7 set to 0
10011000	Mode 0 Port A input, Port C (upper) input, Mode 0 Port B output, Port C (lower) output
10101000	Mode 1 Port A output, Port C (upper) input, Mode 0 Port B output, Port C (lower) output

Port A can operated in one of three modes – 0, 1 and 2. These are set by bits D5 and D6. If they are set to 00 then Mode 0 is selected, 01 to Mode 1 and 10 to Mode 2. Port B can be used in two modes (Mode 0 and 1) and is set by bit D2. Examples of bit definitions and the mode of operation are given in Table 4.2.

4.2.1 Mode 0

Mode 0 is the simplest mode with no handshaking. In this mode the bits on Port C can be programmed as inputs or outputs.

4.2.2 Mode 1

This mode gives handshaking for the synchronization of data. Handshaking is normally required when one device is faster than another. Figure 4.5 shows a typical handshaking operation in which the originator of the data asks the recipient if it is ready to receive data. If it is not then the recipient sends back a 'not ready for data' signal. When it is ready it sends a 'ready for data' signal and the originator then sends the data.

If Ports A and B are inputs then the bits on Port C have the definitions given in Table 4.3.

When inputting data, the $\overline{\text{STB}}$ going low (active) writes data into the port. After this data is written into the port, the IBF line automatically goes high. This automatically remains high until the data is read from the port.

If any of the ports are outputs, then the bit definitions of Port C are given in Table 4.4.

In this mode, when data is written to the port the $\overline{\text{OBF}}$ line goes low, which indicates that data is ready to be read from the port. The $\overline{\text{OBF}}$ line will not go high until the $\overline{\text{ACK}}$ is pulled low. Handshaking modes will be discussed in more detail in Chapter 6.

4.2.3 Mode 2

This mode allows bi-directional I/O. The signal lines are given in Table 4.5.

Table 4.3   Mode 1 handshaking lines for inputting data.

Signal	Port A	Port B
Strobe ($\overline{\text{STB}}$)	PC4	PC2
Input Buffer full (IBF)	PC5	PC1

Table 4.4   Mode 1 handshaking lines for outputting data.

Signal	Port C	Port B
Output Buffer Full ($\overline{\text{OBF}}$)	PC7	PC1
Acknowledge ($\overline{\text{ACK}}$)	PC6	PC2

Table 4.5   Mode 2 operation for bi-directional I/O.

Signal	Port A
$\overline{\text{OBF}}$	PC7
$\overline{\text{ACK}}$	PC6
$\overline{\text{STB}}$	PC4
IBF	PC5

4.3 Digital I/O programs

The programs in this section are written in C and Pascal (and some in 8088 assembly language). Borland products have a useful utility to obtain help on a procedure or function. To get this help, first place the cursor on the word, for which help is required, then press the Cntrl and F1 keys (see Figure 4.6). The help screen normally informs the user as to which #include file (in C) or uses file (in Pascal) is required and its basic syntax.

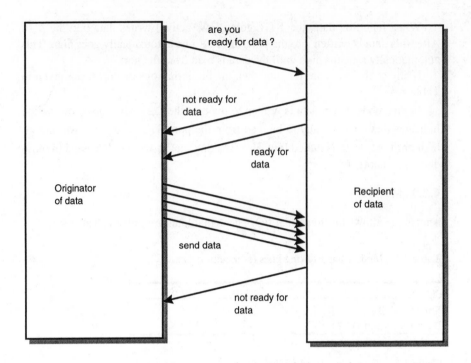

Figure 4.5 Simple handshaking of data.

Program 4.1 outputs the binary code for 0 to 255 to Port B with a one-second delay between changes. The program exits when the output reaches 255. The C function `outportb(PORT,BYTE)` and the Pascal equivalent `port[PORT]:=BYTE` send a single byte `BYTE` to the port at the address `PORT`, in this case to Port B. Both functions are non-standard and if another compiler (and/ or libraries) is used they must be replaced by their equivalents. Figure 4.7 shows a typical set-up to test the program where Port B has been connected to eight light-emitting diodes (LEDs).

In C a macro is defined using the `#define` statement. Program 4.1 uses these to define each of the port addresses. This helps to document the program and makes it easier to make global changes. For example, a different base address is relatively easy to set up, as a single change to `BASE_ADDRESS` automatically updates all port defines in the program. In this case the base address is `1F0h`. This address should be changed to the required base address of the DIO card.

The program uses the functions `sleep()` and `outportb()` which are prototyped in the include file *dos.h*. An `unsigned char` data type is used for the parameter `i` as the `outportb()` function requires an 8-bit unsigned value to be passed to it. If the program is being used with a debugger it may be better to declare `i` as an integer as the actual bit-pattern is easier to interpret as an integer rather than as a character.

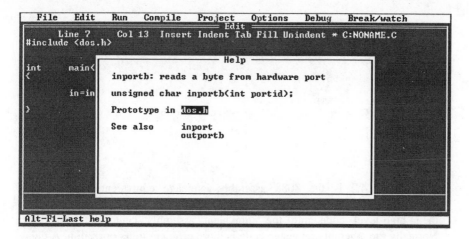

Figure 4.6 Borland on-line help screen.

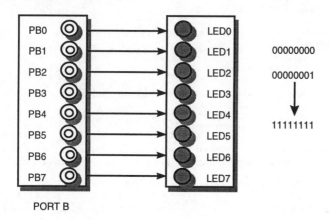

PORT B

Figure 4.7 Possible system set-up.

📄 Program 4.1

```
/* ppi_1.c                                                    */
/* Program that will count from 0 to 255                      */
/* and display it to PORT B. One second between counts        */

#define    BASE_ADDRESS   0x1F0 /* change this as required    */
#define    PORTA          BASE_ADDRESS
#define    PORTB          (BASE_ADDRESS+1)
#define    PORTC          (BASE_ADDRESS+2)
#define    CNTRL_REG      (BASE_ADDRESS+3)

#include   <dos.h>      /* required for outportb() */

int    main(void)
{
/* NOTE: It may be better to define i is an integer (int)   */
/* as it is easier to display the value in the debugger     */
```

```
unsigned char  i=0;

    outportb(CNTRL_REG,0x90);
        /*set A input, B output*/

    for (i=0;i<=255;i++)
    {
        outportb(PORTB,i);
        sleep(1);                  /* wait 1 second */
    }
    return(0);

}
```

Program 4.2 is the 8088 assembly language equivalent and uses the instruction out to send a byte to Port A. The C and Pascal compilers convert their high-level code into the equivalent assembly language instructions. Normally the assembly language code is more efficient in its operation. A delay routine has been added which uses the system timer. This will be discussed in more detail in Section 8.5.4.

📄 Program 4.2

```
code          SEGMENT
              ASSUME cs:code

BASEADDRESS EQU      01F0H ; change this as required
PORTA       EQU      BASEADDRESS
PORTB       EQU      BASEADDRESS+1
CNTRLREG    EQU      BASEADDRESS+3

;   program to output to Port B counts in binary until from 00000000
;   to 11111111 with approximately 1 second delay between changes
start:
            mov dx,CNTRLREG      ; set up PPI with
            mov al,90h           ; Port B as Output
            out dx,al

            mov al,00h
loop:
            mov dx,PORTB
            out dx,al            ; output to Port B

            call delay
            inc al
            cmp al,0ffh
            jnz loop             ; repeat until all 1s

            mov ah,4cH           ; program exit
            int 21h              ;

        ; ROUTINE TO GIVE 1 SECOND DELAY USING THE PC TIMER

DELAY:      push ax
            push bx

            mov ax,18            ; 18.2 clock ticks per second;

            ; Address of system timer on the PC is 0000:046C (low word)
            ; and 0000:046E (high word)
```

```
        mov bx,0
        mov es,bx

        ; Add the number of required ticks of the clock (ie 18)
        add ax,es:[46CH]
        mov bx,es:[46EH]

loop2:
        ; Compare current timer count with AX and BX
        ;   if they are equal 1 second has passed

        cmp bx,es:[46EH]
        ja loop2
        jb over
        cmp ax,es:[46CH]
        jg loop2

over:   pop bx
        pop ax
        ret

code    ENDS
        END     start
```

Program 4.3 is the Turbo Pascal equivalent of Program 4.1 and runs in a similar manner. The delay() function delays the program by a number of milliseconds (1/1000 sec), in this case one second. As with the C program the port addresses have been defined as constants using the const reserved word. The control register is programmed with the bit pattern 10010000b; this is 90h as a hexadecimal.

🖹 Program 4.3

```
program ppi_1(input,output);
uses crt;

{   ppi_1.pas                                                      }
{   Program to count from 255 to 0 and display this to Port B     }
{   with a one second delay in between                            }

const   BASE_ADDRESS=$01F0; { change this if required             }
        PORTA=BASE_ADDRESS;
        PORTB=BASE_ADDRESS+1;
        PORTC=BASE_ADDRESS+2;
        CNTRL_REG=BASE_ADDRESS+3;
var     i:integer;

begin
    i:=0;

    port[CNTRL_REG]:=$90;      { set A input, B output }

    for i:=0 to 255 do
    begin
        port[PORTB]:=i;
        delay(1000);
    end;

end.
```

It can be difficult to exit from a program once it has started so the next program allows the user to quit if a key is pressed on the keyboard. The kbhit() function (or the keypressed statement in Pascal) returns a TRUE when a key is pressed. It is prototyped in *conio.h*. Program 4.4 contains this function and the decimal number 256 is replaced with its hexadecimal equivalent 0x100 ($100 in Pascal). Binary data is often easier to convert and display as hexadecimal than in a decimal from.

📄 Program 4.4

```
/* ppi_2.c                                                           */
/* Program to count from 0 to 255  and display it to Port B          */
/* one second between counts                                         */
#define      BASE_ADDRESS    0x1F0     /* change this as required    */
#define      PORTA           BASE_ADDRESS
#define      PORTB           (BASE_ADDRESS+1)
#define      PORTC           (BASE_ADDRESS+2)
#define      CNTRL_REG       (BASE_ADDRESS+3)

#include     <dos.h>         /* required for outportb()    */
#include     <conio.h>       /* required for kbhit()       */

int    main(void)
{
int    i=0;

   outportb(CNTRL_REG,0x90);   /* set A input, B output */

   do
   {
      outportb(PORTB,i++);
      sleep(1);   /* wait 1 second */
   } while (!kbhit() && (i!=0x100) ); /* 0x100 is 256 in decimal */

   return(0);
}
```

Program 4.5 is the Pascal equivalent and uses the repeat...until keypressed; statement. Note that the program will not stop until a key has been pressed or the value of i becomes 256.

📄 Program 4.5

```
program ppi_2(input,output);
uses crt;
{  ppi_2.pas                                                        }
{  Program to count from 0 to 255   and display it to Port B        }
{  with one second between counts                                   }
const    BASE_ADDRESS=$01F0; { change this if required              }
         PORTA=BASE_ADDRESS;
         PORTB=BASE_ADDRESS+1;
         PORTC=BASE_ADDRESS+2;
         CNTRL_REG=BASE_ADDRESS+3;

var      i:integer;
begin
   i:=0;
   port[CNTRL_REG]:=$90;              { set A input, B output }
```

```
      repeat
         port[PORTB]:=i;
         i:=i+1;
         delay(1000);
      until (keypressed or (i=$100));
end.
```

Program 4.6 reads the binary input from Port A and sends it to Port B. It will stop only when all the input bits on port A are 1s. It shows how a byte can be read from a port and then outputted to another port. Port A is used, in this example, as the input and Port B as the output. Figure 4.8 shows how Port A could be connected to input switches and Port B to the light-emitting diodes (LEDs). Loading the bit pattern 90h into the control register initializes the correct set-up for Ports A and B.

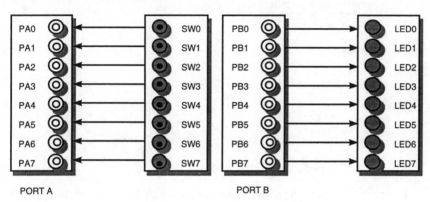

Figure 4.8 Typical system set-up.

🖹 Program 4.6

```
/* ppi_3.c                                                       */
/* Program that will read from PORT A and send these            */
/* bits to PORT B. All 1's on PORT A will stop program.         */
#define     BASE_ADDRESS   0x1F0 /* change this as required     */

#define     PORTA            BASE_ADDRESS
#define     PORTB            (BASE_ADDRESS+1)
#define     PORTC            (BASE_ADDRESS+2)
#define     CNTRL_REG        (BASE_ADDRESS+3)

#include <dos.h>      /* required for inportb() and outportb() */
#include <conio.h>    /* required for kbhit()                  */

int   main(void)
{
int   i;
    outportb(CNTRL_REG,0x90);/*set A input, B output*/
    do
    {
        i=inportb(PORTA);
        outportb(PORTB,i);
    } while (!kbhit() && (i!=0xFF) );
```

```
        return(0);
}
```

The Turbo Pascal equivalent is similar and is given in Program 4.7.

📄 Program 4.7
```
program ppi_3(input,output);

uses    crt;
{ ppi_3.pas                                             }
{ Program that will read from port A and send           }
{ to PORT B. Program will stop with all 1s.             }

const   BASE_ADDRESS=$01F0; { change this if required }
        PORTA=BASE_ADDRESS;
        PORTB=BASE_ADDRESS+1;
        PORTC=BASE_ADDRESS+2;
        CNTRL_REG=BASE_ADDRESS+3;

var   i:integer;

begin
    port[CNTRL_REG]:=$90; { set A input, B output }

    repeat
        i:=port[PORTA];
        port[PORTB]:=i;
    until (keypressed or (i=$FF));

end.
```

Program 4.8 shows how the same program can be executed using 8088 assembly language.

📄 Program 4.8
```
code        SEGMENT
            ASSUME cs:code
; program to read from Port A and send to
; Port B. Program stops with all 1's
start:
        mov dx,1f3h
        mov al,90h
        out dx,al
loop:
        mov dx,1f0h
        in al,dx            ; read from Port A

        mov dx,1f1h
        out dx,al           ; output to Port B

        cmp al,ffh
        jnz loop:           ; repeat until all 1s
        mov ah,4cH          ; program exit
        int 21h             ;

code        ENDS
            END     start
```

4.4 Bitmask operation

A technique known as bitmasking is used to identify individual bits by setting all other bits, other than the bit of interest, to a 0. It uses the AND bitwise operator (&), which yields a 0 for a bit if one of the bit operands is a 0. If one of the bit operands is a 1 it yields the value of the other operand bit. Figure 4.9 shows an example of masking the third least significant bit (b_2). In this case, the bit mask used is 0x04; this is then bitwise ANDed with the operand. There can only be two possible results from this operation: a 0 (if b_2 is 0) or 4 (if b_2 is 1). An X indicates a 'don't care' state in which a bit can take on any binary value (that is, 0 or 1).

Program 4.9 reads a byte from Port A and displays which bits are set. It waits two seconds between every poll of the port. The if statement is used with bitmask values of 128 (0x80 or 1000 0000b), 64 (0x40 or 0100 0000b), and so on, to determine which of the bits in a decimal integer are set.

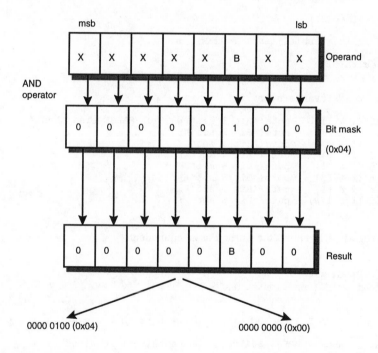

Figure 4.9   Bitmask operation.

📄 Program 4.9

```
/* ppi_4.c                                         */
/* Program that reads from PORT A and displays     */
/* the bits that are set                           */
```

```
#define      BASE_ADDRESS     0x1F0 /* change this as required    */
#define      PORTA            BASE_ADDRESS
#define      PORTB            (BASE_ADDRESS+1)
#define      PORTC            (BASE_ADDRESS+2)
#define      CNTRL_REG     (  BASE_ADDRESS+3)

#include     <dos.h>  /* needed for outportb */
#include     <conio.h>
#include     <stdio.h>

void  TestBitPattern(int i);

int   main(void)
{
int    i;
   outportb(CNTRL_REG,0x90);          /*set A input, B output*/
   do
   {

      clrscr();

      i=inportb(PORTA);
      TestBitPattern(i);

      sleep(2);

   } while (!kbhit() && (i!=0xFF) );

   return(0);
}

void  TestBitPattern(int i)
{
   if (i & 1)      puts("Bit 1 set");  /*0 -FALSE else TRUE*/
   if (i & 2)      puts("Bit 2 set");
   if (i & 4)      puts("Bit 3 set");
   if (i & 8)      puts("Bit 4 set");
   if (i & 16)     puts("Bit 5 set");
   if (i & 32)     puts("Bit 6 set");
   if (i & 64)     puts("Bit 7 set");
   if (i & 128)    puts("Bit 8 set");
}
```

Program 4.10 shows the Turbo Pascal equivalent.

📄 Program 4.10

```
program ppi_4(input,output);

uses crt;
{ Reads from PORT A and displays the bits that are set }

const    BASE_ADDRESS=$01F0; { change this if required   }
         PORTA=BASE_ADDRESS;
         PORTB=BASE_ADDRESS+1;
         PORTC=BASE_ADDRESS+2;
         CNTRL_REG=BASE_ADDRESS+3;

var      i:integer;

procedure TestBitPattern(i:integer);
begin
```

```pascal
    if ((i and 1)=1)         then writeln('Bit 1 set');
    if ((i and 2)=2)         then writeln('Bit 2 set');
    if ((i and 4)=4)         then writeln('Bit 3 set');
    if ((i and 8)=8)         then writeln('Bit 4 set');
    if ((i and 16)=16)       then writeln('Bit 5 set');
    if ((i and 32)=32)       then writeln('Bit 6 set');
    if ((i and 64)=64)       then writeln('Bit 7 set');
    if ((i and 128)=128)     then writeln('Bit 8 set');
end;

begin
    port[CNTRL_REG]:=$90;   { set A input, B output }

    repeat

      clrscr;
      i:=port[PORTA];
      TestBitPattern(i);
      delay(1000);

    until (keypressed or (i=255));
end.
```

4.5 Program enhancements

Programs 4.11 and 4.12 are similar to Programs 4.9 and 4.10 but have some enhancements. A loop has been added to test each of the bits in the inputted value. The statement:

```c
for (bitmask=1;bitmask<256;bitmask<<=1, bit++)
```

sets bitmask to 1, 2, 4, 8, 16, 32, 64 and 128 each time round the loop. This is because the initial value is set to 1 (00000001b) and each time round the loop the binary value is shifted left by one bit position (bitmask<<=1 is equivalent to bitmask=bitmask<<1). In Turbo Pascal the shift left operator is shl.

📄 Program 4.11
```c
/* ppi_5.c                                                    */
/* Reads from PORT A and display the bits that are set        */
#include <stdio.h>

#define     BASE_ADDRESS    0x1F0 /* change this as required */
#define     PORTA           BASE_ADDRESS
#define     PORTB           (BASE_ADDRESS+1)
#define     PORTC           (BASE_ADDRESS+2)
#define     CNTRL_REG       (BASE_ADDRESS+3)
    /* Ctrl Register bit set-up   */
#define   MODE0             0x80
#define   PORTAIN           0x10
#define   PORTBIN           0x02
#define   PORTCUIN          0x08
#define   PORTCLIN          0x10
#define   SLEEPDELAY        2

#include <dos.h>              /* needed for outportb()      */
```

```c
#include <conio.h>          /* needed for clrscr()        */

void  TestBitPattern(unsigned char);/* ANSI-C function prototype*/

int   main(void)
{
unsigned char i,status;

    status=PORTAIN | MODE0;
    outportb(CNTRL_REG,status);      /* set A input, B output */
    do
    {
        clrscr();
        i=inportb(PORTA);
        TestBitPattern(i);
        sleep(SLEEPDELAY);
    } while (!kbhit() );

    return(0);
}

void  TestBitPattern(unsigned char i)
{
int    bitmask,bit=1;
    for (bitmask=1;bitmask<256;bitmask<<=1, bit++)
        if (i & bitmask) printf("Bit %d set\n",bit);
}
```

Program 4.12 is the Turbo Pascal equivalent.

🗎 Program 4.12

```pascal
program ppi_5(input,output);
uses crt;
{* ppi_5.pas                                              *}
{* Program that will read from PORT A and display         *}
{* the bits that are set.                                 *}

const    BASE_ADDRESS=$01F0; { change this if required }
         PORTA=BASE_ADDRESS;
         PORTB=BASE_ADDRESS+1;
         PORTC=BASE_ADDRESS+2;
         CNTRL_REG=BASE_ADDRESS+3;
         MODE0     =$80;    { Port A mode 0              }
         PORTAIN    =$10;    { Port A input              }
         PORTBIN    =$02;    { Port B input              }
         PORTCUIN   =$08;    { Port C upper input        }
         PORTCLIN   =$10;    { Port C lower input        }
         SLEEPDELAY =1000;   { one second                }

var i:integer;

procedure  TestBitPattern(i:integer);
var          j,bit:integer;
begin
    bit:=1; { bit stores the bit powers ie 1,2,4,8..128}

    for j:=1 to 8 do  { test for 8 bits }
    begin
        if ((i and bit)=bit) then writeln('Bit ',j,' is set');
        bit:=bit shl 1;
    end;
end;
```

```
begin
    port[CNTRL_REG]:=PORTAIN + MODE0;   { set A input, B output }

    repeat

        clrscr;

        i:=port[PORTA];

        TestBitPattern(i);

        delay(SLEEPDELAY);

    until (keypressed);

end.
```

4.6 Traffic light controller

A simple traffic light system can be set up by connecting Port B to a RED, AMBER and GREEN light. In Program 4.13 PB0 is connected to RED, PB1 to AMBER and PB2 to GREEN. The required sequence is given in Table 4.6. After sequence number 4 the program returns to sequence number 1 and so on. A one-second delay between changes is also required.

The sequence is set up in an array with the following declaration:

```
int  sequence[MAXSEQ]={0x01,0x03,0x04,0x02};
```

This sets sequence[0] to 0000 0001b, sequence[1] to 0000 0011b, and so on. Any fixed sequence can be set up in this way. The use of array indexing allows a fast and easy-to-read method of setting up the required sequence.

The number of values in the sequence is set up with the macro MAXSEQ. This macro allows all parts of the program to reference properly the last value in the array.

Figure 4.10 shows how the traffic light connects to Port B. A '1' on PB0 sets the RED light on, else it will be off.

Table 4.6   Traffic light sequence.

Sequence number	Light sequence	Bit pattern sent to Port B
1	RED	0000 0001 (01h)
2	RED and AMBER	0000 0011 (03h)
3	GREEN	0000 0100 (04h)
4	AMBER	0000 0010 (02h)
1	RED	0000 0001 (01h)
2	RED and AMBER	0000 0011 (03h)
3	GREEN	0000 0100 (04h)
	and so on.	

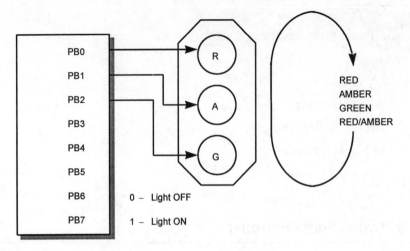

Figure 4.10 Traffic light setup.

📄 Program 4.13

```
/* ppi_6.c                                                  */
/* Traffic Light Controller                                 */
#include <stdio.h>
#define    BASE_ADDRESS    0x1F0 /* change this as required */
#define    PORTA           BASE_ADDRESS
#define    PORTB           (BASE_ADDRESS+1)
#define    PORTC           (BASE_ADDRESS+2)
#define    CNTRL_REG       (BASE_ADDRESS+3)
#define    MAXSEQ          4

#include <dos.h>        /* needed for outportb()   */
#include <conio.h>      /* needed for clrscr()     */

int    main(void)
{
int    sequence[MAXSEQ]={0x01,0x03,0x04,0x02}, status,i;

    status=0x90;
    outportb(CNTRL_REG,status);/* set A input, B output */
    do
    {
        for (i=0;i<MAXSEQ;i++)
        {
            outportb(PORTB,sequence[i]);
            sleep(1);
        }
    } while (!kbhit() );
    return(0);
}
```

The Turbo Pascal equivalent is given in Program 4.14. Unfortuately, in Turbo Pascal it is not possible to initialize an array with a defined sequence.

Program 4.14

```
program ppi_6(input,output);
uses crt;
const BASE_ADDRESS=$01F0; { change this if required }
      PORTA=BASE_ADDRESS;
      PORTB=BASE_ADDRESS+1;
      PORTC=BASE_ADDRESS+2;
      CNTRL_REG=BASE_ADDRESS+3;
      MAXSEQ=4;
type arrtype=array[1..MAXSEQ] of integer;
var  i:integer;
     sequence:arrtype;

begin
   port[CNTRL_REG]:=$90;    { set A input, B output }
   { Sequence is 0000 0001, 0000 0011, 0000 0100, 0000 0010 }
   sequence[1]:=$01; sequence[2]:=$03;
   sequence[3]:=$04;sequence[4]:=$02;
   repeat
      for i:=1 to MAXSEQ do
      begin
          port[PORTB]:=sequence[i];
          delay(1000);
      end;
   until (keypressed);

end.
```

4.7 Generation of gray code

This example shows how bits in a value can be masked and operated on to give the required functionality. Gray code is used to represent binary values. It has an advantage over binary in that only a single bit changes when counting from 0 to 9. Table 4.7 shows the conversion between decimal, binary and gray code.

Program 4.15 shows how the gray code sequence is set up using an array, that is:

```
int    gray_code[MAXSEQ]={0x00,0x01,0x03,0x02,0x06,
                          0x07,0x05,0x04,0x0C,0x0D};
```

Table 4.7 Gray code conversion.

Decimal	Binary	Gray code
0	0000	0000
1	0001	0001
2	0010	0011
3	0011	0010
4	0100	0110
5	0101	0111
6	0110	0101
7	0111	0100
8	1000	1100
9	1001	1101

The bit patterns stored in the array `gray_code` will thus be 000000000b, 00000001b, 00000011b, 000000010b, and so on. These values are outputted to Port B with a half-second delay between outputs.

📄 **Program 4.15**

```
/* ppi_7.c                                                    */
/* Program to output Gray code                                */

#define       BASE_ADDRESS    0x1F0 /* change this as required    */

#define       PORTA           BASE_ADDRESS
#define       PORTB           (BASE_ADDRESS+1)
#define       PORTC           (BASE_ADDRESS+2)
#define       CNTRL_REG       (BASE_ADDRESS+3)
#define       MAXSEQ          10

#include      <dos.h>   /* required for outportb() */
#include      <stdio.h>

int   main(void)
{
int   i;
int   gray_code[MAXSEQ]={0x00,0x01,0x03,0x02,0x06,0x07,0x05,0x04,
                         0x0C,0x0D};

    outportb(CNTRL_REG,0x90);         /*set A input, B output*/
    for (i=0;i<MAXSEQ;i++)
    {
        outportb(PORTB,gray_code[i]);
        delay(500);
    }

    return(0);
}
```

The gray code can also be generated mathematically. If the binary number is made up of four bits $B_4B_3B_2B_1$, then the gray code for $G_4G_3G_2G_1$ will be:

$$G_1 = B_1 \oplus B_2$$
$$G_2 = B_2 \oplus B_3$$
$$G_3 = B_3 \oplus B_4$$
$$G_4 = B_4$$

where $\oplus$ is the exclusive-OR (EX-OR) operator.

In C the EX-OR operator is ^ and in Pascal it is xor. The following code masks the bits of a value i and scales the variables bit1, bit2, bit3 and bit4 to give a 0 or a 1.

```
        bit1=(i&1);        /* mask LSB and scale to 0 or 1      */
        bit2=(i&2)>>1;     /* mask 2nd bit and scale to 0 or 1  */
        bit3=(i&4)>>2;     /* mask 3rd bit   and scale to 0 or 1 */
        bit4=(i&8)>>3;     /* mask 4th bit   and scale to 0 or 1 */
```

Once the bits have been masked and scaled to a 0 or a 1 they can be used with the EX-OR, the shift left and with the OR operator to produce the required result, as given below.

```
code=bit1^bit2 | (bit2^bit3)<<1 | (bit3^bit4)<<2 | bit4<<3;
```

Program 4.16 uses these operations to produce a gray code sequence.

📄 **Program 4.16**

```
/* ppi_8.c                                                     */
/* Program to output Gray code                                 */

#define      BASE_ADDRESS      0x1F0 /* change this as required */
#define      PORTA             BASE_ADDRESS
#define      PORTB             (BASE_ADDRESS+1)
#define      PORTC             (BASE_ADDRESS+2)
#define      CNTRL_REG         (BASE_ADDRESS+3)

#include     <dos.h>   /* needed for outportb */
#include     <conio.h>
#include     <stdio.h>

#define      MAXSEQ            10

int      main(void)
{
int       i,bit1,bit2,bit3,bit4,code;

    outportb(CNTRL_REG,0x90);         /*set A input, B output    */

    for (i=0;i<MAXSEQ;i++)
    {
        bit1=(i&1);         /* mask LSB and scale to 0 or 1       */
        bit2=(i&2)>>1;      /* mask 2nd bit and scale to 0 or 1   */
        bit3=(i&4)>>2;      /* mask 3rd bit  and scale to 0 or 1  */
        bit4=(i&8)>>3;

        code=bit1^bit2 | (bit2^bit3)<<1 | (bit3^bit4)<<2 | bit4<<3;

        outportb(PORTB,code);

        delay(500);

    }

    return(0);

}
```

4.8 Creating an emulator function

Developing a program which interfaces to hardware can cause problems as not all computers have DIO boards installed in them. It is possible to overcome this problem by substituting calls to the interface hardware with test 'stub' routines. These emulate the input/output functions calls, as shown in Figure 4.11.

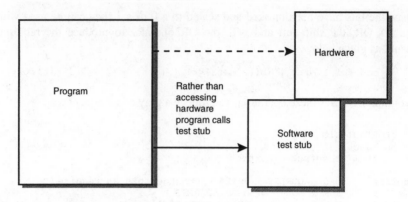

Figure 4.11 Program calling test stub.

4.8.1 Outputting a byte

The emboldened text in Program 4.17 shows a simple emulator routine for
`inportb()`. It determines if the output is being sent to PORT A, B, C or the
control register, and will display their bit pattern. The program uses the emulator
routine to test the traffic light program.

📄 Program 4.17

```
/* ppi_6.c                                                */
#include <stdio.h>
#include <dos.h>             /* required for outportb()     */
#include <conio.h>           /* required for kbhit()        */

#define     BASE_ADDRESS    0x1F0 /* change this as required */
#define     PORTA           BASE_ADDRESS
#define     PORTB           (BASE_ADDRESS+1)
#define     PORTC           (BASE_ADDRESS+2)
#define     CNTRL_REG       (BASE_ADDRESS+3)
#define     MAXSEQ          4

#ifdef   outportb()
#undef   outportb()
void  outportb(int portid,unsigned char val);
void  outportb(int portid,unsigned char val)
{
int      bitmask;
   if (portid==PORTA) printf("PORT A=");
   else if (portid==PORTB) printf("PORT B=");
   else if (portid==PORTC) printf("PORT C=");
   else if (portid==CNTRL_REG) printf("Control Register=");

   for (bitmask=128;bitmask>=1;bitmask>>=1)
      if (val & bitmask) printf("1");
      else printf("0");
   puts("");
}
#endif
```

```
int    main(void)
{
int    sequence[MAXSEQ]={0x01,0x03,0x04,0x02}, status,i;

    status=0x90; /* 1001 0000 */
    outportb(CNTRL_REG,status);/* set A input, B output */
    do
    {
        for (i=0;i<MAXSEQ;i++)
        {
            outportb(PORTB,sequence[i]);
            sleep(1);
        }
    } while (!kbhit() );
    return(0);
}
```

Test run 4.1 shows a sample run.

🖳 Test run 4.1

```
Control Register=10010000
PORT B=00000001
PORT B=00000011
PORT B=00000100
PORT B=00000010
PORT B=00000001
PORT B=00000011
PORT B=00000100
PORT B=00000010
PORT B=00000001
PORT B=00000011
PORT B=00000100
PORT B=00000010
```

4.8.2 Inputting a byte

The highlighted text in Program 4.18 shows a simple emulator routine for
inportb(). When the emulator routine is called the user is prompted for the
bit to be toggled. If the function key F1 is pressed then the least significant bit is
toggled. Function key F2 toggles the next most significant bit and so on to
function key F8 which toggles the most significant bit.

📄 Program 4.18
```
#define      BASE_ADDRESS    0x1F0 /* change this as required */

#define      PORTA           BASE_ADDRESS
#define      PORTB           (BASE_ADDRESS+1)
#define      PORTC           (BASE_ADDRESS+2)
#define      CNTRL_REG       (BASE_ADDRESS+3)

#include <dos.h>
#include <stdio.h>

#ifdef    inportb()
#undef    inportb()
```

```
unsigned char  inportb(int portid);
enum      fkeys {F1=59,F2,F3,F4,F5,F6,F7,F8,F9,F10};

int       PORTAcontents=0,PORTBcontents=0,PORTCcontents=0;

unsigned char inportb(int portid)
{
char      ch,contents;

   printf("Select function key to toggle bit >>");

   if (portid==PORTA) contents=PORTAcontents;
   else if (portid==PORTB) contents=PORTBcontents;
   else if (portid==PORTC) contents=PORTCcontents;

   ch=getch();

   if (ch==0) ch=getch();
   if (ch==F1) contents=contents ^ 1;
   if (ch==F2) contents=contents ^ 2;
   if (ch==F3) contents=contents ^ 4;
   if (ch==F4) contents=contents ^ 8;
   if (ch==F5) contents=contents ^ 16;
   if (ch==F6) contents=contents ^ 32;
   if (ch==F7) contents=contents ^ 64;
   if (ch==F8) contents=contents ^ 128;

   if (portid==PORTA) PORTAcontents=contents;
   else if (portid==PORTB) PORTBcontents=contents;
   else if (portid==PORTC) PORTCcontents=contents;

   return(contents);
}
#endif


int    main(void)
{
int    in;

   outportb(CNTRL_REG,status);/* set A input, B output */
   clrscr();
   do
   {
      in=inportb(PORTA);
      printf("Input is %d\n",in);
   } while (in!=255);

   return(0);

}
```

4.9 Exercises

4.1   Write a program that sends a 'walking-ones' code to Port B. The
         delay between changes should be one second. A 'walking-ones' code
         is as follows:

```
00000001
00000010
00000100
00001000
  :  :
10000000
00000001
00000010
```
and so on.

Hint: Either use the shift left operator that is << or shl, or set up an array with the required sequence, for example:

```
int sequence[8]={0x01,0x02,0x04,0x08,0x10,0x20,0x40,0x80};
```

Modify the program so that the delay is programmable (in milliseconds).

4.2 Write separate programs which output the patterns in (a) and (b). The sequences are as follows:

(a)	(b)
00000001	10000001
00000010	01000010
00000100	00100100
00001000	00011000
00010000	00100100
00100000	01000010
01000000	10000001
10000000	01000010
01000000	00100100
00100000	00011000
00010000	00100100
::	and so on.
00000001	
00000010	
and so on.	

4.3 Write separate programs which output the following sequences:

(a)	(b)
1010 1010	1111 1111
0101 0101	0000 0000
1010 1010	1111 1111
0101 0101	0000 0000
and so on.	and so on.

(c)	(d)
0000 0001	0000 0001
0000 0011	0000 0011
0000 1111	0000 0111
0001 1111	0000 1111
0011 1111	0001 1111
0111 1111	0011 1111
1111 1111	0111 1111

```
0000 0001          1111 1111
0000 0011          0111 1111
0000 0111          0011 1111
0000 1111          0001 1111
0001 1111          0000 1111
and so on.         and so on.
```

(e)   The inverse of (d) above.

4.4   Write a program that reads a byte from Port A and display the equivalent Gray code to Port B.

4.5   Write a program that reads a byte from Port A and display the equivalent ASCII code to the screen. Table 4.8 shows some examples.

Table 4.8   Conversions.

Character	Binary	Hex	Decimal
'0'	0011 0000b	30h	48
'1'	0011 0001b	31h	49
	.	.	.
	.	.	.
	.	.	.
'?'	0011 1111b	3Fh	63
'@'	0100 0000b	40h	64
'A'	0100 0001b	41h	65
'B'	0100 0010b	42h	66
	.	.	.
	.	.	.
	.	.	.
'a'	0110 0001b	61h	97
'b'	0110 0010b	62h	98
	and so on.		

4.6   Write a program that reads a byte from Port A and send the 1s complement representation to Port B. Note that 1s complement is all bits inverted. *Hint*: In C the 1s complement operator is a tilda (~) and in Pascal it is not.

4.7   Change the program in Exercise 4.6 so that it gives the 2s complement value on Port B. *Hint*: Either complement all the bits of the value and add 1 or send the negated value.

4.8   Modify the program in Exercise 4.1 so that the frequency of the walking-ones is controlled via port A. Table 4.9 shows how the value inputted from port A varies the delay between steps.

Table 4.9 Timing.

Value on Port A	Time between steps
0	No sequence
1	1 second
2	0.5 seconds
3	0.333... seconds
4	0.25 seconds
8	0.125 seconds
.	.
255	1/255 seconds

4.9   Write a program that flashes each of the following bits on Port B at the given frequency. The rate is specified in Table 4.10.

Table 4.10 Bit timings.

Bit	Frequency (Hz)	Comment
0	0.125	1 flash every 8 seconds
1	0.25	1 flash every 4 seconds
2	0.5	1 flash every 2 seconds
3	1	1 flash every second
4	2	2 flashes every second
5	4	4 flashes every second
6	8	8 flashes every second
7	16	16 flashes every second

Hint: The required sequence is:

Sequence	Required bit pattern
0	00000000
1	10000000
2	01000000
3	11000000
4	00100000
5	10100000
6	01100000
7	11100000
8	00010000
.	
.	
.	
255	11111111

Notice that if the bit pattern of the sequence number is turned around then the required pattern is achieved, that is, if bit 0 is swapped with bit 7, bit 1 with bit 6 and so on. The following statement swaps the bits of the variable i and put the result into outval.

```
outval=((seq&1)<< 7) + ((seq&2)<< 5) + ((seq&4)<<3) +
       ((seq&8)<<1) + ((seq&16)>>1) + ((seq&32)>>3) +
       ((seq&64)>>5) + ((seq&128)>>7);
```

The code (seq&1)<<7 masks the least significant bit of the variable seq and then shifts it seven positions to the left. An example conversion is shown next:

seq	bit pattern of seq	bit pattern of outval
1	00000001	10000000
54	00110110	01101100
129	10000001	10000001

4.10   Binary coded decimal (BCD) is used mainly in decimal displays and is equivalent to the decimal system where a 4-bit code represents each decimal number. The first 4 bits represent the units, the next 4 the tens, and so on. Write a program that outputs to port B a BCD sequence with a one-second delay between changes. A sample BCD table is given in Table 4.11. The output should count from 0 to 99.

Table 4.11   BCD conversion.

Digit	BCD
00	00000000
01	00000001
02	00000010
03	00000011
04	00000100
05	00000101
06	00000110
07	00000111
08	00001000
09	00001001
10	00010000
11	00010001
.	.
.	.
.	.
97	10010111
98	10011000
99	10011001

Hint: One possible implementation is to use two variables to represent the units and tens. These would then be used in a nested loop. The resultant output value will then be (tens<<4)+ units. An outline of the loop code is given next.

```
   for (ten=0;tens<10;tens++)
     for (units=0;units<10;units++)
     {


     }
```

4.10 Projects

4.10.1 Project 1: Security system 1

A household security system is controlled by a PC-based system. There are six switch sensors connected to the following:

- Sensor 1: Front door ('0' – closed, '1' – open)
- Sensor 2: Back door
- Sensor 3: Window 1
- Sensor 4: Window 2
- Sensor 5: Window 3
- Sensor 6: Window 4

Each sensor gives a '0' output when a door or window is closed and a '1' when open. There is also a system shut down switch. If the system is to be shut-down this outputs a '1'. A schematic of the layout and the connections to the DIO are shown in Figure 4.12.

Requirements
(1) If any door or window is opened then a message will be displayed on the screen to inform the user there has been a break-in and its location. The message will not clear until the Alarm accept signal is switched to give a '1'.
(2) The system ON/OFF switch will disable the system if the input is a '1'.
(3) If a break-in is detected the alarm output should flash on and off at a frequency of one flash per two seconds (that is, ON for one second and OFF for a second). This will not stop until the Alarm accept signal is a '1'.
(4) If a break-in is detected the system should still monitor all inputs and display messages.
(5) The Alarm accept signal is generated via a push button switch and must be pressed until the Alarm goes off.

4.10.2 Project 2: Security system 2

Modify Project 1 so that the system sets a bit on Port B to indicate that a window or door has been opened (this could be used to connect to an LED on a status panel). Any bit which is set should not be reset until the Alarm accept is pressed. A system schematic is given in Figure 4.13.

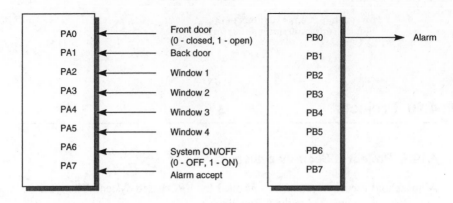

Figure 4.12 System connections.

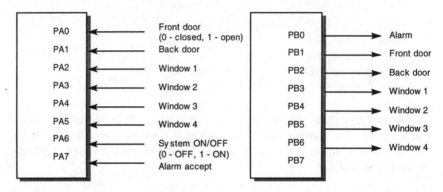

Figure 4.13 System connections.

4.10.3 Project 3: Traffic light controller 1

Design a PC-based control system for a road junction with a single traffic light and a pedestrian crossing. The sequence and timing of each of the individual lights is outlined in Table 4.12.

The traffic light has a pedestrian button which when activated causes the normal sequence to be interrupted and the traffic light goes to RED in a safe manner. For example, if the button is pressed when the sequence is at RED AMBER then the system should follow the normal sequence until it gets back to a RED only then should the pedestrian light become active. A WALK light will be active when pedestrians are allowed to cross the road. This should stay active for four seconds, followed by a flashing WALK light for another four seconds (on for one second and off for one second). When this goes OFF a DON'T WALK light should be ON. The system connections are shown in Figure 4.14 and the system constraints are:

(1) The pedestrian button is a push button type and may only be pressed for a

short time. It can also be pressed at any time in the sequence. The minimum time for a button press is 0.5 seconds. Thus the program must be able to scan the pedestrian button at least twice a second and remember if it has been pressed.

(2) The system should act in a predictable manner, that is, RED/AMBER must always follow RED, GREEN follows RED/ AMBER, AMBER follows GREEN and RED follows AMBER. Sequence timings should also be unaffected by the pedestrian switch status.

(3) Safety is the most critical factor. The DON'T WALK light should always be on when the AMBER or GREEN lights are on and the WALK should only be on when the RED light is on.

Table 4.12 Traffic light timings.

Sequence No.	Sequence	Timing (seconds)
1	RED	6
2	RED/AMBER	1
3	GREEN	4
4	AMBER	2
1	RED	6
2	RED/AMBER	1
	and so on.	

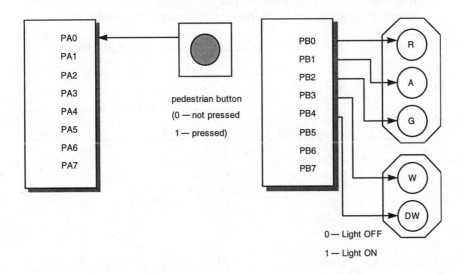

Figure 4.14 System connections.

4.10.4 Project 4: Traffic light controller 2

Design a PC-based control system for a road junction with two traffic lights. The sequence and timing of each of the individual lights is outlined in Table 4.13.

Each traffic light has a pedestrian button which, when activated, causes the normal sequence to be interrupted and the traffic lights to go to RED in a safe manner. For example if the button is pressed when the sequence is at RED/AMBER then the system should follow the normal sequence until it gets back to a RED, only then should the pedestrian light become active. A WALK light actives when pedestrians are allowed to cross the road. This should be active for four seconds, followed by a flashing WALK light for another four seconds (on for one second and off for one second). When this goes OFF the DON'T WALK light should be ON. The system connections are shown in Figure 4.15 and the system constraints are:

(1) The pedestrian button is a push button type and may only be pressed for a short time. It can also be pressed at any time in the sequence. The minimum time for a button press is 0.5 seconds. Thus the program must be able to scan the pedestrian button at least twice a second and remember if it has been pressed.

(2) The system should act in a predictable manner, that is, RED/AMBER must always follow RED, GREEN follows RED/ AMBER, AMBER follows GREEN and RED follows AMBER. Sequence timings should also be unaffected by the pedestrian switch status.

(3) Safety is the most critical factor. The DON'T WALK light should always be on when the AMBER or GREEN lights are on and the WALK should only be on when the RED light is on.

(4) If any one of the pedestrian buttons are pressed then both traffic lights should go to RED and pedestrians at both junctions will be allowed to cross.

(5) The WALK/ DON'T WALK lights are common to both traffic lights.

Table 4.13   Traffic light timings.

Sequence No.	Sequence (traffic light 1)	Sequence (traffic light 2)	Timing (seconds)
1	RED	RED	6
2	RED	RED/AMBER	1
3	RED	GREEN	4
4	RED	AMBER	2
5	RED	RED	6
6	RED/AMBER	RED	1
7	GREEN	RED	4
8	AMBER	RED	2
1	RED	RED	6
2	RED	RED/AMBER	1
	and so on.	and so on.	

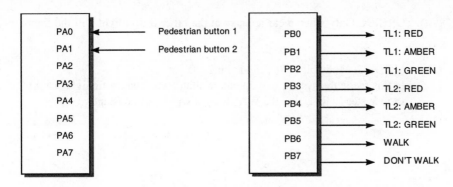

Figure 4.15 System connections.

4.10.5 Project 5 : Traffic light controller 3

Design a PC-based stand-alone system for a road junction with two traffic lights, as specified in Project 4. The system set-up is shown in Figure 4.16. It works in a number of modes which are programmed using two switches connected to Mode bit 1 and Mode bit 2. Each traffic light also has a radar detector attached. Radar 1 monitors the traffic on traffic light 1 and radar 2 on traffic light 2. If a car is waiting at a traffic light then the radar returns a '1' else it will give a '0'.

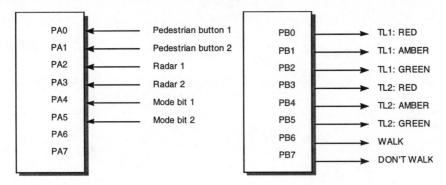

Figure 4.16 System set-up.

There are three different modes of operation, these are set by Mode bit 1 and Mode bit 2. The modes are:

(1) MODE 0: Mode bit 1='0', Mode bit 2='0'
In this mode the system operates as in Project 4.

(2) MODE 1: Mode bit 1='0', Mode bit 2='1'
In this mode the radar gives priority to the traffic light at which there are cars waiting. If there are no cars at one of the traffic lights, then this traffic light should show a steady RED and the other remains a constant

GREEN. Only when a car appears at the other traffic light will the lights change.

(3)   MODE 2: Mode bit 1='1', Mode bit 2='0'
       In this mode the system will operate a shutdown. The traffic lights should show a steady RED and the WALK light will be on constantly.

5
Programmable timer/counter

5.1 Introduction

Many events require to be timed or the number of occurrences of the event monitored. The PC could achieve this by connecting an input to a PPI and then continually monitoring the input. A transition from a low to a high (or vice versa) could signal the start of an event and the opposite transition its end. This is time-consuming as the PC would have to monitor the input continually. It may also not be able to monitor the event fast enough to capture a short event. An event may be as short as a fraction of a second and as long as many years. A better solution is to use an IC that is specially designed to count or time pulses. Using this IC allows the PC to conduct other tasks and simply interrogate the IC when it has time.

Figure 5.1 shows some applications of a counter. The speed of a motor can

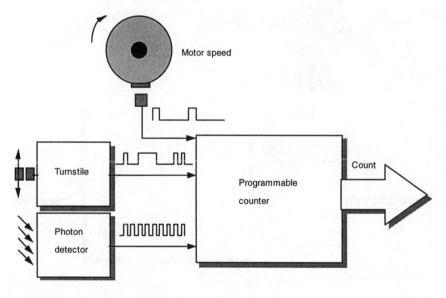

Figure 5.1   Some applications of a programmable counter.

be determined if a sensor is attached to the rotor so that a pulse is produced for each revolution. From these pulses the speed can be determined (for example, 10 pulses per second translates to 10 rev/sec). The counter could also be connected to a turnstile to count the number of people entering a building, or count the number of cars passing a junction and so on.

Some applications of a programmable timer are shown in Figure 5.2. It shows the control of a motor (for example, ON for a certain time), controlling the frequency of an alarm signal and a timer for street lights (for example, ON for 12 hours and OFF for 12 hours).

PC systems can be fitted with an 8253 PTC (programmable timer/counter) integrated circuit (IC) to give timing and counting capabilities. Each IC has 24 pins and contains three timer/counters, each of which can be programmed with differing functions. Typically, they are fitted onto a multifunction DIO interface card, as shown in Figure 5.3, or are fitted to a counter/timer I/O board. The base address at which these ICs map into the isolated memory is normally set by in-line switches or wire jumpers. Connection to external equipment is typically achieved via a D-type connector or two 50-way IDC connectors.

The connections to each timer/counter are:

- CLOCK INPUT
- GATE
- OUTPUT

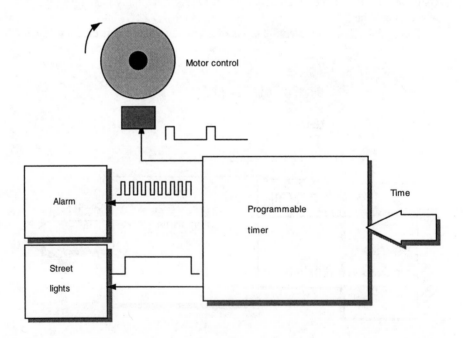

Figure 5.2   Some applications of a programmable timer.

The input line is CLOCK INPUT, the output is OUTPUT and the timer is disabled/enabled by the GATE line. When the GATE is high the timer is enabled, else it is disabled. If the GATE is not connected the input level floats. This is sensed as a HIGH input and the counter will be active.

Each counter has a 16-bit counter register which gives a count range of 0000000000000000b (0 or 0000h) to 1111111111111111b (65 535 or FFFFh) and it always counts down. A diagram of a counter is given in Figure 5.4.

A single control register programs the three timer/ counters on each IC. Its address is set with respect to the base address, as given in Table 5.1.

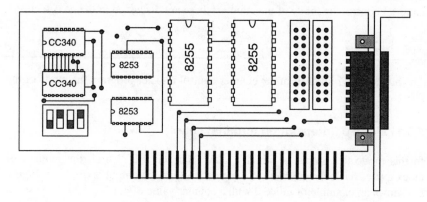

Figure 5.3   DIO with PTC ICs.

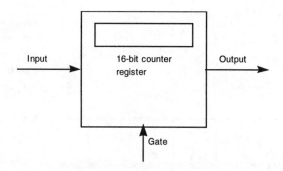

Figure 5.4   Diagram of counter/timer circuit.

Table 5.1   PTC addresses.

Function	Address	Used as
Counter 0 Read/Write Buffer	BASE_ADDRESS	16-bit register
Counter 1 Read/Write Buffer	BASE_ADDRESS+1	16-bit register
Counter 2 Read/Write Buffer	BASE_ADDRESS+2	16-bit register
Counter Control Register	BASE_ADDRESS+3	To program the counters

5.2 Control register

The control register programs the functionality of each of the three counters/timers. Figure 5.5 shows the format of this register. The counter to be programmed is set up by setting bits SC1 and SC0. If a PC card is used then only 8 bits can be loaded to or read from the PTC at a time. Thus to access the 16-bit counter register there must be two read or write operations. The method of access is controlled by bits RL1 and RL0. If these are set to 11 then the first byte written/read to/from the counter register is the LSB (least significant byte). The next write/read accesses the MSB (the most significant byte). Mode bits M2, M1 and M0 control the mode of the counter; these are discussed in the next section.

5.3 Modes

The bits M2, M1 and M0 in the counter control register program the mode of the PTC.

5.3.1 Mode 0 (interrupt on terminal count)

In this mode the output is initially LOW and stay LOW until the number of clock cycles has been counted. If the gate is LOW the output is disabled. Figure 5.6 shows an example of mode 0 with a counter value of 4.

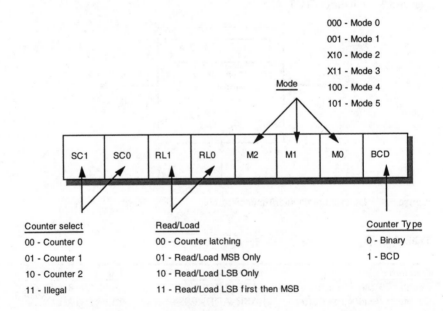

Figure 5.5   Timer control register bit definition.

5.3.2 Mode 1 (programmable one-shot)

The programmable one-shot mode is similar to mode 0, but the output starts initially HIGH. The output goes LOW at the start of the count and remains LOW until the count finishes. It then goes HIGH. The count is initiated by a LOW to HIGH transition on the GATE input. A LOW or HIGH level on the GATE after this has no effect on the count. Figure 5.7 shows an example of mode 1 with a counter value of 4.

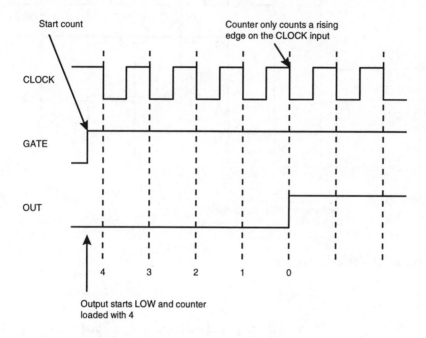

Figure 5.6   Mode 0 operation.

5.3.3 Mode 2 (rate generator)

In this mode the inputted Clock pulses are divided by the value in the counter register. The output goes LOW for one cycle and HIGH for the rest of the cycle. Figure 5.8 shows an example of mode 2 with a counter value of 4. In this case the output is HIGH for three cycles and LOW for one. As with mode 1 the count is initiated by a LOW to HIGH transition on the GATE.

5.3.4 Mode 3 (square wave generator)

The square wave generator is similar to mode 2 but the output is a square wave when the value in the counter is even or is HIGH for an extra cycle more when the value of the count is odd. Figure 5.9 shows an example of mode 3 with a counter value of 4. In this case the output is LOW for 2 cycles and HIGH for 2 cycles.

If the counter is loaded with 5 the output is HIGH for 3 cycles and LOW for 2. As with mode 1 the count is initiated by a LOW to HIGH transition on the GATE.

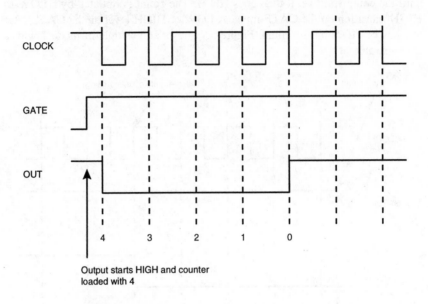

Output starts HIGH and counter loaded with 4

Figure 5.7   Mode 1 operation.

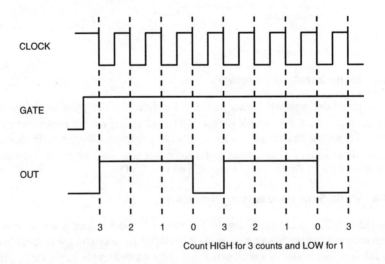

Count HIGH for 3 counts and LOW for 1

Figure 5.8   Mode 2 operation.

68   *Programmable timer/counter*

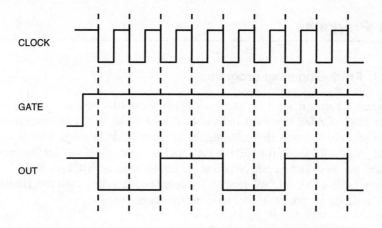

Count HIGH for 2 counts and LOW for 2

Figure 5.9 Mode 3 operation.

5.3.5 Mode 4 (software triggered strobe)

This mode is similar to mode 2 except that the GATE does not initiate the count. The output goes HIGH for the count and goes LOW for one clock cycle. The output then goes back to HIGH.

5.3.6 Mode 5 (hardware triggered strobe)

This mode is similar to mode 2 except that the GATE input has no effect on the count. It starts counting after the rising edge of the input and then goes LOW for one clock period when the count is reached.

Table 5.2 summarizes the control that the gate has on the mode.

Table 5.2 Gate control.

Mode	GATE LOW	GATE LOW-HIGH transition	GATE HIGH	Output signal
0	Disable	None	Enable	see Figure 5.6
1	None	Initiate counting	None	see Figure 5.7
2	Disable. Set output HIGH	Initiate counting	Enable	see Figure 5.8
3	Disable. Set output HIGH	Initiate counting	Enable	see Figure 5.9
4	Disable	None	Enable	As mode 2
5	None	Start count	None	As mode 2

5.4 Programs

5.4.1 Producing timer programs

Program 5.1 uses mode 3 to produce a square wave of a frequency which is the input clock divided by an entered value. This clock input can be taken from an electronic clock output (for example, 25 kHz) or could be taken from a switch input. An oscilloscope (or LED if the input is relatively slow) can be used to display the input and output. Note that the GATE must be HIGH in order for the counter to be active, a LOW disables the count and sets the output to a HIGH.

The mode of counter 0 is set up using the statement:

```
outportb(CNTRL_REG, 0x36);
```

which loads the bit pattern 0011 0110b into the control register. Taking each of the bits in turn, starting from the most significant bit, then 00 sets up counter 0, 11 specifies that the LSB will be loaded into counter register then the MSB, 011 selects mode 3 and 0 specifies a binary count.

The statement:

```
outportb(COUNTER0, d & 0x00FF);
```

masks off the least significant byte (LSB) of the variable d and puts it into the LSB of the counter register. The most significant byte of d is then loaded into the MSB of the counter by the following statement:

```
outportb(COUNTER0, d >> 8);
```

This uses the shift right operator (>>) to move the MSB bits eight positions to the right (that is, into the LSB positions).

📄 Program 5.1

```
/* This program divides the input clock on counter 0    */
/* by an entered value. The GATE is set to a HIGH and    */
/* the output is OUT0.                                    */

#include <stdio.h>
#include <dos.h>

#define   BASE_ADDRESS   0x1F8 /* change for system used on */
#define   COUNTER0       BASE_ADDRESS
#define   COUNTER1       (BASE_ADDRESS+1)
#define   COUNTER2       (BASE_ADDRESS+2)
#define   CNTRL_REG      (BASE_ADDRESS+3)

void   set_up_PTC(int);   /* ANSI C prototype definitions   */
int    main(void)
{
int    Divide;

    puts("Enter the value the clock to be divided by>");
```

```
        scanf("%d",&Divide);
        set_up_PTC(Divide);

        puts("The Programmable counter is programmed");
        return(0);
}

void set_up_PTC(int d)
{
        outportb(CNTRL_REG, 0x36);
            /*0011 0110 - Binary Select (0)                           */
            /*Mode Select 3 (011) Square wave generator               */
            /*Read/Load Low Byte then High Byte (11)                  */
            /*Counter 0 selected (0)                                  */

        outportb(COUNTER0, d & 0x00FF);/*Load low byte into counter*/
        outportb(COUNTER0, d >> 8);  /*Load high byte into counter  */
}
```

Once the hardware is programmed, there it performs the same task until either it is reprogrammed or the power is taken away. The program can end and the hardware continues to divide the input. Program 5.2 is the Turbo Pascal equivalent program. Program 5.3 uses mode 2 to produce a rate generator and Program 5.4 gives the Pascal equivalent.

📄 Program 5.2

```
program ptc(input,output);
{   This program divides the input clock on counter 0      }
{   by an entered value. The GATE is set to a HIGH and     }
{   the output is OUT0.                                    }
const
        BASE_ADDRESS    =   $1F8; { change if required          }
        COUNTER0        =   BASE_ADDRESS;
        COUNTER1        =   BASE_ADDRESS+1;
        COUNTER2        =   BASE_ADDRESS+2;
        CNTRL_REG       =   BASE_ADDRESS+3;

var     divide:integer;

procedure set_up_PTC(d:integer);
begin
    port[CNTRL_REG] := $36;
        {011 0110 - Binary Select (0)                        }
        {Mode Select 3 (011) Square wave generator           }
        {Read/Load Low Byte then High Byte (11)              }
        {Counter 0 selected (0)                              }

    port[COUNTER0] := d and $00FF;   { Low byte counter      }
    port[COUNTER0] := d shr 8;       { High byte counter     }
end;

begin

    writeln('Enter the value the clock to be divided by>');
    readln(Divide);

    set_up_PTC(Divide);
    writeln('The Programmable counter is programmed');

end.
```

📄 Program 5.3

```
/*    This program divides the input clock on counter 0        */
/*    by an entered value to produce a rate generator.         */
/*    The GATE is set to a HIGH and the output is OUT0.         */
/*    The output goes LOW for one cycle then HIGH for the rest  */

#define     BASE_ADDRESS     0x1F8 /* change for system used on    */
#define  COUNTER0     BASE_ADDRESS
#define  COUNTER1     (BASE_ADDRESS+1)
#define  COUNTER2     (BASE_ADDRESS+2)
#define  CNTRL_REG       (BASE_ADDRESS+3)

#include <stdio.h>
#include <dos.h>

void        set_up_PTC(int);  /* ANSI C prototype definition   */

int   main(void)
{
int    Divide;
    puts("Enter value clock to be divided by>>");
    scanf("%d",&Divide);
    set_up_PTC(Divide);
    puts("The Programmable counter is programmed");

    return(0);
}

void  set_up_PTC(int d)
{
    outportb(CNTRL_REG, 0x34);
        /*0011 0100 - Binary Select (0)                         */
        /*Mode Select 2 (010) Rate generator                    */
        /*Read/Load Low Byte then High Byte (11)                */
        /*Counter 0 selected (0)                                */

    outportb(COUNTER0, d & 0x00FF);/*Load low byte into counter*/
    outportb(COUNTER0, d >> 8);   /*Load high byte into counter   */
}
```

📄 Program 5.4

```
program ptc_2(input,output);
{ This program will divide an inputted clock by an         }
{ entered value on counter 0 to give a rate generator.     }
{ The input is CLK0 and the GATE is set to a HIGH,         }
{ the output will be OUT0. Note the output will go LOW     }
{ for one cycle HIGH for the rest.                         }

const
     BASE_ADDRESS =   $1F8; { change if required }
     COUNTER0    =  BASE_ADDRESS;
     COUNTER1    =  BASE_ADDRESS+1;
     COUNTER2    =  BASE_ADDRESS+2;
     CNTRL_REG   =  BASE_ADDRESS+3;

var divide:integer;

procedure set_up_PTC(d:integer);
begin
    port[CNTRL_REG] := $34;
        {0011 0100 - Binary Select (0)                          }
```

72   *Programmable timer/counter*

```
        {Mode Select 2 (010) Rate generator            }
        {Read/Load Low Byte then High Byte (11)         }
        {Counter 0 selected (0)                         }
    port[COUNTER0] := d and $00FF;   { Low byte counter  }
    port[COUNTER0] := d div 256;     { High byte counter }
end;

begin
    writeln('Enter the val the clock is to be divided by>');
    readln(Divide);
    set_up_PTC(Divide);
    writeln('The Programmable counter is programmed');
end.
```

Program 5.5 is an assembly language program, divide by 10 counter.

📄 Program 5.5

```
code            SEGMENT
                ASSUME cs:code
BASEADDRESS     EQU     01F8H      ; change this as required
COUNTER0        EQU     BASEADDRESS
COUNTER1        EQU     BASEADDRESS+1
CNTRLREG        EQU     BASEADDRESS+3
; 8088 program to set up divide by 10 counter.
start:
        mov dx,CNTRLREG   ; Control Reg.
        mov al,36h        ; see ptc_1.c
        out dx,al          ; Square wave, etc.
        mov dx,COUNTER0
        mov dx,10         ; Low byte
        out al,dx
        mov al,00         ; High byte
        out al,dx
        mov ah,4cH        ; program exit
        int 21h           ;
code    ENDS
        END     start
```

Program 5.6 contains bit definitions for the control register assignments. This allows the set_up_PTC() to be passed the required status parameters. For example, to program counter 2 with mode 3, binary count and load/read LSB then MSB, the function call would be:

```
set_up_PTC(MODE3, C2, BINARY, R_L_LSB_MSB, divide);
```

This makes the set_up_PTC() function more general purpose as it can now be used to program each of the counters.

📄 Program 5.6

```
#include <stdio.h>
#include <dos.h>
#define  BASE_ADDRESS   0x1F8 /* change for system used on */
#define  COUNTER0       BASE_ADDRESS
#define  COUNTER1       (BASE_ADDRESS+1)
#define  COUNTER2       (BASE_ADDRESS+2)
#define  CNTRL_REG      (BASE_ADDRESS+3)
```

```
enum      c_modes        {MODE0=0,MODE1,MODE2,MODE3,MODE4,MODE5};
enum      counters       {C0=0,C1,C2};
enum      counttype      {BINARY,BCD};
enum      readloadtype   {COUNTLATCH=0,R_L_MSB,R_L_LSB,R_L_LSB_MSB};

void      set_up_PTC(int mode,int counter, int ctype, int ltype,
                     int d);

int   main(void)
{
int   divide;

    puts("Enter number of clock cycles to be counted>");
    scanf("%d",&Divide);
    set_up_PTC(MODE1, C2, BINARY, R_L_LSB_MSB, divide);
    puts("The Programmable counter is programmed");
    return(0);
}

void  set_up_PTC(int mode,int counter, int ctype, int ltype, int d)
{
/* mode      - mode of counter, i.e. mode 0-5         */
/* counter - counter to be programmed 0-2             */
/* ctype     - count type Binary or BCD               */
/* ltype     - type of load e.g. LSB first then MSB   */
/* d          - divide value                          */
int   c_register=0;

    c_register=ctype | (mode<<1) | (ltype<<4) | (counter<<6);
    outportb(CNTRL_REG, c_register);
    outportb(COUNTER0, d & 0x00FF);
    outportb(COUNTER0, d >> 8);
}
```

An alternative method to the bit shifting used in Program 5.5 is to define
each of the control register values with their associated bit values. For example:

```
enum      c_modes        {  MODE0=0x00,MODE1=0x02,MODE2=0x40,
                            MODE3=0x06,MODE4=0x08,MODE5=0x0A};
enum      counters       {  C0=0x00,C1=0x40,C2=0x80};
enum      counttype      {  BINARY=0x00,BCD=0x01};
enum      readloadtype   {  COUNTLATCH=0x00,R_L_MSB=0x10,
                            R_L_LSB=0x20,R_L_LSB_MSB=0x30};
```

The set_up_PTC() function would then only use the OR bitwise operator to
determine the control register value, as shown next.

```
void  set_up_PTC(int mode,int counter,
                 int ctype, int ltype, int d)
{
int       c_register=0;

    c_register=ctype | mode | ltype | counter;

    outportb(CNTRL_REG, c_register);

    outportb(COUNTER0, d & 0x00FF);
    outportb(COUNTER0, d >> 8);
}
```

5.4.2 Pulse counting programs

In the following programs the PTC counts a number of clock pulses on counter 0. These pulses could be generated by many means, such as from switches, clock pulses, and so on. The counter always counts down and is initialized with 1111 1111 1111 1111b with the lines:

```
outportb(CNTRL_REG, 0x30);
outportb(COUNTER0,0xff);    /* load LSB */
outportb(COUNTER0,0xff);    /* load MSB */
```

and this is latched into the counter register using the statement:

```
outportb(CNTRL_REG, 0x00);
```

The getcount() function contains the statements given next. It reads the LSB and MSB of the counter register. Then scales them so that the MSB is placed above the LSB. This is achieved by shifting the bits in the MSB by eight positions to the left. The scaled value is then subtracted from the initialized value to produce the final count.

```
lsb=inportb(portid);
msb=inportb(portid);
return(0xffff-(lsb+(msb<<8)));
```

Program 5.7

```
/* Program which will determine the number of       */
/* clock pulses on Counter 0                         */
#include <stdio.h>
#include <dos.h>
#include <conio.h>    /* required for clrscr() and kbhit()   */

#define  BASE_ADDRESS    0x1F8 /* change for system used on   */
#define  COUNTER0        BASE_ADDRESS
#define  COUNTER1        (BASE_ADDRESS+1)
#define  COUNTER2        (BASE_ADDRESS+2)
#define  CNTRL_REG       (BASE_ADDRESS+3)

int      getcount(int portid);
void     set_up_PTC(void);

int      main(void)
{
int      count;

    set_up_PTC();

    do
    {
        clrscr();
        count=getcount(COUNTER0);
        printf("count is %d\n",count);
        delay(1000);
    } while (!kbhit());
    return(0);
}
```

```c
void   set_up_PTC(void)
{
    outportb(CNTRL_REG, 0x30);

    outportb(COUNTER0,0xff);        /* reset counter */
    outportb(COUNTER0,0xff);        /* reset counter */

    outportb(CNTRL_REG, 0x00);      /* latch counter */
}
int      getcount(int portid)
{
int       lsb,msb;
    /* Count starts from 0xffff and then counts down      */
    lsb=inportb(portid);
    msb=inportb(portid);
    return(0xffff-(lsb+(msb<<8)));
}
```

📄 Program 5.8

```pascal
program ptc5(input,output);
{ Program which will determine the number of           }
{ clock pulses on Counter 0                            }
uses crt;

const
      BASE_ADDRESS =  $1F8; { change if required          }
      COUNTER0      =  BASE_ADDRESS;
      COUNTER1      =  BASE_ADDRESS+1;
      COUNTER2      =  BASE_ADDRESS+2;
      CNTRL_REG     =  BASE_ADDRESS+3;

var count:integer;

function getcount(portid:integer):integer;
var       lsb,msb:integer;
begin
   lsb:= port[portid];
   msb:= port[portid];
   getcount:= $ffff-((msb shl 8) + lsb);
end;

procedure set_up_PTC;
begin
   port[CNTRL_REG] := $30;
   port[COUNTER0]  := $ff; { reset counter register      }
   port[COUNTER0]  := $ff; { reset counter register      }
   port[CNTRL_REG] := $00; { latch counter value         }
end;

begin
      set_up_PTC;
      repeat
         clrscr;

         count:=getcount(COUNTER0);
         writeln('Count is ',count);
         delay(1000);

      until keypressed;
end.
```

5.5 Exercises

Note: For some of the timing programs a fast clock input may be required. For example, if a system is to produce a 1 second clock then a 1kHz clock input can be used. The timer will then divide the input clock by 1000, giving the required 1 Hz frequency. Typical clock frequencies are 1 kHz, 10 kHz, 100 kHz and 1 MHz.

5.1   Write a program that determines the input clock rate per minute. The screen should be updated at least every 15 seconds. For example, a sample could be taken every 15 seconds then scaled to show the number of clock pulses per minute (ppm). A sample run is shown in Test run 5.1.

🖥 Test run 5.1

```
Input Rate >> 60 ppm
Input Rate >> 44 ppm
Input Rate >> 32 ppm
```

5.2   Write a program that samples an electronic clock signal (such as 10 kHz, 100 kHz, and so on) and displays the clock frequency to the screen. The program should continually monitor the input and display the updated value every five seconds. Test run 5.2 is an example of a 10 kHz input clock.

🖥 Test run 5.2

```
Frequency >> 9654 Hz
Frequency >> 10030 kHz
Frequency >> 10100 kHz
```

5.3   Write a program that makes an LED (light emitting diode) ON at the start of the count, then goes OFF for one second and back ON after one second.

5.4   Write a program that generates an output frequency of 1 kHz. This could be achieved by inputting a 100 kHz clock and dividing by 100.

5.5   Write a program that generates a single shot pulse duration of two seconds. The output must be HIGH initially then go LOW for the two seconds and HIGH again.

5.6   Write a program that generates an output which is LOW for 40 µs then HIGH for 200 µs; this then repeats.

6
Analogue to Digital Conversion

6.1 Analogue/ digital systems

The analogue/ digital (A/D) conversion bridges the gap between the digital and analogue worlds. Figure 6.1 shows a typical analogue/digital system. Inputs to the system take the form of physical, chemical or biological stimulus; a transducer converts these into electrical signals. Examples of transducers are pressure sensors, thermocouples (to measure temperature), light detectors, and so on. The amplitude of the electrical signals produced by transducers is normally relatively small. In order for them to be inputted into a digital converter they must then be amplified to produce the required electrical level. An analogue-to-digital converter (ADC) then converts the signal into a digital form. A computer, or processor, can then store and/ or process these digital values to generate electrical signals via a digital-to-analogue converter (DAC). Note that an analogue/ digital system does not need to have inputs and outputs. It could consist of purely of analogue inputs or purely of analogue outputs.

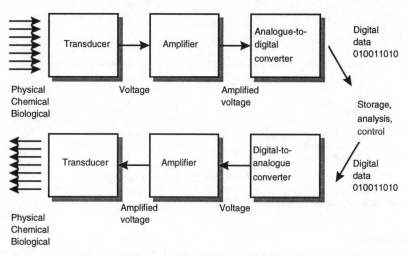

Figure 6.1   Analogue/ digital system.

6.2 Transducers and sensors

A transducer converts one form of energy into another. This section discusses some of the available measurement techniques, and typical sensors and transducers.

6.2.1 Temperature

There are several methods of converting temperature into an electrical signal; these include thermocouples, thermistors, infra-red sensors and temperature ICs.

Thermocouple
Thermocouples are probes with two metals joined at a junction. The number of free electrons in a metal depends on the temperature and its type. If two dissimilar metals join then the contact produces a voltage difference that varies directly with temperature (over a given range).

The sensor consists of a measuring and a reference junction (often know as the hot and cold junctions). The resultant voltage relates to the temperature difference between the two, as shown in Figure 6.2.

Figure 6.3 shows a typical thermocouple conversion. In this case the conversion factor is 50°C per 2 mV or 25°C/mV. The output from the thermocouple is normal amplified to give a voltage between 0 and +5 V.

There are three main types used, these are type K (–50°C to +1000°C), type T (–100°C to +325°C) and type J (–25 °C to +625°C). Type J uses nickel-chromium/nickel-aluminium, type T copper/copper-nickel and type J iron/copper-nickel. The accuracy of a thermocouple is around ± 1°C.

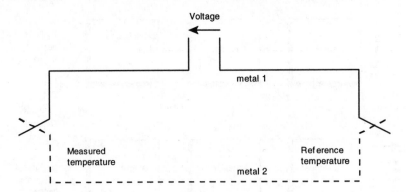

Figure 6.2   A thermocouple.

Thermistor
A thermistor is a specially designed resistor that has a predictable change in resistance over a large temperature range. They either have a negative temperature coefficient (ntc) or a positive temperature coefficient (ptc). Most

semiconductors have a ntc, as their resistance increases with a decrease in temperature and viceversa. For a measured resistance a simple look-up table for the thermistor determines its temperature.

Thermistors are generally either a bead type (contained in glass or a metal enclosure) or disk type. They are normally specified as their resistance at 25°C. Standard thermistors include 1 KΩ, 4.7 KΩ, 10 KΩ, 47 KΩ, 220 KΩ, 470 KΩ and 350 KΩ. Each has a standard calibration table that maps resistance to temperature. For example, a typical 1 KΩ thermistor has a resistance of 100 KΩ at –60°C, 10 KΩ at –30 °C, 1 KΩ at 25°C and 100 Ω at +100°C. Typical tolerances are ± 10%.

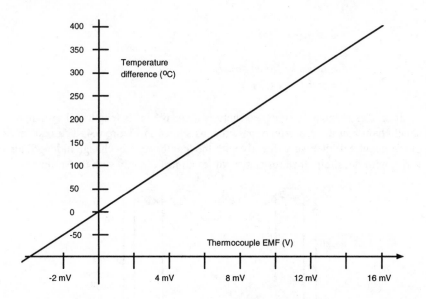

Figure 6.3 Typical thermocouple conversion.

Infra-red sensor
The infra-red energy emitted from an object varies with its temperature. By measuring this infra-red an estimation of its temperature is achieved. This technique generates a colour map of the object whose colours are compared to the colours of a known object at a constant reference temperature. It is an extremely useful method if the object is extremely hot (such as the sun or a furnace) as the sensor does not touch the object (non-obtrusive testing). It is also used to detect minute signals, such as detecting tumours, searching for survivors under rubble and to take thermal pictures of houses to detect heat loss.

Temperature sensor IC
A typical temperature sensor IC is the LM35. This provides a linear voltage change of 10 mV per °C and has an accuracy of around ± 0.4°C.

6.2.2 Pressure measurements

Pressure measurements are used in many applications, such as in sound recording, in measuring the stress on bridges, on weighing machines, and so on.

Stain gauge

The resistance of a conductor relates to its resistivity, its length and its cross-sectional area. It is given by:

$$R = \frac{\rho L}{A}$$

where R = resistance (Ω)
L = length (m)
A = cross sectional area (m^2)
ρ = resistivity (Ω.m)

If an elastic metal is stretched there is a change in its length and a relatively small change in the cross-sectional area, as shown in Figure 6.4. The resistance of the metal will then vary directly with the length. As this change in length also varies with the strain, then resistance varies almost directly with the strain.

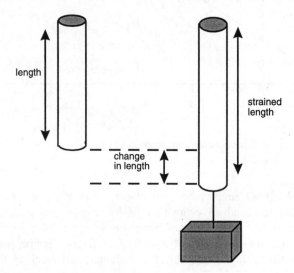

Figure 6.4   Metal conductor under strain.

A strain gauge is useful in measuring pressure, force, torque and movement. Typically, they consist of an aluminium or copper-nickel foil track on a polyester printed circuit board (PCB), as shown in Figure 6.5. A strain gauge amplifier then converts the change in resistance to a voltage level. The most common metal used for the foil is a copper-nickel alloy as the change in its resistance is virtually proportional to the strain.

Capacitive transducer

A parallel plate capacitor has a capacitance that varies directly with the area of the plates and inversely with the distance between the plates. It is given by:

$$C = \frac{\varepsilon_0 A}{d} \quad F$$

where $\varepsilon_0 = 8.854 \times 10^{-12}$ $F.m^{-1}$

Distance or displacement can either be measured by varying the distance between the plates and keeping the cross-sectional area constant or by varying the cross-sectional area and keeping the distance between the plates constant. To measure distance one of the plates is fixed and the other moves parallel to the fixed plate. As the cross-sectional area remains constant then the capacitance of the plates varies directly by the distance between them, as shown in Figure 6.6.

When measuring displacement one of the plates is fixed and the other moves laterally. The common cross-sectional area of the plates will thus vary. Since the distance between the plates is constant then the capacitance varies indirectly with the displacement, as shown in Figure 6.7.

A capacitive transducer is typically used as a pressure sensor. If one plate is fixed and the other is able to move then the capacitance varies with the applied pressure. By a similar method an inductive transducer, which depends on magnetic fields, can be constructed. These tend to be less linear than equivalent capacitive methods and are mainly used to detect the presence of a metal object.

Piezo-electric crystals

When a force is applied to a quartz crystal it produces a small emf (voltage level). This varies directly with the force and has a conversion factor which is constant over a wide range (typically 0.05 $(V/m)/(N/m^2)$). Piezo-electric crystals are extremely accurate and have a high resolution. They are typically used in applications to measure relatively small changes of pressure, such as vibration monitors and pressure sensors, and to convert sound to electrical energy, typically in microphones and pick-ups on acoustic guitars. Problems can occur as the generated signal is extremely small and can be affected by pick-up noise, poor connections and unsuitable cabling.

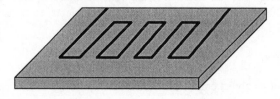

Figure 6.5 Bounded strain gauge.

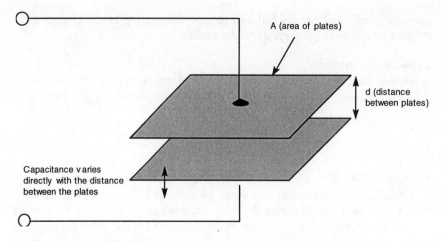

A (area of plates)

d (distance between plates)

Capacitance varies directly with the distance between the plates

Figure 6.6   Variation of capacitance with respect to distance between plates.

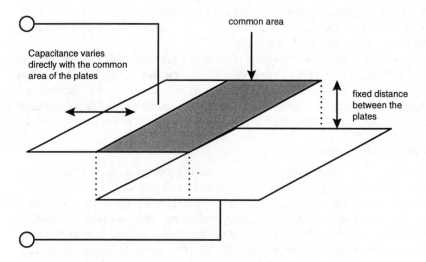

common area

Capacitance varies directly with the common area of the plates

fixed distance between the plates

Figure 6.7   Variation of capacitance with respect to plate displacement.

Piezo-electric cells can also detect and transmit high frequency sound such as ultrasound. This is used in applications to detect objects, to transmit messages, in echo-search sensors, and so on.

6.2.3 Position

The position of an object can be detected either by:

- Bouncing pulses off the object with radio waves, optical or ultrasonic waves and measuring the delay between the transmitted and returned pulse – if the speed of propagation is known then the distance is simply the propagation velocity multiplied by half the time taken for the wave to propagate to the object and back;

- Passive electrical methods such as capacitive, resistive or inductive transducers.

6.2.4 Sound

Sound can be detected by converting a change in air pressure into an electrical signal. Typically a capacitive transducer is used if the sound waves are relatively strong and piezo-electric transducers for small changes; these are shown in Figure 6.8.

6.2.5 Acceleration and velocity

Velocity is the change in distance with respect to time. A change of velocity with respect to time gives acceleration. Velocity and acceleration measurements normally consist of either strain gauges or position monitors to detect a change of position of an object of a test mass.

6.2.6 Light

Photo-current: Photodiodes and phototransistors

Photodiodes and phototransistors convert light energy (photons) into an electrical current. The symbols for these are given in Figure 6.9. Their operation is based on the fact that the number of free electrons generated in a semiconductor material is proportional to the incident light intensity. A photodiode operates in a reverse biased mode. The reverse bias current produced is a measure of the incident light intensity. With the correct semiconductor doping they can operate in the infra-red, visible light and ultra-violet regions. A basic gallium arsenside (GaAs) photodiode detects infra-red. If doped with phosphide it can be made to detect orange-red light. Gallium phosphide detects green visible light.

Photo-conductive cell

The resistance of a photo-conductive cell varies with the amount of incident light. Typically this type of sensor is used in an automatic street lighting system.

Photo-voltaic cell

The voltage produced by a photo-voltaic cell varies with the amount of incident light. A typical cell is made from selenium and is used in many camera light meters.

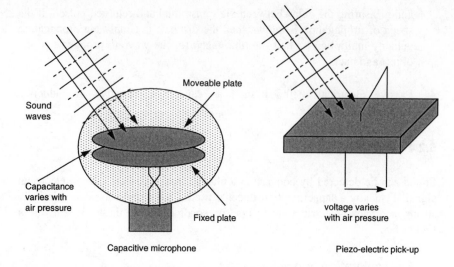

Figure 6.8 Capacitive and piezo-electric transducers.

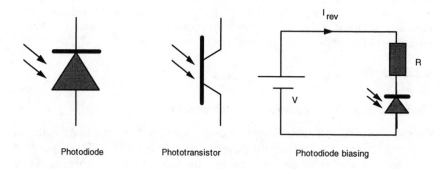

Figure 6.9 Photodiode and phototransistor.

6.2.7 Flow

There are three main methods used to measure flow:

(1) Turbine – A turbine flowmeter consists of a small axial turbine connected to a magnetic pick-up, as shown in Figure 6.10. The output digital frequency of the pick-up varies with the flow rate. This can be converted to a voltage via a frequency-to-voltage converter.

(2) Electromagnetic – An electromagnetic flowmeter uses Faraday's principle of magnetic induction. The induced voltage between a pair of insulated electrodes varies as the speed of the liquid passing between them. The advantage of this method is that it is non-obtrusive but it tends to be bulky to fit. It also requires the liquid to be a good conductor of electricity.

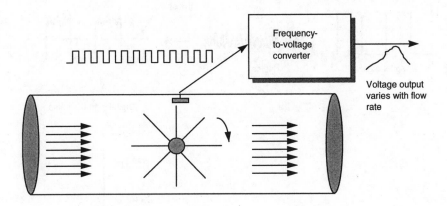

Figure 6.10 Turbine flow rate transducer.

(3) Doppler – A Doppler detector uses the Doppler-shift principle to detect flow rates. The frequency difference between transmitted and reflected ultrasonic waves is a measure of the flow rate.

6.3 Comparison of analogue and digital technology

The main advantage of digital technology over analogue is that digital signals are less affected by noise. Any unwanted distortion added to a signal is described as noise. This could be generated by external equipment producing airborne static, from other signals coupling into the signal's path (cross-talk), from within electrical components, from recording and playback media, and so on. Figure 6.11 shows an example digital signal with noise added to it. The comparator outputs a HIGH level (a '1') if the signal voltage is greater than the threshold voltage, else it outputs a LOW. If the noise voltage is less than the threshold voltage then the noise will not affect the recovered signal. Even if the noise is greater than this threshold there are techniques which can reduce its effect. For example, extra bits can be added to the data either to detect errors or to correct the bits in error.

Large amounts of storage are required for digital data. For example, 70 minutes of hi-fi quality music requires over 600 MB of data storage. The data once stored tends to be reliable and will not degrade over time (extra data bits can also be added to correct or detect any errors). Typically, the data is stored either as magnetic fields on a magnetic disk or as pits on an optical disk.

The accuracy of digital systems depends on the number of bits used for each sample, whereas an analogue system's accuracy depends on component tolerance. Analogue systems also produce a differing response for different systems whereas a digital system has a dependable response.

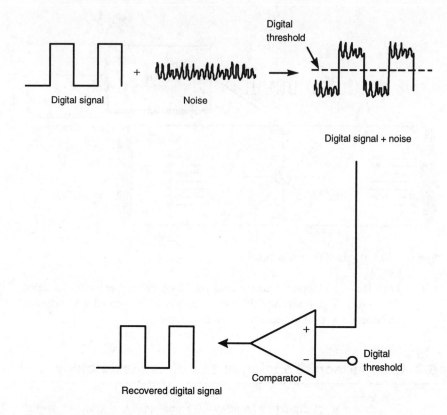

Figure 6.11 Recovery of a digital signal with noise added to it.

It is very difficult (if not impossible) to recover the original analogue signal after it is affected by noise (especially if the noise is random). Most methods of reducing noise involve some form of filtering or smoothing of the signal.

An advantage of analogue technology is that it is relatively easy to store. For example, video and audio signals are stored as magnetic fields on tape and a picture is stored on photographic paper. These media tend to add noise to the signal when they are stored and when they are recovered (such as tape hiss). Unfortunately, it is also not possible to detect if an analogue signal has an error in it. A comparison of digital and analogue technology is given in Table 6.1.

6.3.1 Sampling theory

As a signal may be continually changing, a sample of it must be taken at given time intervals. The rate at which the signal is sampled depends on its rate of change. For example, the temperature of the sea does not vary much over a short time period but a video image of a sports match will. To encode a signal digitally it is normally sampled at fixed time intervals. Sufficient information is then extracted to allow the signal to be processed or reconstructed.

Table 6.1 Comparison of analogue and digital technology.

	DIGITAL	ANALOGUE
Noise	Less prone to noise.	Prone to all forms of noise.
Correcting errors	Extra bits can be added to data to correct or detect any errors.	Errors cannot be corrected they can only be filtered.
Storage	Easy to store, but large data storage is required. Bulk storage is now available, such as 680 MB for a CD and several GB's on hard-disks. The data once stored tends not to degrade over time. Note that over 1 MB of storage is required to store a 35 mm photograph.	Relatively easy to store, such as magnetic, physical tracks, photographic, and so on. The stored signal tends to degrade over time.
Processing	Easy to process data in a binary form and can be done in real-time or off-line.	Less easy to process. It must normally be done in real-time.
Signal transmission	Relatively easy to transmit data with little degradation. Good quality cables, such as optical fibre or co-axial are normally required.	Signal degrades over long distances and is it distorted by the electrical characteristics of the cable.
Signal bandwidth	Almost unlimited.	Limited by noise.
Accuracy	Depends on the number of bits used to code samples. For example, 16-bit coding gives an accuracy of $\pm 0.0008\%$, whereas 8 bits gives $\pm 0.2\%$.	Depends on the tolerance of the circuit components.
Flexibility	Analogue circuit functions can now be replaced by digital processors. These have can have a fixed functionality or can be programmed in a high-level language.	Analogue circuits are normally fixed and cannot be reprogrammed.

If a signal is to be reconstructed as the original signal it must be sampled at a rate defined by the Nyquist Criterion. This states that the sampling rate must be at least twice the highest frequency of the signal. For example, a hi-fi audio signal has a maximum frequency of 20 kHz; this signal must be sampled at least 40 000 times per second (40 kHz), that is, once every 25 µs (note that professional audio systems use a sample frequency of 44.1 kHz). Figure 6.12 shows a signal sampled every T_S seconds.

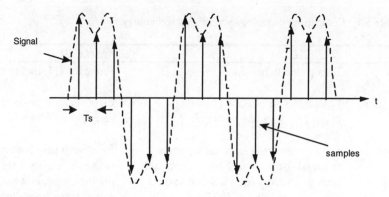

Figure 6.12 The sampling process.

6.3.2 Quantization

Before coding an analogue signal into a digital form it must first be quantized into discrete steps of amplitude. Once quantized, the instantaneous values of the continuous signal can never be exactly restored. This leads to random error called quantization error. Figure 6.13 shows a quantization process. Notice that the 11th and 12th sample are both coded as binary 0001 although they differ in amplitude.

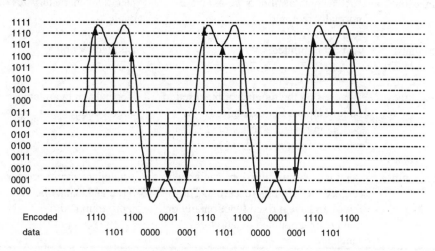

Figure 6.13 Sampling and quantization.

6.3.3 Coding of samples

The more quantization levels the smaller the level-gap and the more actuate the final coded value will be. Figure 6.14 shows an example of uni-polar and bi-polar three-bit coding. In uni-polar coding the signal is always a positive, whereas in bi-polar conversion the signal has positive and negative values. The

full range of the input signal fits between 0 and FS (full scale) for uni-polar and
−FS/2 to FS/2 for bi-polar. Typically, this the range will be between 0 and 5, 10
or 15 V for uni-polar and ±5 or ±15 V for bi-polar. The number of
quantization level depends on the number of bits used. In this case with three
bits there will be eight different coded values from 000 to 111.

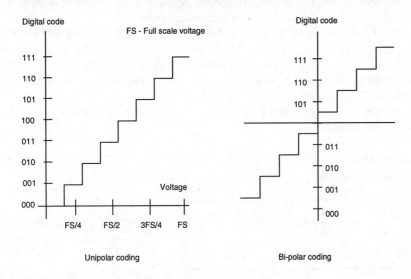

Figure 6.14   Three bit uni-polar and bi-polar coding.

6.3.4 Quantization error

The maximum error between the original level and the quantized level occurs
when the original level falls exactly halfway between two quantized levels. The
maximum error will be a half of the smallest increment or

$$\text{Max error} = \pm\frac{1}{2}\frac{\text{Full scale}}{2^{N}}$$

Table 6.2   Number of quantization levels as a function of bits.

Bits (N)	Quantization levels	Accuracy (%)
1	2	50
2	4	25
3	8	12.5
4	16	6.25
8	256	0.2
12	4 096	0.012
14	16 384	0.003
16	65 536	0.00076

6.4 Digital-to-analogue converters (DAC)

A digital-to-analogue converter (DAC) converts digital data into a corresponding analogue voltage, or current. Most DACs operate in parallel, that is, the bits are loaded in parallel and, since there is no clocking device, the required output is achieved once the circuit has settled.

The basic concept of the DAC is that the bits are used to switch ON or OFF weighted voltages, or currents. These are then added and the output is an analogue level relating to the digital input. The most significant bit is weighted with half the full-scale voltage and so on. A basic voltage summator DAC is shown in Figure 6.15.

An electronic switch can be produced electronically by a transistor called a field-effect transistor (FET).

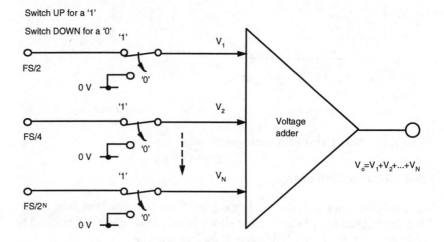

Figure 6.15   DAC with voltage summator.

6.5 Analogue-to-digital converters (ADC)

Analogue-to-digital conversion tends to be more difficult than digital-to-analogue conversion. This section discusses the most popular type, the successive approximation ADC.

An ADC takes a finite time to compute the digital value. It must be told when to start the computation and return a signal back to the computer to inform it that it has finished. When this signal is returned, the computer reads the ADC output. The main signal lines to control this handshaking are shown in Figure 6.16.

The SC (start conversion) line goes active HIGH to inform the ADC to compute a digital value. Once it finishes, the $\overline{\text{EOC}}$ goes active LOW, indicating that the value on the output of the ADC is correct. The bar above the $\overline{EOC}$ signal line shows that the signal is active LOW. A timing diagram of this conversion cycle is shown in Figure 6.17.

6.5.1 Successive approximation ADC

The successive-approximation method is the most common type of ADC because of its speed, accuracy and ease of implementation. It operates by making a comparison between the input voltage and a generated compared voltage. A sequencer and a DAC produces a comparison voltage, as shown in Figure 6.18.

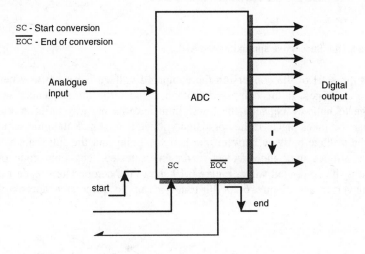

Figure 6.16 ADC block diagram.

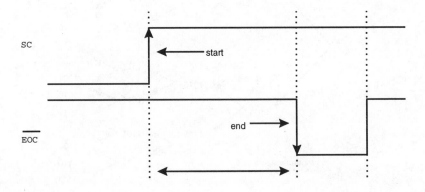

Figure 6.17 ADC control.

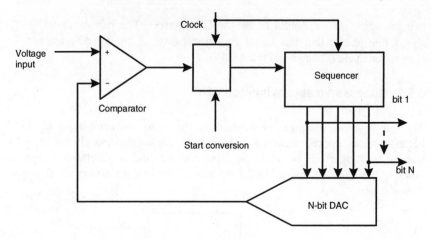

Figure 6.18 Successive approximation ADC.

At the start of the conversion the compared voltage is set halfway between the input ranges. If the compared voltage is too large the sequencer sets the voltage to halfway between the lower limit and the halfway point and a new comparison takes place. If the compared voltage is too small then the sequencer sets the voltage halfway between the halfway point and the full-scale voltage. This continues until the smallest increment is tested. The final code on the output is the computed value. Figure 6.19 shows the comparisons made for a 4-bit convertor and Figure 6.20 illustrates a sample successive approximation cycle.

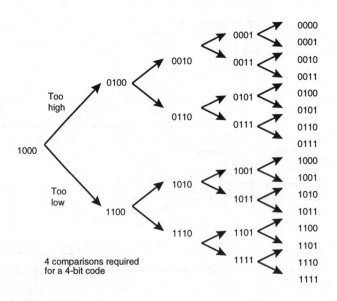

Figure 6.19 Sequencer operation.

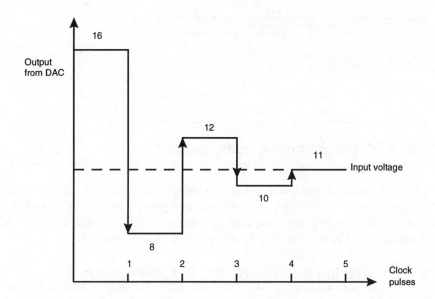

Figure 6.20 Sample conversion for successive approximation ADC.

It can be shown that the number of comparisons required is equal to the number of bits in the coded sample. Thus, the number of clock cycles required for a successive approximation ADC to compute its value is equal to the number of output bits.

6.5.2 Parallel output ADC

An N-bit parallel converter (or flash converter) uses a resistor ladder to generate 2^N-1 quantization voltage levels from the lsb (least significant bit) to (2^N-1) times the lsb. Each of these is compared with the input voltage using 2^N-1 comparators. If the voltage on the + input of a comparator is greater than the − then the output is HIGH, else it is LOW. Voltage threshold levels are fed into the + input and the input voltage into the − input. Thus, the output from the comparators gives a HIGH if the input voltage is greater than the applied threshold voltages and a LOW when it is lower. A decoder then translates the output from the comparators into a binary code. Figure 6.21 shows an example of a 3-bit parallel ADC with 7 comparators. Table 6.3 lists the number of comparators required for a given ADC resolution. It can be seen that a 16-bit ADC requires 65 535 voltage levels and comparators.

The flash ADC does not require a clock input and its speed is only limited by the settling time of the signals. It is normally used in high speed applications, such as the colour decoding on VGA/ SVGA monitors, radar applications, and so on.

Table 6.3 Number of comparators as a function of the number of bits.

Bits	Number of comparators
1	1
3	7
4	15
8	255
12	4 095
16	65 535

6.6 ADC programming using cards

There are two main methods of connecting an ADC to a computer. The first is to use a plug-in card that has registers which can be programmed (as DIO and PTC cards). This normally has more than one analogue input channel (usually 16 channels on one card). The other method is to use the PPI interface.

6.7 Interfacing an ADC via the PPI using mode 0

Two control lines synchronize the data between the computer and ADC. These are SC (start conversion) and $\overline{EOC}$ (end of conversion). The SC line is an input to the ADC and is used to start the computation. The $\overline{EOC}$ line is an output from the ADC and indicates that the output has a valid value. A bar above a signal line indicates that it is active low, whereas no bar indicates an active high signal.

Thus the SC line is active high, that is, a high starts computation; whereas the $\overline{EOC}$ line is an active low, that is, when the ADC has computed the digital value it goes low. The PPI can be used to control and monitor these ADC handshaking lines by connecting them to two bits on Port C, as shown in Figure 6.22. Port C can be used to control SC and monitor $\overline{EOC}$.

The $\overline{EOC}$ line is an input to the PPI and SC is an output. The computer starts the ADC computing a value by setting SC high. Next the computer monitors the $\overline{EOC}$ line until it goes low. Then the computer reads from the port at which the ADC output is connected, in this case, Port A.

Port C can be split into an input and output with Port C (upper) and Port C (lower). In this case, Port C (lower) is an input (as it connect to $\overline{EOC}$) and Port C (upper) an output (as it connects to SC). The sequence of operations on the ADC is as follows:

[1] Set SC (PC4) high.   [2]Monitor $\overline{EOC}$ (PC0) until it goes low.
[3] Read from Port A.   [4]Set SC (PC4) low.
[5] Delay for a small time period.   [6]Goto [1].

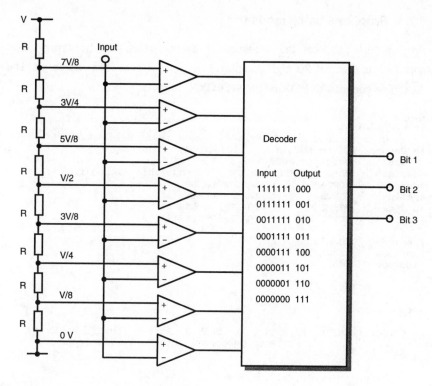

Figure 6.21 3-bit parallel (or flash) ADC.

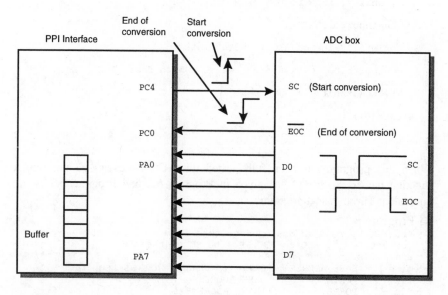

Figure 6.22 Interfacing to an ADC using PPI.

6.7.1 Programs using mode 0

Program 6.1 conducts the sequence of events which has been previously specified, that is, set SC high, monitor $\overline{EOC}$ until it goes low, and so on. The $\overline{EOC}$ line connects to PC0 and the SC to PC4.

📄 Program 6.1

```
/* Program to read an analogue voltage from an 8-bit ADC    */
/* Connect PC0 to EOC on ADC, PC4 to SC on the ADC          */
/* and ADC output to PORT A                                 */
#define      BASE_ADDRESS   0x1F0 /* change this as required */
#define      PORTA          BASE_ADDRESS
#define      PORTB          (BASE_ADDRESS+1)
#define      PORTC          (BASE_ADDRESS+2)
#define      CNTRL_REG      (BASE_ADDRESS+3)

#include     <conio.h>
#include     <stdio.h>
#include     <dos.h>

int     main(void)
{
int     in;

    outportb(CNTRL_REG,0x91);  /* Mode 0, Port C (lower) input */
                    /* Port C (upper) output, Port A input    */
    do
    {
        outportb(PORTC,0x10); /* set SC HIGH */
        do
        {
            /* loop until EOC is LOW */
        } while ((inportb(PORTC) & 0x01) !=0);

        in=inportb(PORTA);

        printf("Value on ADC is %d\n",in);

        outportb(PORTC,0x00); /* set SC LOW to reset ADC   */
        delay(1);
    } while (!kbhit());

    return(0);

}
```

When this program has been fully tested the ADC code can be put into a function named getad(), as given in Program 6.2 and Program 6.3 is the equivalent Turbo Pascal program.

📄 Program 6.2

```
/* Program to read an analogue voltage from an 8-bit ADC     */
/* Connect PC0 to EOC on ADC, PC4 to SC on the ADC           */
/* and ADC output to PORT A                                  */
#define      BASE_ADDRESS   0x1F0 /* change this as required  */
#define      PORTA          BASE_ADDRESS
#define      PORTB          (BASE_ADDRESS+1)
#define      PORTC          (BASE_ADDRESS+2)
```

```c
#define    CNTRL_REG        (BASE_ADDRESS+3)
#include   <conio.h>
#include   <stdio.h>
#include   <dos.h>

int        getad(void);

int        main(void)
{
int        in;
    outportb(CNTRL_REG,0x91);  /* Mode 0, Port C (lower) input */
                        /* Port C (upper) output, Port A input */
    do
    {
       in=getad();
       printf("Value on ADC is %d\n",in);
    } while (!kbhit());
    return(0);
}

int    getad(void)
{
int    in;

    outportb(PORTC,0x10); /* set SC HIGH */

    do
    {
            /* loop until EOC is LOW   */
    } while ((inportb(PORTC) & 0x01) !=0);

    in=inportb(PORTA);

    outportb(PORTC,0x00);          /* set SC LOW to reset ADC */

    return(in);
}
```

🖹 Program 6.3

```pascal
program atod(input,output);
{ Program to read an analogue voltage from an 8-bit ADC     }
{ Connect PC0 to EOC on ADC, PC4 to SC on the ADC           }
{ and ADC output to PORT A                                  }

uses crt;

const    BASE_ADDRESS    =$01F0; { change this as required }
         PORTA           =BASE_ADDRESS;
         PORTB           =BASE_ADDRESS+1;
         PORTC           =BASE_ADDRESS+2;
         CNTRL_REG       =BASE_ADDRESS+3;

var          inbyte:integer;

function    getad:integer;
var      inp:integer;
begin

   port[PORTC]:=$10; { set SC HIGH }

   repeat
   until ((port[PORTC] and 1)=0); { loop until EOC is low }
```

```
   inp:=port[PORTA];
   port[PORTC]:=0; { set SC LOW to reset ADC }
   getad:=inp;
end;

begin

   port[CNTRL_REG]:=$91;
      { Mode 0, PORT A input, Port C (upper) output  }
      { Port C (lower) input                         }

   repeat
      inbyte:=getad;
      writeln('Value on ADC is ',inbyte);
   until keypressed;

end.
```

6.8 Interfacing an ADC via the PPI using mode 1

The main problem with mode 0 operation is that the computer must continually monitor the EOC line. An improved technique is to allow the PPI to inform the ADC that the data in the port buffer has not been read yet. This is achieved by operating the PPI in mode 1. In this mode PORT C is used for handshaking lines, the definition of these is outlined in Table 6.4.

When inputting data to the computer, the external device sets the $\overline{STB}$ line LOW (active). Data is then read into the input port buffer. Next the PPI automatically set the IBF line high. This remains high until the PC has read from the buffer. This line is used to stop the external device from sending any more data to the PPI. Once the data is read from the buffer then the IBF goes low. This informs the external device that it can send more data.

Figure 6.23 shows the set-up which relates to the following programs. It shows a typical handshaking operation; unfortunately an inverter is required between the IBF and SC lines to allow the signals to match up properly.

When the port buffer is empty the PC5 line (IBF) is inactive, or low. This connects, through the inverter, to the SC of the ADC. Initially it will be high, causing the ADC to start computing a value. When it finishes the $\overline{EOC}$ line goes low. This line connects directly to PC4 ($\overline{STB}$) causing the data on the Port A to be loaded into the port buffer. The PPI then automatically sets PC5 (IBF) high (causing SC to go low, thus resetting the ADC). This then stays high until the PC has read from the port buffer. When it does the IBF line goes low causing the SC to go high. This causes the ADC to start computing a new value, and so on.

Table 6.4 Mode 1 handshaking lines for inputting data.

Signal	PORT A	PORT B
Strobe ($\overline{STB}$)	PC4	PC2
Input Buffer Full (IBF)	PC5	PC1

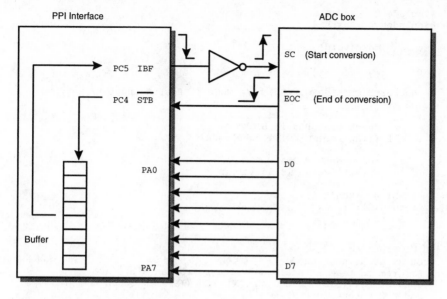

Figure 6.23   Interfacing to an ADC using PPI.

6.8.1 Programs using mode 1

As has been seen in mode 1, when PC4 ($\overline{\text{STB}}$) goes low the output from the ADC is read into the input port buffer. When this happens the PC5 (IBF) line automatically goes high. This indicates that the input buffer is full. Thus, the PC tests this line to determine if there is a valid value in the input port buffer. The statement:

```
if ( (inportb(PORTC) & 0x20)==0x20)
```

reads a byte from Port C and masks off the PC5 (IBF) bit. If this bit is a 1 then the line is high and the data in the port buffer is valid. Program 6.4 uses this technique and can be used to test the ADC module. More complex programs can be developed from this simple test program. Program 6.5 is the Turbo Pascal equivalent.

📄 Program 6.4
```
/* Program to read an analogue voltage from an 8-bit ADC        */
/* Connect PC4 (STB) to EOC on ADC, PC5 (IBF) to SC on the ADC  */
/* and ADC output to PORT A                                     */
#define      BASE_ADDRESS   0x1F0 /* change this as required     */

#define      PORTA          BASE_ADDRESS
#define      PORTB          (BASE_ADDRESS+1)
#define      PORTC          (BASE_ADDRESS+2)
#define      CNTRL_REG      (BASE_ADDRESS+3)

#include     <conio.h>
```

```c
#include    <stdio.h>
#include    <dos.h>

int     main(void)
{
int     in;

    outportb(CNTRL_REG,0xB0);  /* Mode 1, Port A input */
    do
    {
        /* check that PC5 is HIGH `*/
        if ((inportb(PORTC) & 0x20)==0x20)
        {
            in=inportb(PORTA);
            printf("Value is %d \n",in);
        }
    } while (!kbhit());
    return(0);
}
```

📄 Program 6.5

```pascal
program atod(input,output);
{ Program to read an analogue voltage from an 8-bit ADC        }
{ Connect PC4 (STB) to EOC on ADC, PC5 (IBF) to SC on the ADC  }
{ and ADC output to PORT A                                     }
uses        crt;

const   BASE_ADDRESS   =$01F0; { change this as required }
        PORTA          =BASE_ADDRESS;
        PORTB          =BASE_ADDRESS+1;
        PORTC          =BASE_ADDRESS+2;
        CNTRL_REG      =BASE_ADDRESS+3;

var     inbyte:integer;
begin

    port[CNTRL_REG]:=$B0; { Mode 1, PORT A input }
    repeat
        { check that PC5 is HIGH }
        if ((port[PORTC] and $20)=$20) then
        begin
            inbyte:=port[PORTA];
            writeln('Input = ',inbyte);
        end;
    until keypressed;
end.
```

Once the ADC sampling code has been well tested it can be put into a function named getad(), as shown in Programs 6.6 and 6.7. Program 6.7 is the Turbo Pascal equivalent.

📄 Program 6.6

```c
/* Program to read an analogue voltage from an 8-bit ADC     */
/* Connect PC4 (STB) to EOC on ADC, PC5 (IBF) to SC on the   */
/* ADC and ADC output to PORT A                              */
#define     BASE_ADDRESS   0x1F0     /* change this as required   */
#define     PORTA          BASE_ADDRESS
#define     PORTB          (BASE_ADDRESS+1)
#define     PORTC          (BASE_ADDRESS+2)
```

```
#define      CNTRL_REG      (BASE_ADDRESS+3)
#define      SC             0x20          /* bit 5 of Port C      */
#include     <conio.h>
#include     <stdio.h>
#include     <dos.h>

int     getad(void);

int     main(void)
{
int     i;

    outportb(CNTRL_REG,0xB0); /* Mode 1, Port A input */
    do
    {
       i=getad();
       printf("Value on port is %d\n",i);
    } while (!kbhit());

    return(0);
}

int     getad(void)
{
int     in;

    do
    {
         /* loop until PC5 is HIGH (that is, IBF) */
    } while ( (inportb(PORTC) & SC)==0);
    in=inportb(PORTA);
    return(in);
}
```

📄 Program 6.7

```
program atod(input,output);
{ Program to read an analogue voltage from an 8-bit ADC            }
{ Connect PC4 (STB) to EOC on ADC, PC5 (IBF) to SC on the ADC      }
{ and ADC output to PORT A                                         }
uses crt;

const     BASE_ADDRESS    =$01F0; { change this as required }
          PORTA           =BASE_ADDRESS;
          PORTB           =BASE_ADDRESS+1;
          PORTC           =BASE_ADDRESS+2;
          CNTRL_REG       =BASE_ADDRESS+3;
var       inbyte:integer;

function getad(ioport:integer):integer;
begin
   repeat
        { loop until PC5 is HIGH (that is, IBF }
   until ((port[PORTC] and $20)=$20);
   getad:=port[ioport];
end;
begin
   port[CNTRL_REG]:=$B0;       { Mode 1, PORT A input }
   repeat
      inbyte:=getad(PORTA);
      writeln('Value on ADC is ',inbyte);
   until keypressed;
end.
```

6.9 Converting from digital to absolute values

In most cases the digital value read from the ADC must be converted back into a real value, such as pressure or temperature. To determine an absolute temperature it is necessary to characterize the temperature-to-voltage conversion of the sensor and the gain of the amplifier used. Normally, the output voltage from a temperature sensor feeds into an amplifier to either give a uni-polar or bi-polar voltage range.

Two example voltage to temperature conversion graphs are shown in Figure 6.24. The first has a uni-polar voltage range and shows that an output voltage of 5 V represents a temperature of +100°C and 0 V represents 0°C. The conversion between the output voltage (V) and the temperature will thus be:

$$T = 20 \times V \qquad °C$$

The second has a bi-polar voltage range. An output voltage of +5 V represents a temperature of 100°C and –5 V represents 0°C. The conversion between the output voltage (V) and the temperature will thus be:

$$T = 10 \times V + 50 \qquad °C$$

The output voltage of the amplifier feeds into an ADC which has either a uni-polar or bi-polar coding. A graph of the conversion between the digital value and temperature is shown in Figure 6.25. This conversion assumes that the maximum voltage input is coded as a 255 and the minimum as 0. From this graph the conversion between the sampled digital value and the temperature can be found.

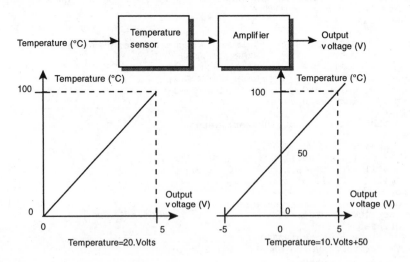

Figure 6.24 Temperature conversion.

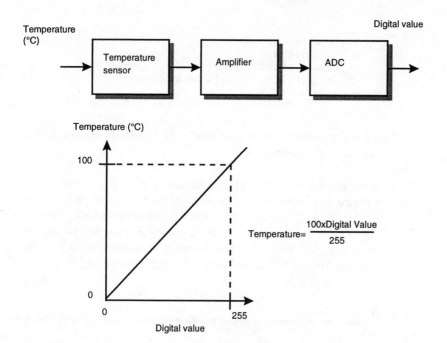

Figure 6.25 Digital value to temperature conversion.

6.10 Exercises

6.1 Write a program that reads from an ADC module on Port A and sends the digital value to Port B.

6.2 Write a program that determines the sampling rate for an ADC connected to a PPI. The program should continually run, with an update to the sampling rate every 10 seconds.

6.3 In the programs with getad() function there is a loop which repeats until the $\overline{\text{EOC}}$ line goes low. This may cause a problem if the ADC is not working correctly, or not connected. If a program does occur then the program stays within getad() indefinitely. Rewrite this routine so that it times-out after a given time interval (for example, a one second time-out). The program should then display an error message that a time-out has occurred. *Hint*: on a time-out a valule of – 1 value to the calling program. This value can then be tested to determine if there has been a time-out. For example:

```
#define      TIMEOUT      -1
int   main(void)
{
    :::::::::etc
    inval=getad();
    if (inval==TIMEOUT) puts("Time-out error");
    else printf("ADC value is %d\n",inval);
    :::::::::etc
}
```

6.4   If a temperature sensor is available, write a problem that displays the absolute temperature.

6.5   If a light sensor is available, interface it to an ADC and write a program that senses if the light intensity is in one of three states: low, medium or high intensity light. A schematic of the system is given in Figure 6.26 and a sample run in Test run 6.1. For example an input digital value of between 0 and 50 could be interpreted as low light, between 51 and 150 as medium light and between 151 and 255 as high intensity light.

🖥 Test run 6.1

```
Light intensity: LOW LIGHT
Light intensity: LOW LIGHT
Light intensity: MEDIUM LIGHT
Light intensity: HIGH INTENSITY LIGHT
Light intensity: MEDIUM LIGHT
```

6.6   Write a program that reads continually from an ADC module on Port A. The value read is then used to determine various thresholds in a level detect circuit; these levels are specified in Table 6.5. A message of the level should be displayed to the screen and the required bit pattern sent to Port B.

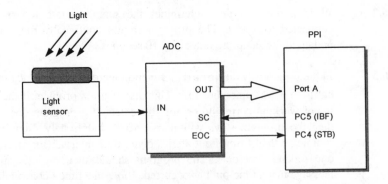

Figure 6.26   Light sensor interfaced to the PPI.

Table 6.5 Specification for Exercise 6.6.

Level	Digital input value from ADC	Output to Port B
1	0–6	0000 0001
2	7–15	0000 0010
3	16–32	0000 0100
4	33–100	0000 1000
5	101–150	0001 0000
6	151–200	0010 0000
7	201–255	0100 0000

6.7 Write a program that determines when a voltage is above or below an entered threshold voltage. Test run 6.2 shows a sample run. Note that the input must be calibrated, that is, an absolute voltage should be assigned to a digital value.

⌨ Test run 6.2

```
Set voltage on channel 0 on ADC to 5 Volts DC >>
Set voltage on channel 0 on ADC to 0 Volts DC >>
******Calibration Complete***************
Enter voltage at which alarm will display >>  2.6
VOLTAGE ABOVE 2.6 Volts
VOLTAGE ABOVE 2.6 Volts
VOLTAGE BELOW 2.6 Volts
```

6.8 Write a program that displays an alarm message if the voltage is more than 2.6 volts. This alarm message should continue until the applied voltage falls below 2 volts.

6.11 Digital-to-analogue conversion

6.11.1 Introduction

A digital-to-analogue converter (DAC) converts a digital value into an analogue voltage. This is normally an easier device to implement than an ADC, and it can be constructed using electronic switches and a voltage summator.

6.11.2 DAC using modules

The PC can interface to a DAC using the PPI ports by simply connecting the output of a PPI port to the DAC input connections. Figure 6.27 shows Port B connected to an 8-bit DAC. Note that there are no requirements for external clocks or hardware synchronization.

Figure 6.28 shows a discrete form of a triangular waveform. Program 6.8 produces a similar waveform with 256 discrete steps. This is achieved by outputting a value from 0 to 255 to the DAC. The triangular effect is made by counting up from 0 to 255 and then down to 0. This process then continues until a key is pressed. If possible, observe the waveform on an oscilloscope and measure the time between consecutive minima. Program 6.9 is the Pascal equivalent.

Port B   8-bit DAC

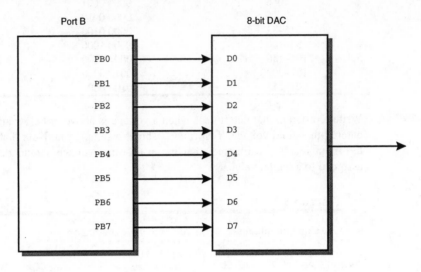

Figure 6.27   DAC controlled via Port B.

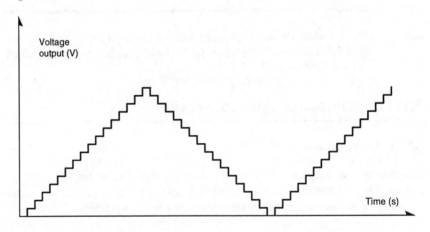

Figure 6.28   Triangular wave.

📄 **Program 6.8**
```
/* Program to generate a triangular waveform    on PORT B.   */
/* Connect DAC to Port B.                                    */

#define      BASE_ADDRESS    0x1F0 /* change this as required    */
#define      PORTA           BASE_ADDRESS
#define      PORTB           (BASE_ADDRESS+1)
#define      PORTC           (BASE_ADDRESS+2)
#define      CNTRL_REG       (BASE_ADDRESS+3)
```

```c
#include    <dos.h>   /* needed for outportb */
#include    <stdio.h>
#include <conio.h>

int       main(void)
{
int       i;

    outportb(CNTRL_REG,0x90);   /* set A input, B output */
    do
    {
        i=0;
        do    /* UP LOOP */
        {
            outportb(PORTB,i++);
        } while (i<256);

        do  /* DOWN LOOP */
        {
            outportb(PORTB,i--);
        } while (i>0);

    } while (!kbhit());        /* repeat until a key has been pressed */

    return(0);
}
```

📄 Program 6.9

```pascal
program dac_1(input,output);
uses crt;

{ Program to generate a triangular waveform on PORT B.    }
{  Connect DAC to Port B.                                  }

const    BASE_ADDRESS    =$01F0; { change this as required  }
         PORTA           =BASE_ADDRESS;
         PORTB           =BASE_ADDRESS+1;
         PORTC           =BASE_ADDRESS+2;
         CNTRL_REG       =BASE_ADDRESS+3;

var      i:integer;

begin
    port[CNTRL_REG]:=$90;   { set A input, B output }
    repeat
        i:=0;
        repeat
            port[PORTB]:=i;
            i:=i+1;
        until (i=255);
        repeat
            port[PORTB]:=i;
            i:=i-1;
        until (i=0);
    until keypressed;
end.
```

Program 6.10 uses the #define statement to define the function putda().
This could be inserted into a header file (for example, port.h).

📄 Program 6.10

```c
/* Program to generate a triangular waveform on PORT B.    */
/* Connect DAC to Port B.                                   */
#define   BASE_ADDRESS        0x1F0 /* change this as required */
#define   PORTA               BASE_ADDRESS
#define   PORTB               (BASE_ADDRESS+1)
#define   PORTC               (BASE_ADDRESS+2)
#define   CNTRL_REG           (BASE_ADDRESS+3)
#define   _putda(_value)      outportb(PORTB,_value)

#include    <dos.h>  /* needed for outportb */
#include    <stdio.h>
#include    <conio.h>

int    main(void)
{
int    i;

    outportb(CNTRL_REG,0x90);   /* set A input, B output */
    do
    {
        i=0;
        do          /* UP LOOP */
        {
            _putda(i);
            i++;
        } while (i<256);

        do          /* DOWN LOOP */
        {
            _putda(i);
            i--;
        } while (i>0);

    } while (!kbhit());  /* repeat until a key has been pressed */
    return(0);
}
```

Programs 6.11 and 6.12 have a getad() module added. These are used to generate a sawtooth wave (or ramp waveform), as shown in Figure 6.29.

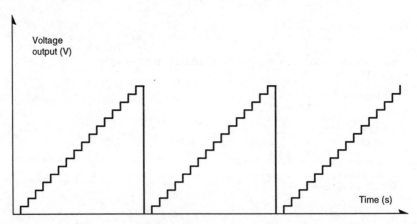

Figure 6.29 Sawtooth waveform.

📄 Program 6.11

```
program dac_2(input,output);
uses crt;
{  Program to generate a sawtooth waveform on PORT B.        }
{  Connect DAC to Port B.                                    }
const   BASE_ADDRESS    =$01F0; { change this as required    }
        PORTA           =BASE_ADDRESS;
        PORTB           =BASE_ADDRESS+1;
        PORTC           =BASE_ADDRESS+2;
        CNTRL_REG       =BASE_ADDRESS+3;
        MAXDAC          =255;         MINDAC    =0;

var   i:integer;

procedure putda(i:integer);
begin
     port[PORTB]:=i;
end;

begin
   port[CNTRL_REG]:=$90;   { set A input, B output }
   repeat
      for i:=MINDAC to MAXDAC do
          putda(i);
   until keypressed;
end.
```

📄 Program 6.12

```
/* Program to generate a sawtooth waveform  on PORT B.       */
/* Connect DAC to Port B.                                    */
#define  BASE_ADDRESS    0x1F0 /* change this as required     */
#define  PORTA           BASE_ADDRESS
#define  PORTB           (BASE_ADDRESS+1)
#define  PORTC           (BASE_ADDRESS+2)
#define  CNTRL_REG       (BASE_ADDRESS+3)
#define  MAXDAC          256
#define  MINDAC          0

#include    <dos.h>  /* needed for outportb() */
#include    <stdio.h>
#include    <conio.h>

void  putda(int value);

int    main(void)
{
int    i;
   outportb(CNTRL_REG,0x90);   /* set A input, B output */
   do
   {
      /* UP LOOP */
      for  (i=MINDAC;i<MAXDAC;i++)
          putda(i);
   } while (!kbhit());
   return(0);
}

void       putda(int value)
{
   outportb(PORTB,value);
}
```

6.9 Write a program that reads from an 8-bit ADC on Port A and sends the digital value to an 8-bit DAC connected to Port B.

6.10 If a controllable light source is available, write a program that controls the brightness of it. A sample run with five light states is shown in Test run 6.3.

6.11 If a speed controllable motor is available, write a program that drives it at a speed which is entered via the keyboard. Determine the voltage-to-speed relationship of the motor and determine the digital value required to be outputted for given speed.

⌨ Test run 6.3

```
Brightness:
1 - LIGHT OFF (DAC value 0)
2 - DIM        (DAC value 50)
3 - NORMAL     (DAC value 100)
4 - BRIGHT     (DAC value 150)
5 - VERY BRIGHT (DAC value 255)
Enter brightness>>>
```

6.12 Determine the fastest time between output changes of an ADC and explain the limitations on the signal output.

6.13 Write a program that acts as a programmable voltage source. Test run 6.4 shows a sample run. Note that the voltage output must be calibrated to a known maximum and minimum.

⌨ Test run 6.4

```
All 1s sent to the D/A, please enter voltage reading> 5
All 0s sent to the D/A, please enter voltage reading> 0.01

Enter voltage to be programmed >>>>   1.2
**** Voltage has been programmed ****
Enter voltage to be programmed >>>>   2.5
**** Voltage has been programmed ****
Enter voltage to be programmed >>>>>
```

6.14 Write a program that produces a single voltage ramp from the minimum to the maximum possible voltage over a period of 10 seconds.

6.15 Write a program that samples an input waveform and outputs it to the DAC. Observe the differences between the input and output.

6.16   Write a program that produces a triangular waveform with a period of 100 mS (10 Hz).

6.17   Output the fastest sine-wave with at least 10 digitized values for one period.

6.13 Project

Design a control system that monitors and controls environmental conditions in a building. A block diagram of the system is shown in Figure 6.30. Inputs to the system are temperature and light intensity. The motor controls the amount of cooling; the higher its speed the greater the cooling in the air conditioning system.

The program should run continuously, displaying input temperature, the light intensity state and the motor speed. A warning alert should be displayed if the temperature exceeds 60°C. The light states are:

- Low light (night time);
- Medium light (normal ambient light);
- High intensity light.

Table 6.6 shows how the motor speed relates to the temperature and the light intensity. At night the air conditioning system is automatically switched off.

Table 6.6   Motor speeds (rpm).

Temperature (°C)	Low light	Medium light	High light
0–10	OFF	15 rpm	30 rpm
10–20	OFF	30 rpm	60 rpm
20–40	OFF	45 rpm	90 rpm
over 40	OFF	60 rpm	120 rpm

Notes

(1)   If only one ADC is available then one of the inputs (such as the temperature) should be entered via the keyboard. The kbhit() function can be used to interrupt the normal program flow and allow the user to enter a value from the keyboard. A possible usage is outlined in Program 6.13 and a sample monitor screen is shown in Figure 6.31.

(2)   If a motor is not available the speed of the motor should still be displayed on the screen.

(3)   Calibration information for all sensors and for the voltage-to-speed conversion of the motor is required.

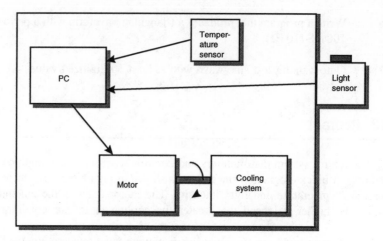

Figure 6.30 Temperature control system.

📄 **Program 6.13**

```
   ::etc., etc., etc.::::::::::::::::::::::::::::::
int   main(void)
{
float temperature;
int      light_input,temp_input;
   ::etc., etc., etc.::::::::::::::::::::::::::::::
  do
  {
   ::etc., etc., etc.::::::::::::::::::::::::::::::
    if (kbhit())
    {
        printf("Enter system temperature >>");
        scanf("%f",&temperature);
    }
    temp_input=getad(PORTA);
    light_input=getad(PORTB);
      ::etc., etc., etc.::::::::::::::::::::::::::::::
  } while (1);
}
```

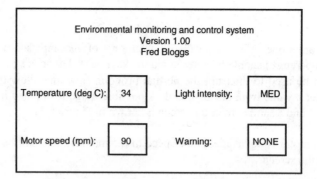

Figure 6.31 Sample monitor screen.

7
Serial Communications

7.1 Introduction

Information can either be sent either in an analogue form (voice signal, transducer signal, and so on) or in a digital form. The transmission of information in a digital format has many advantages over analogue transmission as it:

- Is less susceptible to noise;
- Is less affected by the transmitter, transmission system and receiver;
- Can include extra information to identify or correct errors;
- Allows reprogramming of functionality by software.

Samuel Morse developed the first use of digital transmission when he used a series of dots and dashes (a bit like 1s and 0s) to represented alphabetic characters. This code has since been called Morse code and it was used extensively in telegraph transmissions.

With the growth of computers and the increasing speed of electronic equipment there has been a rapid expansion in the usage of digital communications. Applications now include digital telephone exchanges, wide-area networks, digital radio, electronic mail systems, faxes, interactive video, and so on.

The digital data can either be sent several bits at a time (parallel communications) or one bit at a time (serial communications). Normally to reduce the number of cables used the digital data is transmitted in a serial form. Figure 7.1 shows some of its applications. Typical implementations include serial mouse, printers, plotters, accessing remote instrumentation, scanners, digitizers and modems. Another typical application of serial communication is the transmission of images and text over a telephone network using either a fax or a modem. It is typical in an industrial plant to gather data from instruments, where measurements from devices such as temperature or pressure sensors are sent in a binary form over a serial communication link. This has the advantage over tradition analogue transmission as it is less affected by noise. Remote equipment, such as motors and values, can also be controlled by sending digital codes over a serial link.

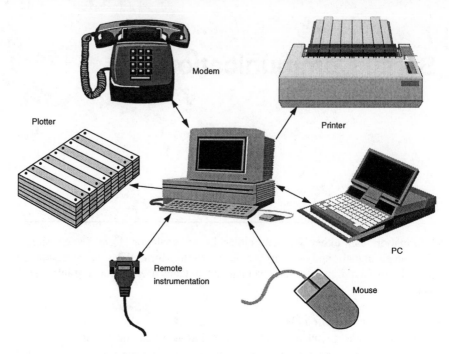

Figure 7.1 Applications of serial communications.

In 1962 the Electronics Industries Association (EIA) introduced the RS-232 standard in an attempt to standardize the interface between Data Terminal Equipment (DTE) and Data Circuit-termination Equipment (DCE). The growing use of PCs has ensured that RS-232 became an industry standard for all low-cost serial interfaces between the DTE (the computer) and the peripheral.

New serial communications standards, such as RS-422 and RS-449, allow very long cable runs and high bit rates. The standard RS-232 only allows a bit rate of 19 600 bps for a maximum distance of 20 metres, but RS-422 allows a bit rate of up to 10 Mbps over distances up to 1 mile, using twisted-pair, coaxial cable or optical fibres. The new standards can also be used to create computer networks.

7.2 Communication terminology

This section discusses some of the terminology used in RS-232 communications.

7.2.1 Parallel and serial interfaces

Figure 7.2 illustrates serial and parallel communications. Typically data is either sent one bit at a time or a byte at a time. The main advantage of sending data one bit at a time is that, in the simplest case, there are only two wires (signal and ground). Unfortunately, it results in much slower data transfer and is also more difficult to interface to. In parallel transmission the data is handshaked between the two nodes by a strobe signal. This strobe informs the receiver that the data on the data lines is valid. In serial communications there are normally no strobe lines thus a start-of-transmission identifier is sent from the transmitter to inform the receiver that data is to be sent.

A serial interface employs a device known as a shift register. At the transmitter a parallel-in-serial-out (PISO) shift register converts the parallel byte into a serial bit stream. A serial-in-parallel-out (SIPO) shift register at the receiver converts it back into a parallel form.

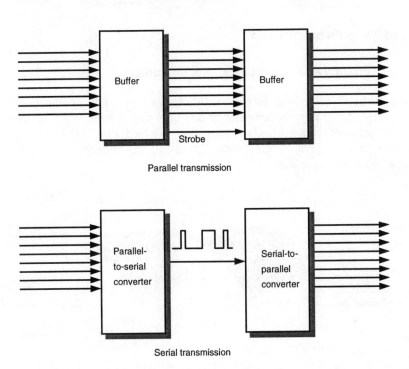

Figure 7.2 Serial and parallel communications.

7.2.2 Connecting two nodes

Two communication nodes can communicate over a serial link, using the methods shown in Figure 7.3, that is:

- Simplex communications – One-way communications in which data can only flow from one node to the other;
- Half-duplex communications – Two-way communications but only one node can communicate at a time;
- Full-duplex communications – Two-way communications in which both devices can communicate simultaneously.

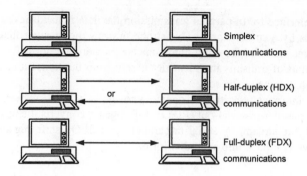

Figure 7.3   Serial communications.

7.2.3   Terminal and communications equipment

Data terminal equipment (DTE) is the end of the data communications
equipment, for example a computer or fax. Data circuit-termination equipment
(DCE) provides communications capability between two DTEs, such as a
modem or connecting cable. Figure 7.4 shows the differing definitions of
communications equipment.

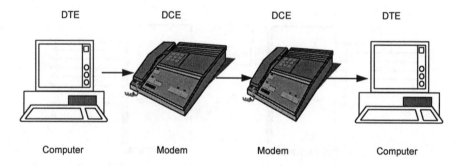

Figure 7.4   Data terminal equipment and Data circuit-terminating equipment.

7.3   ASCII character codes

Data communication is the transmission of digital information from a source to a
destination. Normally this information is sent as codes; which could take the
form of ASCII characters, microprocessor machine codes, control words, and so
on. This section looks at how data is coded to be sent over the RS-232 link.

The three most common character sets currently in use are Baudot code,
American Standards Code for Information Interchange (ASCII) code and the
Extended Binary-Coded Decimal Interchange Code (EBCDIC). RS-232 uses the
ASCII character set.

In an attempt to standardize data communication codes the US adopted the ASCII code. It is now a standard international alphabet. Characters are defined as a 7-bit character code of which 32 are control and 96 are printable. The bits are identified as b_0 (the lsb) to b_6 (the msb). An eighth bit (b_7) can be used as a parity bit to give a degree of error detection. For even parity the parity bit is added so to that it evens up the number of 1s. For odd parity it makes the number of 1s odd.

In RS-232 communications the least significant bit of the ASCII character is sent before all other bits in the character. The final ASCII character bit sent is the parity bit. Figure 7.5 shows an example of the message 'Fred' sent using odd parity.

When ASCII characters are displayed to a screen there are many unseen characters which are not displayed. These include carriage return (CR, 0Dh), space (SP, 20h) and horizontal tab (HT, 09h), and so on. Program 7.1 displays the ASCII characters from 0 to 127.

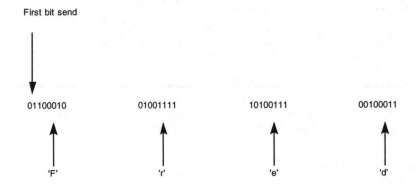

Figure 7.5   Example message showing first bit sent.

📄 Program 7.1

```
#include <stdio.h>
int    main(void)
{
int i;

    for (i=0;i<128;i++)
    {
        printf("<%3d%2c>",i,i);
        if (!(i % 6)) printf("\n");
    }
    return(0);
}
```

Test run 7.1 shows a sample run. Notice that the ASCII character 10 (NL) generates a new line and character 8 (BS) causes a back-space. ASCII character 9 (HT) generates a horizontal tab. Also when the program is run the computer speaker is beeped when the character 7 (BEL) is printed.

```
<   0  >
<   1  _> <   2  _> <  3   _> <   4  _> <  5  _> <  6  _>
<   7  > <  8  > <  9     > < 10
> < 11       _> < 12
>
> < 14  _> < 15   ¤> < 16  _> < 17  _> < 18  _>
< 19  _> < 20   ¶> < 21   §> < 22  _> < 23  _> < 24  _>
< 25  _> < 26   > < 27  _> < 28  _> < 29  _> < 30  _>
< 31  _> < 32   > < 33   !> < 34   "> < 35   #> < 36   $>
< 37  %> < 38   &> < 39   '> < 40  (> < 41  )> < 42   *>
< 43  +> < 44   ,> < 45  -> < 46   .> < 47  /> < 48   0>
< 49  1> < 50   2> < 51   3> < 52  4> < 53  5> < 54   6>
< 55  7> < 56   8> < 57   9> < 58  :> < 59  ;> < 60   <>
< 61  => < 62   >> < 63   ?> < 64  @> < 65  A> < 66   B>
< 67  C> < 68   D> < 69   E> < 70  F> < 71  G> < 72   H>
< 73  I> < 74   J> < 75   K> < 76  L> < 77  M> < 78   N>
< 79  O> < 80   P> < 81   Q> < 82  R> < 83  S> < 84   T>
< 85  U> < 86   V> < 87   W> < 88  X> < 89  Y> < 90   Z>
< 91  [> < 92   \> < 93   ]> < 94  ^> < 95  _> < 96   `>
< 97  a> < 98   b> < 99   c> <100  d> <101  e> <102   f>
<103  g> <104   h> <105   i> <106  j> <107  k> <108   l>
<109  m> <110   n> <111   o> <112  p> <113  q> <114   r>
<115  s> <116   t> <117   u> <118  v> <119  w> <120   x>
<121  y> <122   z> <123   {> <124  |> <125  }> <126   ~>
<127  @>
```

Format codes and control characters are non-printing characters. These codes are decimal 0 to 31. Table 7.1 gives a listing of these.

7.3.1 Format codes

Backspace (BS)

On displays the backspace character (000 1000) erases the previous character sent. Normally the backspace key on a keyboard generates a ^H (Cntrl-H) character (although some keyboards return a ^?).

Horizontal Tab (HT)

The horizontal tab character (000 1001) feeds the current display cursor forward by one tab spacing. Tab settings are normally set by the computer or by a software package. Most keyboards have a TAB key which return a ^I character.

Line Feed (LF), Carriage Return (CR)

The carriage return character (000 1101) returns the cursor display position to the beginning of a line. A line feed (000 1010) forces a new line and moves the cursor position down one place. On UNIX systems a new-line character is normally defined by the CR/LF sequence whereas on PC systems it is defined by the line feed character.

Table 7.1   Non-printing ASCII characters.

ASCII character	ASCII decimal	Binary code	Hex code	Control character	Function
NUL	0	000 0000	00	^@	Null
SOH	1	000 0001	01	^A	Start of Heading
STX	2	000 0010	02	^B	Start of Text
ETX	3	000 0011	03	^C	End of Text
EOT	4	000 0100	04	^D	End of Transmission
ENQ	5	000 0101	05	^E	Enquiry
ACK	6	000 0110	06	^F	Acknowledge
BEL	7	000 0111	07	^G	Bell
BS	8	000 1000	08	^H	Backspace
HT	9	000 1001	09	^I	Horizontal Tab
LF	10	000 1010	0A	^J	Line Feed
VT	11	000 1011	0B	^K	Vertical Tab
FF	12	000 1100	0C	^L	Form Feed
CR	13	000 1101	0D	^M	Carriage Return
SO	14	000 1110	0E	^N	Shift Out
SI	15	000 1111	0F	^O	Shift In
DLE	16	001 0000	10	^P	Data Line Escape
DC1	17	001 0001	11	^Q	Device Control 1
DC2	18	001 0010	12	^R	Device Control 2
DC3	19	001 0011	13	^S	Device Control 3
DC4	20	001 0100	14	^T	Device Control 4
NAK	21	001 0101	15	^U	Negative Acknowledge
SYN	22	001 0110	16	^V	Synchronous Idle
ETB	23	001 0111	17	^W	End of Transmit Block
CAN	24	001 1000	18	^X	Cancel
EM	25	001 1001	19	^Y	End of Medium
SUB	26	001 1010	1A	^Z	Substitute
ESC	27	001 1011	1B	^[, ESC	Escape
FS	28	001 1100	1C	^\	File Separator
GS	29	001 1101	1D	^]	Group Separator
RS	30	001 1110	1E	^6	Record Separator
US	31	001 1111	1F	^_	Unit Separator

Form Feed (FF)

The form feed character (000 1100) causes a line printer to feed to the next page. If it is sent to a display it moves the display cursor one place to the right (the opposite effect to the backspace character).

Vertical Tab (VT)

When sent to a printer the vertical tab (000 1011) character causes the current position to move to the next programmed vertical tab space. If it is sent to a display it moves the current cursor position one line upwards. Normally, a vertical tab is defined by a ^K keystroke.

Many keyboards return the following characters when the arrow keys are pressed. Some displays also interpret these characters as movement commands.

Cursor left	^H
Cursor down	^J

Cursor up	^K
Cursor right	^L

7.3.2 Communication-control characters

End of Text (EXT)
Most computer systems use the end of text character (000 0100) to interrupt a process (^C).

End of Transmission (EOT)
UNIX systems use the end-of-transmission character (000 0101) to signal that the user has finished entering data. It is also as an end-of-file character (^D).

Substitute (SUB)
PC-based DOS systems use the SUB character (001 1010) to define an end-of-file (EOF).

7.3.3 Other Codes

Null (NUL)
The null character (000 0000) is often used to pad the beginning of transmitted characters and to delimit a string of characters. For example if the word 'FRED' can be sent as 'F', 'R', 'E', 'D' , NUL. The control character used to represent the null character is ^@.

Bell (BEL)
When sent to a device with a speaker the bell character (000 0111) generates a tone. The control character used to represent the bell is ^G.

Device control (DC1-DC4)
DC1–DC4 control the operation of displays and printers. A receiver uses the DC1 (^Q) character to inform the transmitter to stop transmitting. The DC3 (^S) character inform the transmitter to start transmitting again. This type of communication is known as software handshaking.

Esc (escape)
Used by some packages to escape from menu options, and so on.

Del (delete)
The delete character (111 1111) erases the character at the current cursor position.

7.3.4 Printable character set

The printable characters are all displayable. They include all upper- and lower-case letters ('a'–'z', 'A'–'Z'), numerical characters ('0'–'9') and other characters such as SPACE, '!' and '#'. The codes for upper- and lower-case letters only differ by one bit position (the b_5 bit), for example:

'A'	100 0001
'a'	110 0001
'B'	100 0010
'b'	110 0010
'Z'	101 1010
'z'	111 1010

Program 7.2 reads a file and displays the integer values of the characters in a file and Test run 7.2 shows a sample run of the program with the file FILE.TXT (as shown in File listing 7.1). The first character in the file, 'T', is ASCII decimal 84, the next, 'h' is decimal 104, and so on. Notice that the new line character is decimal 10, as the program was run on a PC-based system using DOS.

📄 Program 7.2

```c
#include <stdio.h>

int    main(void)
{
FILE   *in;
char   ch, fname[BUFSIZ];

    printf("\nEnter a file to read >> ");

    gets(fname);

    if ( (in=fopen(fname,"r"))==NULL)
        printf("Cannot open file <%s>\n",fname);
    else
    {
        do
        {
            fscanf(in,"%c",&ch);
            printf("%d ",ch);
        } while (!feof(in));
        fclose(in);
    }
    return(0);
}
```

🖥 Test run 7.2

```
Enter a file to read >> file.txt
84 104 105 115 32 105 115 32 97 110 32 101 120 97 109 112
108 101 10 111 102 32 97 110 32 65 83 67 73 10 102 105 108
101 46 10
```

📖 File listing 7.1: Listing of FILE.TXT

```
This is an example
of an ASCII
file.
```

7.4 Electrical characteristics

7.4.1 Line voltages

The electrical characteristics of RS-232 defines the minimum and maximum voltages of a logic '1' and '0'. A logic '1' ranges from –3 V to –25 V, but will typically be around –12 V. A logical '0' ranges from 3 V to 25 V, but will typically be around +12 V. Any voltage between –3 V and +3 V has an indeterminate logical state. If no pulses are present on the line the voltage level is equivalent to a high level, that is –12 V. A voltage level of 0 V at the receiver is interpreted as a line break or a short circuit. Figure 7.6 shows an example transmission.

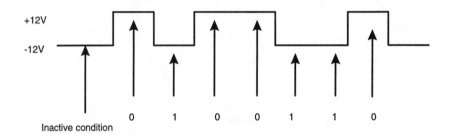

Figure 7.6 RS-232 voltage levels.

7.4.2 DB25S connector

The DB25S connector is a 25-pin D-type connector and gives full RS-232 functionality. Figure 7.7 shows the pin number assignment. A DCE (the terminating cable) connector has a male outer casing with female connection pins. The DTE (the computer) has a female outer casing with male connecting pins. There are three main signal types: control, data and ground. Table 7.2 lists the main connections. Control lines are active HIGH, that is they are HIGH when the signal is active and LOW when inactive.

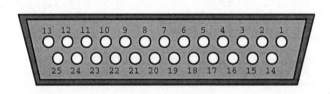

Pin	Signal
2	TxData
3	RxData
4	RTS
5	CTS
6	DSR
7	GND
20	DTR

Figure 7.7 RS-232 DB25S connector.

124 *Serial Communications*

7.4.3 DB9S Connector

The 25-pin connector is the standard for RS-232 connections but as electronic equipment becomes smaller there is a need for smaller connectors. For this purpose most PCs now use a reduced function 9-pin D-type connector rather than the full function 25-way D-type. As with the 25-pin connector the DCE (the terminating cable) connector has a male outer casing with female connection pins. The DTE (the computer) has a female outer casing with male connecting pins. Figure 7.8 shows the main connections.

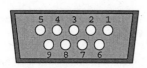

Pin	Signal
2	RxData
3	TxData
4	DTR
5	GND
6	DSR
7	RTS
8	CTS

Figure 7.8   RS-232 DB9S Interface.

7.4.4 PC connectors

All PCs have at least one serial communications port. The primary port is named COM1: and the secondary is COM2:, as illustrated in Figure 7.9. There are two types of connectors used in RS-232 communications, these are the 25- and 9-way D-type. Most modern PCs use either a 9-pin connector for the primary (COM1:) serial port and a 25-pin for a secondary serial port (COM2:), or they use two 9-pin connectors for serial ports. The serial port can be differentiated from the parallel port in that the 25-pin parallel port (LPT1:) is a 25-pin female connector on the PC and a male connector on the cable. The 25-pin serial serial connector is a male on the PC and a female on the cable. The different connector types can cause problems in connecting devices. Thus a 25-to-9 pin adaptor is a useful attachment, especially to connect a serial mouse to a 25-pin connector.

Table 7.2   Main pin connections used in 25-pin connector.

Pin	Name	Abbreviation	Functionality
1	Frame Ground	FG	This ground normally connects the outer sheath of the cable and to earth ground.
2	Transmit Data	TD	Data is sent from the DTE (computer or terminal) to a DCE via TD.
3	Receive Data	RD	Data is sent from the DCE to a DTE (computer or terminal) via RD.

Table 7.2 (Cont.)

Pin	Name	Abbreviation	Functionality
4	Request To Send	RTS	DTE sets this active when it is ready to transmit data.
5	Clear To Send	CTS	DCE sets this active to inform the DTE that it is ready to receive data.
6	Data Set Ready	DSR	Similar functionality to CTS but activated by the DTE when it is ready to receive data.
7	Signal Ground	SG	All signals are referenced to the signal ground (GND).
20	Data Terminal Ready	DTR	Similar functionality to RTS but activated by the DCE when it wishes to transmit data.

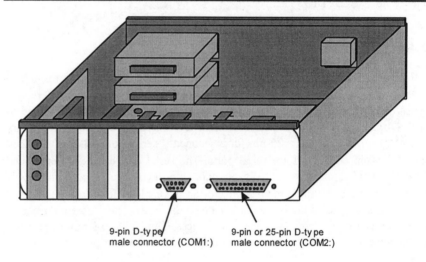

9-pin D-type male connector (COM1:)   9-pin or 25-pin D-type male connector (COM2:)

Figure 7.9   Typical PC connectors.

7.5 Frame format

RS-232 uses asynchronous communications which has a start-stop data format, as shown in Figure 7.10. Each character is transmitted one at a time with a delay between them. This delay is called the inactive time and is set at a logic level high (–12 V) as shown in Figure 7.6. The transmitter sends a start bit to inform the receiver that a character is to be sent in the following bit transmission. This start bit is always a '0'. Next, 5, 6 or 7 data bits are sent as a 7-bit ASCII character, followed by a parity bit and finally either 1, 1.5 or 2 stop bits. Figure

7.11 shows a frame format and an example transmission of the character 'A', using odd parity. The rate of transmission is set by the timing of a single bit. Both the transmitter and receiver need to be set to the same bit-time interval. An internal clock on both sets this interval. These only have to be roughly synchronized and approximately at the same rate as data is transmitted in relatively short bursts.

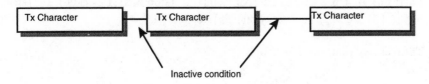

Figure 7.10 Asynchronous communications.

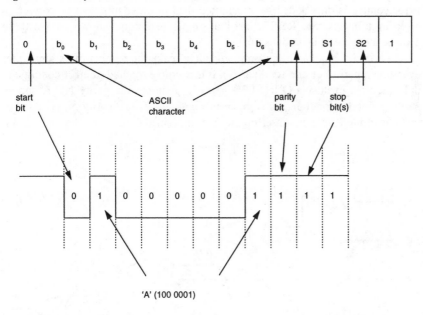

Figure 7.11 RS-232 frame format.

Example

An RS-232 serial data link uses 1 start bit, 7 data bits, 1 parity bit, 2 stop bits, ASCII coding and even parity. Determine the message sent from the following bit stream.

First bit sent
⇓
1111101000001011000001111111111111000001111111100011
00111101010 0111111111111

ANSWER

The format of the data string sent is given next:

{idle} 11111 {start bit} 0 {'A'} 1000001 {parity bit} 0 {stop bits } 11
{start bit} 0 {'p'} 0000111 {parity bit} 1 {stop bits} 11 {idle} 11111111
{start bit} 0 {'p'} 0000111 {parity bit} 1 {stop bits} 11 {idle} 11 {start
bit} 0 {'L'} 0011001 {parity bit} 1 {stop bits} 11

The message sent was thus 'AppL'.

7.5.1 Parity

Error control is data added to transmitted data in order to detect or correct an error in transmission. RS-232 uses a simple technique known as parity to provide a degree of error detection.

A parity bit is added to transmitted data to make the number of 1s sent either even (even parity) or odd (odd parity). It is a simple method of error coding and only requires exclusive-OR (XOR) gates to generate the parity bit. A simple parity generator for four bits is given in Figure 7.12. The parity bit is added to the transmitted data by inserting it into the shift register at the correct bit position.

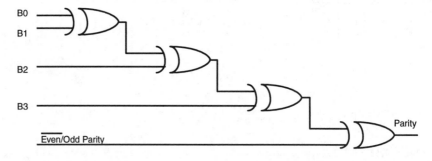

Figure 7.12 Circuit to generate parity bit using EX-OR gates.

A single parity bit can only detect an odd number of errors, that is, 1, 3, 5, and so on. If there is an even number of bits in error then the parity bit will be correct and no error will be detected. This type of error coding is not normally used on its own where there is the possibility of several bits being in error.

7.5.2 Baud rate

One of the main parameters which specify RS-232 communications is the rate of transmission at which data is transmitted and received. It is important that the transmitter and receiver operate at, roughly, the same speed.

For asynchronous transmission the start and stop bits are added in addition to the 7 ASCII character bits and the parity. Thus a total of 10 bits are required to transmit a single character. With 2 stop bits, a total of 11 bits are required. If 10 characters are sent every second and if 11 bits are used for each character, then the transmission rate is 110 bits per second (bps). Table 7.3 lists how the bit rate relates to the characters sent per second (assuming 10 transmitted bits per character). The bit rate is measured in bits per second (bps).

	Bits
ASCII character	7
Start bit	1
Stop bit	2
Total	10

Table 7.3 Bits per second related to characters sent per second.

Speed(bps)	Characters / second
300	30
1200	120
2400	240

In addition to the bit rate, another term used to describe the transmission speed is the baud rate. The bit rate refers to the actual rate at which bits are transmitted, whereas the Baud rate relates to the rate at which signalling elements, used to represent bits, are transmitted. Since one signalling element encodes one bit, the two rates are then identical. Only in modems does the bit rate differ from the baud rate.

7.5.3 Bit stream timings

Asynchronous communications is a stop-start mode of communication and both the transmitter and receiver must be set up with the same bit timings. A start bit identifies the start of transmission and is always a low logic level. Next, the least significant bit is sent followed by the rest of the bits in the character. After this, the parity bit is sent followed by the stop bit(s). The actual timing of each bit relates to the baud rate and can be found using the following formula:

$$\text{Time period of each bit} = \frac{1}{\text{baud rate}} \text{ second}$$

For example, if the baud rate is 9600 Baud (or bps) then the time period for each bit sent is 1/9600 s or 104 µs. Table 7.4 shows some bit timings as related to baud rate. An example of the voltage levels and timings for the ASCII character 'V' is given in Figure 7.13.

Table 7.4 Bit timings related to baud rate.

Baud rate	Time for each bit (μs)
1200	833
2400	417
9600	104
19200	52

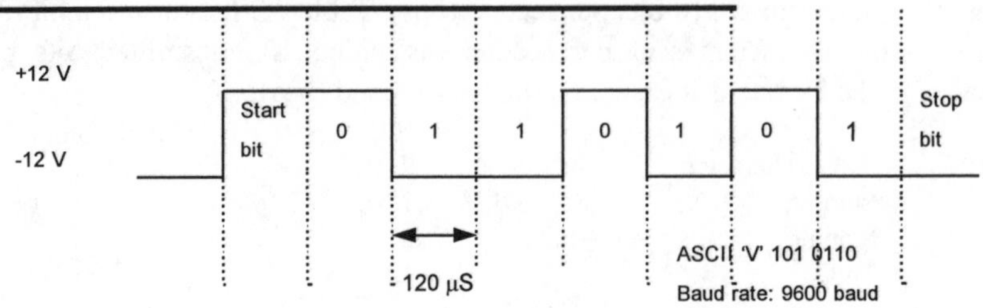

Figure 7.13 ASCII 'V' at RS-232 voltage levels.

7.6 Standards

7.6.1 Standards organizations

The main standards organizations for data communications are the ITU (International Telecommunications Union), the EIA (Electronic Industry Association) and the ISO (International Standards Organisation). The ITU standards related to serial communications, are defined in the V-series specifications and EIA standards as the RS-series.

7.6.2 EIA standard RS-232-C

The RS-232-C standard defines the interfacing of a DTE to a DCE over a distance of up to 50 feet and at a maximum data rate of 20 kbps.

7.6.3 EIA standard RS-449, RS-422A, RS-423A

RS-232 interfaces computer/data terminal equipment separated by a distance up to 50 feet. The EIA has since generated three standards which improve the specification of the interconnection giving higher data rates and longer maximum interconnection lengths. RS-422 and RS-423 define electrical characteristics while RS-499 defines the basic interface standards and refers to the RS-422/3 standards. These standards are:

- RS-422A (electrical characteristics of balanced load voltage digital interface circuits);
- RS-423A (electrical characteristics of unbalanced voltage digital interface circuits);

- RS-449 (general purpose 37-position and 9-position interface for DTE and DCE employing serial binary data interchange).

7.6.4 EIA standard RS-485

RS-485 is an upgraded version of RS-422 and extends the number of peripherals that can be interfaced. It allows for bi-directional multi-point party line communications. This can be used in networking applications. RS-422 and RS-232 facilitate simplex communication, whereas RS-485 allows for multiple receivers on a single line facilitating half-duplex communications. The maximum data rate is unlimited and is set by the rise time of the pulses, but it is usually limited to 10 Mbps. A network using the RS-485 standard can have up to 32 transmitters/receivers with a maximum cable length of 1.2 km, as shown in Figure 7.14.

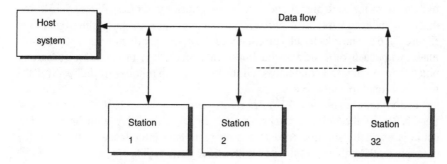

Figure 7.14   RS-485 connecting to multiple nodes.

7.7 Line drivers

Transmission lines have effects on digital pulses in the following ways:

- Attenuation – The transmission line contains series resistance which causes a reduction in the pulse amplitude.
- Pulse distortion – The transmission line insulation produces a shunt capacitance on the signal path and a series resistance and inductance of the conductors. This causes the transmission line to distort the shape of the pulse. The two main effects are the block of high frequencies in the pulse and phase distortion.
- Noise – Noise is any unwanted electrical signals added to a signal. A digital system is less prone to noise as it has only two levels and it takes a relatively large change in voltage to cause an error.

Table 7.5 shows the electrical characteristics of the different serial communication standards. The two main standards agencies are the EIA and the ITU.

Table 7.5 Main serial standards.

EIA	RS-232-C	RS-423-A	RS-422-A	RS-485
ITU	V.28	V.10/X.26	V.11/X.27	
Data rate	20 kbps	300 kbps	10 Mbps	10 Mbps
Max. Distance	15 m	1200 m	1200 m	1200 m
Type	Unbalanced	Unbalanced Differential	Balanced Differential	Balanced Differential
No. of drivers and receivers	1 driver 1 receiver	1 driver 10 receivers	1 driver 10 receivers	32 drivers 32 receivers
Driver voltages	±15 V	± 6 V	±5 V	±5 V
No. of conductors per signal	1	2	2	2

Balanced lines use two lines for each signal line, whereas, unbalanced lines use one wire for each signal and a common return circuit (see Figure 7.15). RS-422 is a balanced interface and uses two conductors to carry the signal (see Figure 7.16). The electrical current in each of the conductors is 180° out-of-phase with each other. Balanced lines are general less prone to noise as any noise induced into the conductors will be of equal magnitude. At the receiver the noise will tend to cancel out.

The voltage levels for RS-232 range from ±3 to ±25 V, whereas, for RS422/RS423 the voltage ranges are ±0.2 to ±6 V. For very high bit rates the cable is normally terminated with the characteristic impedance of the line, for example a 50 Ω cable is terminated with a 50 Ω termination.

RS-422 interface circuits can have up to 10 receivers. They have no ground connection and are thus useful in isolating two nodes. For two-way communications four connections are required, the TX+ and TX- on one node connects to the RX+ and RX- on the other.

Nodes may have a direct RS-422 connection or can be fitted with a special interface adaptor to convert from RS-232 to RS-422 (although the maximum data rate is likely to be limited to the maximum RS-232 rate).

It should also be noted that the maximum connection distance relates to the maximum data rate. If a lower data rate is used then the maximum distance can be increased. For example, in some situations with a good quality cable and in a low noise environment, it is possible to have cable run of 1 km using RS-232 at 1200 bps.

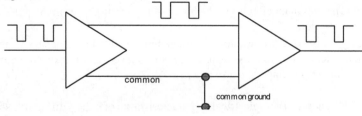

Figure 7.15 Unbalanced digital interface circuit (RS-423).

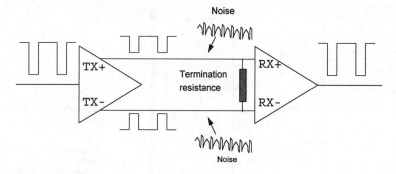

Figure 7.16 Balanced digital interface circuit (RS-422).

7.8 Communications between two nodes

RS-232 is intended to be a standard but not all manufacturers abide by it. Some implement the full specification while others implement just a partial specification. This is mainly because not every device requires the full functionality of RS-232, for example a modem requires many more control lines than a serial mouse.

The rate at which data is transmitted and the speed at which the transmitter and receiver can transmit/receive the data dictates whether data handshaking is required.

7.8.1 Handshaking

In the transmission of data there can be no either handshaking, hardware handshaking or software handshaking. If no handshaking is used then the receiver must be able to read the received characters before the transmitter sends another. The receiver may buffer the received character and store it in a special memory location before it is read. This memory location is named the receiver buffer. Typically, it may only hold a single character. If it is not emptied before another character is received then any character previously in the buffer will be overwritten. An example of this is illustrated in Figure 7.17. In this case the receiver has read the first two characters successfully from the receiver buffer, but it did not read the third character as the fourth transmitted character has overwritten it in the receiver buffer. If this condition occurs then some form of handshaking must be used to stop the transmitter sending characters before the receiver has had time to service the received characters.

Hardware handshaking involves the transmitter asking the receiver if it is ready to receive data. If the receiver buffer is empty it will inform the transmitter that it is ready to receive data. Once the data is transmitted and loaded into the receiver buffer the transmitter is informed not to transmit any more characters until the character in the receiver buffer has been read. The main hardware handshaking lines used for this purpose are:

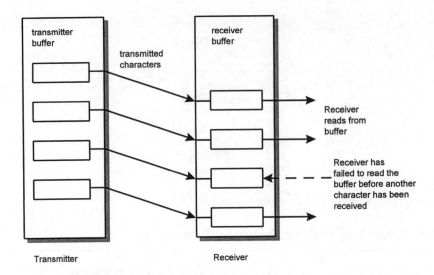

transmitter buffer

receiver buffer

transmitted characters

Receiver reads from buffer

Receiver has failed to read the buffer before another character has been received

Transmitter

Receiver

Figure 7.17 Transmission and reception of characters.

- CTS – Clear To Send;
- RTS – Ready To Send;
- DTR – Data Terminal Ready;
- DSR – Data Set Ready.

Software handshaking involves sending special control characters. These include the DC1-DC4 control characters.

7.8.2 RS-232 pocket tester and break-out boxes

An RS-232 pocket tester is useful in determining which handshaking lines are active and which are inactive. They are normally self-powered and have 25-pins which are wired straight through so that it can be connected in-line from one device to another. The lines connect monitored are pins 2, 3, 4, 5, 6, 8 and 20 which monitor the lines TD, RD, RTS, CTS, DSR, CD and DTR. They are dual colour LEDs and a Green light indicates a high input (a 0, or a SPACE) and red indicates a low input (a 1 or a MARK).

A break-out box allows any of the signal lines to be connected to either side of the connection. An RS-232 pocket tester and micro break-out box are illustrated in Figure 7.18.

7.8.3 RS-232 set-up

Figure 7.19 shows a sample set-up taken from the Terminal program available with Microsoft Windows. The selectable baud rates are 110, 300, 600, 1200, 2400, 4800, 9600 and 19200 baud. Notice that the flow control can either be set to software handshaking (Xon/Xoff), hardware handshaking or none.

The parity bit can either be set to none, odd, even, mark or space. A mark in the parity option sets the parity bit to a '1' and a space sets it to a '0'.

In this case COM1: is set at 1200 baud, 8 data bits, no parity, 1 stop bit and no parity checking. Notice that with this package a parity error is ignored unless the Parity Check box is activated.

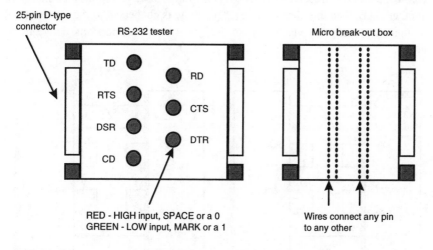

Figure 7.18 RS-232 tester and micro break-out box.

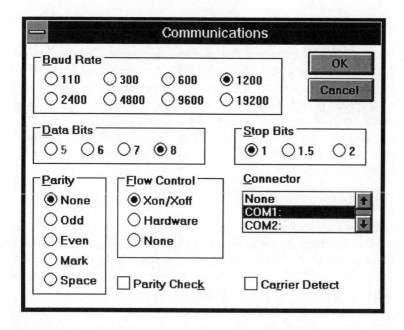

Figure 7.19 Sample communications set-up screen from Microsoft Terminal.

7.8.4 Simple no-handshaking communications

In this form of communication it is assumed that the receiver can read the received data from the receive buffer before another character is received. Data is sent from a TD pin connection of the transmitter and is received in the RD pin connection at the receiver. When a DTE (such as a computer) connects to another DTE, then the transmit line (TD) on one is connected to the receive (RD) of the other and vice versa. Figure 7.20 shows the connections between the nodes.

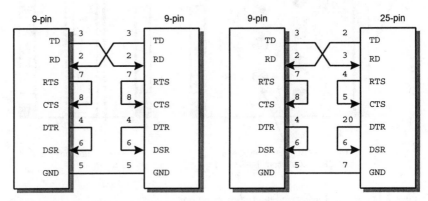

Figure 7.20   RS-232 connections with no hardware handshaking.

7.8.5 Software handshaking

There are two ASCII characters that start and stop communications. These are X-ON (^S , Cntrl-S or ASCII 11) and X-OFF (^Q, Cntrl-Q or ASCII 13). When the transmitter receives an X-OFF character it ceases communications until an X-ON character is sent. This type of handshaking is normally used when the transmitter and receiver can process data relatively quickly. Normally, the receiver will also have a large buffer for the incoming characters. When this buffer is full it transmits an X-OFF. After it has read from the buffer the X-ON is transmitted, see Figure 7.21.

7.8.6 Hardware handshaking

Hardware handshaking stops characters in the receiver buffer from being overwritten. The control lines used are all active HIGH. Figure 7.22 shows how the nodes communicate. When a node wishes to transmit data it asserts the RTS line active (that is, HIGH). It then monitors the CTS line until it goes active (that is, HIGH). If the CTS line at the transmitter stays inactive then the receiver is busy and cannot receive data, at the present. When the receiver reads from its buffer the RTS line will automatically goes active indicating to the transmitter that it is now ready to receive a character.

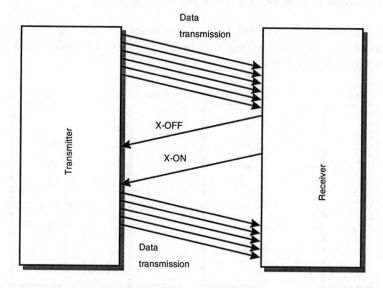

Figure 7.21 Software handshaking using X-ON and X-OFF.

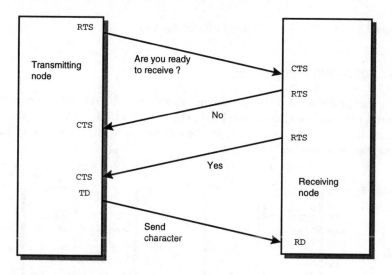

Figure 7.22 Handshaking lines used in transmitting data.

Receiving data is similar to the transmission of data, but, the lines DSR and DTR are used instead of RTS and CTS. When the DCE wishes to transmit to the DTE the DSR input to the receiver will become active. If the receiver cannot receive the character it will set the DTR line inactive. When it is clear to receive it sets the DTR line active and the remote node then transmits the character. The DTR line will be set inactive until the character has been processed.

7.8.7 Two-way communications with handshaking

For full handshaking of the data between two nodes the RTS and CTS lines are crossed over (as are the DTR and DSR lines). This allows for full remote node feedback (see Figure 7.23).

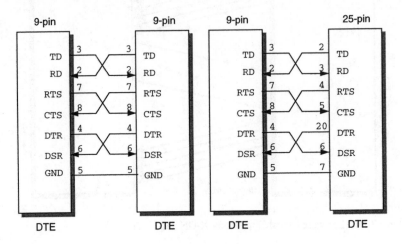

Figure 7.23 RS-232 communications with handshaking.

7.8.8 DTE-DCE connections

A further problem occurs in connecting two nodes. A DTE-DTE connection requires crossovers on their signal lines, whereas DTE-DCE connections require straight-through lines. An example connection for a computer to modem connection is shown in Figure 7.24.

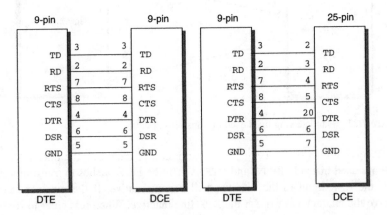

Figure 7.24 DTE to DCE connections.

7.9 Programming RS-232

Normally, serial transmission is achieved via the RS-232 standard. Although 25 lines are defined usually only a few are used. Data is sent along the TD line and received by the RD line with a common ground return. The other lines, used for handshaking, are RTS (Ready to Send) which is an output signal to indicate that data is ready to be transmitted and CTS (Clear to Send), which is an input indicating that the remote equipment is ready to receive data.

The 8250 IC is commonly used in serial communications. It can either be mounted onto the motherboard of the PC or fitted to an I/O card. This section discusses how it is programmed.

7.9.1 Programming the serial device

The main registers used in RS-232 communications are the Line Control Register (LCR), the Line Status Register (LSR) and the Transmit and Receive buffers (see Figure 7.25). The Transmit and Receive buffers share the same addresses.

The base address of the primary port (COM1:) is normally set at 3F8h and the secondary port (COM2:) at 2F8h. A standard PC can support up to four COM ports. These addresses are set in the BIOS memory and the address of each of the ports is stored at address locations 0040:0000 (COM1:), 0040:0002 (COM2:), 0040:0004 (COM3:) and 0040:0008 (COM4:). Program 7.3 can be used to identify these addresses. The statement:

```
ptr=(int far *)0x0400000;
```

initializes a far pointer to the start of the BIOS communications port addresses. Each address is 16 bits thus the pointer points to an integer value. A far pointer is used as this can access the full 1 MB of memory, a non-far pointer can only access a maximum of 64 kB. Direct memory accessing will be covered in more detail in Chapter 8.

📄 Program 7.3
```
#include <stdio.h>
#include <conio.h>
int    main(void)
{
int    far *ptr; /* 20-bit pointer */

   ptr=(int far *)0x0400000; /* 0040:0000 */ clrscr();

   printf("COM1: %04x\n",*ptr);
   printf("COM2: %04x\n",*(ptr+1));
   printf("COM3: %04x\n",*(ptr+2));
   printf("COM4: %04x\n",*(ptr+3));

   return(0);
}
```

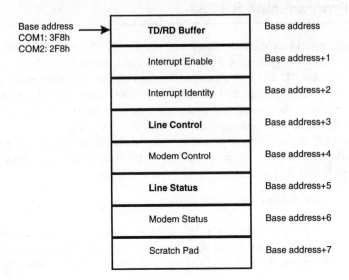

Base address COM1: 3F8h COM2: 2F8h	→	TD/RD Buffer	Base address
		Interrupt Enable	Base address+1
		Interrupt Identity	Base address+2
		Line Control	Base address+3
		Modem Control	Base address+4
		Line Status	Base address+5
		Modem Status	Base address+6
		Scratch Pad	Base address+7

Figure 7.25 Serial communication registers.

Test run 7.3 shows a sample run. In this case there are four COM ports installed on the PC. If any of the addresses is zero then that COM port is not installed on the system.

⌨ Test run 7.3

```
COM1:  03f8
COM2:  02f8
COM3:  03e8
COM4:  02e8
```

7.9.2 Line Status Register (LSR)

The LSR determines the status of the transmitter and receiver buffers. It can only be read from, and all the bits are automatically set by hardware. The bit definitions are given in Figure 7.26. When an error occurs in the transmission of a character one (or several) of the error bits is (are) set to a '1'.

One danger when transmitting data is that a new character can be written to the transmitter buffer before the previous character has been sent. This overwrites the contents of the character being transmitted. To avoid this the status bit S_6 is tested to determine if there is still a character still in the buffer. If there is then it is set to a '1', else the transmitter buffer is empty.

To send a character:

> *Test Bit 6 until set;*
> *Send character;*

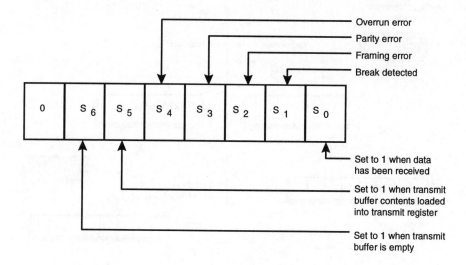

Figure 7.26 Line Status Register.

A typical Pascal routine is:

```
repeat
    status := port[LSR] and $40;
until (status=$40);
```

When receiving data the S_0 bit is tested to determine if there is a bit in the receiver buffer. To receive a character:

Test Bit 0 until set;
Read character;

A typical Pascal routine is:

```
repeat
        status := port[LSR] and $01;
until (status=$01);
```

Figure 7.27 shows how the LSR is tested for the transmission and reception of characters.

7.9.3 Line Control Register (LCR)

The LCR sets up the communications parameters. These include the number of bits per character, the parity and the number of stop bits. It can be written to or read from and has a similar function to that of the control registers used in the PPI and PTC. The bit definitions are given in Figure 7.28.

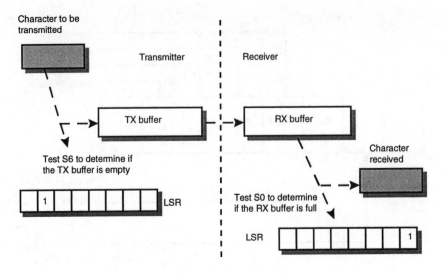

Figure 7.27 Testing of the LSR for the transmission and reception of characters.

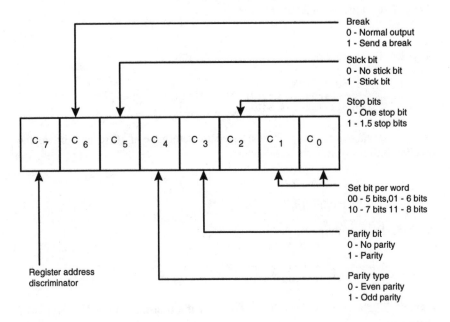

Figure 7.28 Line Control Register.

The msb, C_7, must to be set to a '0' in order to access the transmitter and receiver buffers, else if it is set to a '1' the baud rate divider is set up. The baud rate is set by loading an appropriate 16-bit divisor into the addresses of transmitter/receiver buffer address and the next address. The value loaded depends on the crystal frequency connected to the IC. Table 7.6 shows divisors for a crystal frequency is 1.8432 MHz. In general the divisor, N, is related to the baud rate by:

$$Baud\ rate = \frac{Clock\ frequency}{16 \times N}$$

For example, for 1.8432 MHz and 9600 baud $N = 1.8432 \times 10^6/(9600 \times 16) = 12$ (000Ch).

Table 7.6 Baud rate divisors.

Baud rate	Divisor (value loaded into Tx/Rx buffer)
110	0417h
300	0180h
600	00C0h
1200	0060h
1800	0040h
2400	0030h
4800	0018h
9600	000Ch
19200	0006h

7.9.4 Register addresses

The addresses of the main registers are given in Table 7.7. To load the baud rate divisor, first the LCR bit 7 is set to a '1', then the LSB is loaded into divisor LSB and the MSB into the divisor MSB register. Finally, bit 7 is set back to a '0'. For example, for 9600 baud, COM1 and 1.8432 MHz clock then 0Ch is loaded in 3F8h and 00h into 3F9h.

When bit 7 is set at a '0' then a read from base address reads from the RD buffer and a write operation writes to the TD buffer. An example is this is shown in Figure 7.29.

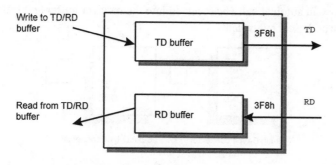

Figure 7.29 Read and write from TD/RD buffer.

Table 7.7 Serial communications addresses.

Primary	Secondary	Register	Bit 7 of LCR
3F8h	2F8h	TD buffer	'0'
3F8h	2F8h	RD buffer	'0'
3F8h	2F8h	Divisor LSB	'1'
3F9h	2F9h	Divisor MSB	'1'
3FBh	2FBh	Line Control Register	
3FDh	2FDh	Line Status Register	

7.9.5 Programming RS232 via DOS

The DOS command mode (or md for DOS Version 6.0) can be used to set the parameters of the serial port. The general format is shown next, options in square brackets ([ ]) are optional.

```
MODE COMn[:]baud[, parity[ ,word_size[ ,stopbits[ ,P]]]]
```

The mode command can also be used for other functions such as setting up the parallel port, text screen, and so on.

```
C:\DOCS\NOTES>mode /?
Configures system devices.
MODE COMm[:] [BAUD=b] [PARITY=p] [DATA=d] [STOP=s] [RETRY=r]
```

For example

```
C>  mode com2:2400,e,8,1
```

sets up COM2: with 2400 Baud, even parity, 8 data bits and 1 stop bit.

```
C>  mode com1:9600
```

changes the Baud rate to 9600 on COM1.

7.10 RS-232 programs

Program 7.4 uses a loop back on the TD/RD lines so that a character sent by the computer will automatically be received into the receiver buffer and Program 7.5 is the Turbo Pascal equivalent.

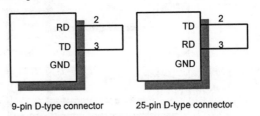

9-pin D-type connector   25-pin D-type connector

Figure 7.30   System connections.

This set-up is useful in testing the transmit and receive routines. The character to be sent is entered via the keyboard. A *CNTRL-D* (^D) keystroke exits the program. Figure 7.30 shows system connections for a 9- and 25-pin connector.

📄 Program 7.4

```
/* This program transmits a character from COM1: and receives */
/* it via this port. The TD is connected to RD.               */

#define  COM1BASE    0x3F8
#define  COM2BASE    0x2F8
#define  TXDATA      COM1BASE
#define  LCR         (COM1BASE+3) /*   0x3FB line control    */
#define  LSR         (COM1BASE+5) /*   0x3FD line status     */

#include <conio.h>   /* required for getch()                 */
#include <dos.h>     /* required for inportb() and outportb() */
#include <stdio.h>

/* Some ANSI C prototype definitions   */
void     setup_serial(void);
void     send_character(int ch);
int      get_character(void);

int      main(void)
{
int      inchar,outchar;

    setup_serial();
    do
    {
        puts("Enter char to be transmitted (Cntrl-D to end)");
        outchar=getch();
        send_character(outchar);
        inchar=get_character();
        printf("Character received was %c\n",inchar);
    } while (outchar!=4);
    return(0);
}

void     setup_serial(void)
{
    outportb( LCR, 0x80);
    /* set up bit 7 to a 1  to set Register address bit   */

    outportb(TXDATA,0x0C);
    outportb(TXDATA+1,0x00);
    /* load TxRegister with 12, crystal frequency is 1.8432MHz */

    outportb(LCR, 0x0A);
    /* Bit pattern loaded is 00001010b, from msb to lsb these are:*/
    /* 0 - access TD/RD buffer ,  0 - normal output             */
    /* 0 - no stick bit  , 0 - even parity                      */
    /* 1 - parity on,  0 - 1 stop bit                           */
    /* 10 - 7 data bits                                         */
}

void send_character(int ch)
{
char  status;
```

```
        do
        {
            status = inportb(LSR) & 0x40;
        } while (status!=0x40);
        /*repeat until Tx buffer empty ie bit 6 set*/

        outportb(TXDATA,(char) ch);
}

int    get_character(void)
{
int    status;
    do
    {
        status = inportb(LSR) & 0x01;
    } while (status!=0x01);
    /* Repeat until bit 1 in LSR is set */

    return( (int)inportb(TXDATA));
}
```

📄 Program 7.5

```
program RS232_1(input,output);
{      This program transmits a character from COM1: and receives }
{      it via this port. The TD is connected to RD.               }
uses   crt;
const   TXDATA   =    $3F8;    LSR      =    $3FD;
        LCR      =    $3FB;    CNTRLD   =    #4;
var     inchar, outchar:char;

procedure   setup_serial;
begin
    port[LCR] := $80;     { set up bit 7 to a 1                    }
    port[TXDATA] := $0C;
    port[TXDATA+1] := $00;
    { load TxRegister with 12, crystal frequency is 1.8432 MHz     }
    port[LCR] := $0A
    { Bit pattern loaded is 00001010b, from msb to lsb these are:}
    { Access TD/RD buffer, normal output, no stick bit           }
    { even parity, parity on, 1 stop bit, 7 data bits            }
end;

procedure   send_character(ch:char);
var         status:byte;
begin
    repeat
        status := port[LSR] and $40;
    until (status=$40);
        {repeat until bit Tx buffer is empty                     }
    port[TXDATA] := ord(ch); {send ASCII code                    }
end;

function    get_character:char;
var         status,inbyte:byte;
begin

    repeat
        status := port[LSR] and $01;
    until (status=$01);
    inbyte := port[TXDATA];
    get_character:= chr(inbyte);
end;
```

```
begin
   setup_serial;

   repeat
      outchar:=readkey;
      send_character(outchar);
      inchar:=get_character;
      writeln('Character received was ',inchar);
   until (outchar=CNTRLD);

end.
```

In the next two programs a transmitter and receiver program are used to transmit data from one PC to another. Program 7.6 should run on the transmitter PC and Program 7.7 runs on the receiver. The cable connections for 9-pin to 25-pin, 9-pin to 9-pin and 25-pin to 25-pin connectors are given in Figure 7.31.

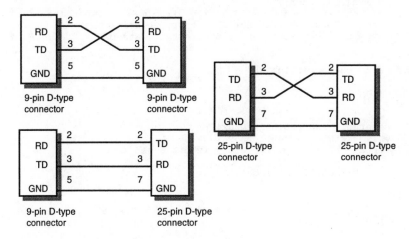

Figure 7.31   Connection from one PC to another.

📄 Program 7.6

```
/*    send.c                                              */
#define   TXDATA    0x3F8
#define   LSR       0x3FD
#define   LCR       0x3FB

#include <stdio.h>
#include    <conio.h>    /* included for getch                */
#include    <dos.h>      /* included for inputb and outputb  */

void     setup_serial(void);
void     send_character(int ch);

int      main(void)
{
int      ch;

   puts("Transmitter program. Please enter text (Cntl-D to end)");
   setup_serial();
```

```
        do
        {
           ch=getche();
           send_character(ch);
        } while (ch!=4);

        return(0);
}

void  setup_serial(void)
{
        outportb( LCR, 0x80);
        /* set up bit 7 to a 1  to set Register address bit         */

        outportb(TXDATA,0x0C);
        outportb(TXDATA+1,0x00);
        /* load TxRegister with 12, crystal frequency is 1.8432MHz   */

        outportb(LCR, 0x0A);
        /* Bit pattern loaded is 00001010b, from msb to lsb these are:*/
        /* Access TD/RD buffer, normal output, no stick bit          */
        /* even parity, parity on, 1 stop bit, 7 data bits           */
}

void  send_character(int ch)
{
char   status;
        do
        {
           status = inportb(LSR) & 0x40;
        } while (status!=0x40);
        /*repeat until Tx buffer empty ie bit 6 set*/

        outportb(TXDATA,(char) ch);
}
```

📄 Program 7.7

```
/*      receive.c                                                  */

#define  TXDATA    0x3F8
#define  LSR       0x3FD
#define  LCR       0x3FB

#include <stdio.h>
#include    <conio.h>    /* included for getch              */
#include    <dos.h>      /* included for inputb and outputb */

void      setup_serial(void);
int       get_character(void);

int       main(void)
{
int       inchar;
        setup_serial();
        do
        {
           inchar=get_character();
           putchar(inchar);
        } while (inchar!=4);
        return(0);

}
```

```
void setup_serial(void)
{
    outportb( LCR, 0x80);
    /* set up bit 7 to a 1 to set Register address bit          */

    outportb(TXDATA,0x0C);
    outportb(TXDATA+1,0x00);
    /* load TxRegister with 12, crystal frequency is 1.8432MHz   */

    outportb(LCR, 0x0A);
    /* Bit pattern loaded is 00001010b, from msb to lsb these are:*/
    /* Access TD/RD buffer, normal output, no stick bit          */
    /* even parity, parity on, 1 stop bit, 7 data bits           */
}

int     get_character(void)
{
int     status;
    do
    {
        status = inportb(LSR) & 0x01;
    } while (status!=0x01);

    /* Repeat until bit 1 in LSR is set */
    return( (int)inportb(TXDATA));

}
```

7.11 Using BIOS

The previous section discussed how the 8250 IC is programmed. Some machines may use a different IC, such as the 8251. An improved method of programming the RS-232 device is to use the BIOS commands. These are device independent and contain programs that can control the RS-232 hardware. The function used, in C, is

```
int bioscom(int cmd,char abyte,int port)
```

where

    port   corresponds to the port to use, 0 for COM1:, 1 for COM2:;
    cmd   0 – set communications parameters to the value given by abyte;
            1 – send a character;
            2 – receive a character;
            3 – return status of communications.

When cmd is set to 0 the device is programmed. In this mode the definition of the bits in abyte is given in Figure 7.32. For example if the function call is bioscom(0,0x42,0) then the RS-232 parameters for COM1: will be 300 baud, no parity, 1 stop bit and 7 data bits.

If cmd is set to 3 then the return value from the function is a 16-bit unsigned integer. Bits 8 to 15 are defined as:

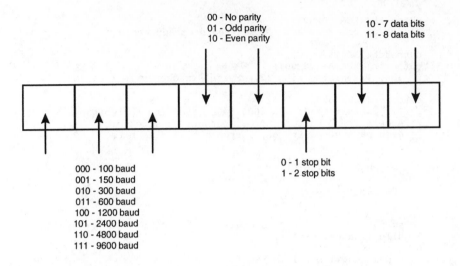

Figure 7.32 Bit definitions for bioscom() function.

Bit 15 – Time out
Bit 14 – Transmit shift register empty (character sent)
Bit 13 – Transmit holding register empty
Bit 12 – Break detect
Bit 11 – Framing error
Bit 10 – Parity error
Bit 9 – Overrun error
Bit 8 – Data ready

Program 7.8 uses combios() to create a transmit/receive program. To test it either loop the TD to the RD or connect two PCs together. The BIOS functions use the RTS and CTS lines in their operation. Thus, connect the RTS to the CTS on the transmitter and receiver or connect the RTS of the transmitter to the CTS of the receiver and the CTS on the transmitter to the RTS of the receiver (see Figure 7.20).

📄 Program 7.8

```
#include <stdio.h>
#include <bios.h>
#include <conio.h>

#define   COM1            0
#define   COM2            1

#define   DATA_READY      0x100
#define   DATABITS7       0x02
#define   DATABITS8       0x03

#define   STOPBIT1        0x00
```

```
#define    STOPBIT2           0x04

#define    NOPARITY           0x00
#define    ODDPARITY          0x08
#define    EVENPARITY         0x18

#define    BAUD110            0x00
#define    BAUD150            0x20
#define    BAUD300            0x40
#define    BAUD600            0x60
#define    BAUD1200           0x80
#define    BAUD2400           0xA0
#define    BAUD4800           0xC0
#define    BAUD9600           0xE0

#define    ESC                0x1B

int        main(void)
{
int        RS232_setting,status,in,ch;

    RS232_setting=BAUD2400 | STOPBIT1 | NOPARITY | DATABITS7;

    bioscom(0,RS232_setting,COM1);

    puts("RS-232 COMBIOS press ESC to exit");

    do
    {
        status = bioscom(3, 0, COM1);

        if (kbhit())
        {
            ch = getch();
            bioscom(1, ch, COM1); /* send character */
        }
        if (status & DATA_READY)
            if ((in = bioscom(2, 0, COM1) & 0x7F) != 0) /* receive char */
                putch(in);
    } while (ch!=ESC);

    return 0;
}
```

7.12 Exercises

7.1   Write a program that continuously sends the character 'A' to the serial
            line. Observe the output on an oscilloscope and identify the bit pattern
            and the baud rate.

7.2   Write a program that continuously sends the characters from 'A' to
            'Z' to the serial line. Observe the output on an oscilloscope.

7.3   Complete Table 7.8 to give the actual time to send 1000 characters
            for the given baud rates. Compare these values with estimated values.

Table 7.8 Baud rate divisors.

Baud rate	Time to send 1000 characters (sec)
110	
300	
600	
1200	
2400	
4800	
9600	
19200	

Note that approximately 10 bits are used for each character thus 960 characters/sec will be transmitted at 9600 baud.

7.4   Modify Program 7.3 or 7.4 so that the program prompts the user for the baud rate when the program is started. A sample run is shown in Test run 7.4.

🖥 Test run 7.4

```
Enter baud rate required:
1    110
2    150
3    300
4    600
5    1200
6    2400
7    4800
8    9600
>> 8
RS232 transmission set to 9600 baud
```

7.5   Modify the setup_serial() routine so that the RS232 parameters can be passed to it. These parameters should include the comport (either COM1: or COM2:), the baud rate, the number of data bits and the type of parity. An outline of the modified function is given in Program 7.9.

📄 Program 7.9

```
#define      COM1BASE 0x3F8
#define      COM2BASE 0x2F8
#define      COM1        0
#define      COM2        1
enum      baud_rates  {BAUD110,BAUD300,BAUD600,BAUD1200,
                       BAUD2400,BAUD4800,BAUD9600};
enum      parity      {NO_PARITY,EVEN_PARITY,ODD_PARITY};
enum      databits    {DATABITS7,DATABITS8};
#include <conio.h>
#include <dos.h>
#include <stdio.h>
```

```
/* Some ANSI C prototype definitions   */
void   setup_serial(int comport, int baudrate, int parity,
                          int databits);
void   send_character(int ch);
int    get_character(void);

int    main(void)
{
int    inchar,outchar;

    setup_serial(COM1,BAUD2400,EVEN_PARITY,DATABITS7);
    :::::::::::etc.
}


void   setup_serial(int comport, int baudrate,
                          int parity, int databits)
{
int    tdreg,lcr;

    if (comport==COM1)
    {
        tdreg=COM1BASE;
        lcr=COM1BASE+3;
    }
    else
    {
        tdreg=COM2BASE;
        lcr=COM2BASE+3;
    }
    outportb( lcr, 0x80);
    /* set up bit 7 to a 1  to set Register address bit   */

    switch(baudrate)
    {
    case BAUD110: outportb(tdreg,0x17);outportb(tdreg+1,0x04);
          break;
    case BAUD300: outportb(tdreg,0x80);outportb(tdreg+1,0x01);
          break;
    case BAUD600: outportb(tdreg,0x00);outportb(tdreg+1,0xC0);
          break;
    case BAUD1200: outportb(tdreg,0x00);outportb(tdreg+1,0x40);
            break;
    case BAUD2400: outportb(tdreg,0x00);outportb(tdreg+1,0x30);
            break;
    case BAUD4800: outportb(tdreg,0x00);outportb(tdreg+1,0x18);
            break;
    case BAUD9600: outportb(tdreg,0x00);outportb(tdreg+1,0x0C);
        break;
    }
        :::::::::: etc.
}
```

7.6   One problem with Programs 7.5 and 7.6 is that when the return key is pressed only one character is sent. The received character will be a carriage return which returns the cursor back to the start of a line and not to the next line. Modify the receiver program so that a line feed will be generated automatically when a carriage return is received. Note a carriage return is an ASCII 13 and line feed is a 10.

7.7 Modify the get_character() routine so that it returns an error flag if it detects an error or if there is a time-out. Table 7.9 lists the error flags and the returned error value. An outline of the C code is given in Program 7.10. If a character is not received within 10 seconds an error message should be displayed.

📄 Program 7.10

```
#include <stdio.h>
#include <dos.h>

#define   TXDATA    0x3F8
#define   LSR       0x3FD
#define   LCR       0x3FB

void      show_error(int ch);
int       get_character(void);

enum      RS232_errors   {PARITY_ERROR=-1, OVERRUN_ERROR=-2,
                          FRAMING_ERROR=-3, BREAK_DETECTED=-4, TIME_OUT=-5};

int       main(void)
{
int       inchar;
    do
    {
        inchar=get_character();

        if (inchar<0) show_error(inchar);
        else printf("%c",inchar);
    } while (inchar!=4);

    return(0);
}

void      show_error(int ch)
{
    switch(ch)
    {
    case PARITY_ERROR: printf("Error: Parity error/n"); break;
    case OVERRUN_ERROR: printf("Error: Overrun error/n"); break;
    case FRAMING_ERROR: printf("Error: Framing error/n"); break;
    case BREAK_DETECTED: printf("Error: Break detected/n");break;
    case TIME_OUT: printf("Error: Time out/n"); break;
    }
}

int   get_character(void)
{
int   instatus;
    do
    {
        instatus = inportb(LSR) & 0x01;
        if (instatus & 0x02) return(BREAK_DETECTED);
                        :::: etc
    } while (instatus!=0x01 );

    return( (int) inportb(TXDATA) );

}
```

Table 7.9 Error returns from get_character().

Error condition	Error flag return	Notes
Parity error	−1	
Overrun error	−2	
Framing error	−3	
Break detected	−4	
Time-out	−5	get_character() should time-out if no characters are received with 10 seconds.

Test the routine by connecting two PCs together and set the transmitter with differing RS232 parameters.

7.13 Projects

7.13.1 Project 1: Half-duplex link

Design and implement a half-duplex link between two computers, that is, only one computer can talk at a time. The same program should run on both computers but one should automatically go into talk mode when a key is pressed on the keyboard and the other as a listener. When the talker transmits an ASCII code 04 (^D) the mode of the computers should swap, that is, the talker should listen and the listener should talk. Figure 7.33 shows a sample conversation.

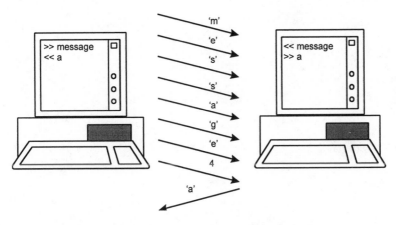

Figure 7.33 System operation.

7.13.2 Project 2: Full-duplex link

Design and implement a *simulated* full-duplex link between two computers, that is, both computers can talk and listen at the same time. The same program should run on both computers. *Hint*: one possible implementation is to loop within the `get_character()` routine and break out of it if a character is received from the line or if a character has been entered from the keyboard. If a character is entered from the keyboard it should be sent and the program then returns to the `get_character()` routine.

7.13.3 Project 3: Simulated software handshaking

Set up two PCs so that one PC transmits characters to the other and the receiving PC displays them. If the space bar is pressed on the receiver PC then it should send an X-OFF character to the transmitter. The transmitter should then display a message informing the user that the receiver is busy. When the spacebar is pressed again on the receiver it should transmit an X-ON character and the transmitter is free to transmit more characters to the receiver. So it continues, with the receiver using the space bar to toggle its busy/idle state.

7.13.4 Project 4: File transfer

Design and implement a program that transfers a file between two PCs. The name of the file should be initially sent following a NULL character (to delimit the filename). Next, the contents of the file are sent and finally an EOF character.

8
Accessing Memory Directly

8.1 Introduction

Computers need memory to run programs and also to store data. The 80386, 80486 and Pentium processors run in one of two modes, either virtual or real. When using the virtual mode they act as a pseudo-8086 16-bit processor, this mode is also named the protected mode. In the real-mode they can use the full capabilities of their address and data bus. The mode and their addressing capabilities depend on the software and thus all DOS-based programs use the virtual mode.

The 8086 has a 20-bit address bus so that when the PC is running 8086-compatible code it can only address up to 1 MB of memory. It also has a segmented memory architecture and can only directly address 64 kB of data at a time. A chunk of memory is known as a segment and hence the phrase 'segmented memory architecture'.

Memory addresses are normally defined by their hexadecimal address. A 4-bit address bus can address 16 locations from 0000b to 1111b. This can be represented in hexadecimal as 0h to Fh. An 8-bit bus can address up to 256 locations from 00h to FFh.

Two important addressing capabilities for the PC relate to a 16- and a 20-bit address bus. A 16-bit address bus addresses up to 64 kB of memory from 0000h to FFFFh and a 20-bit address bus addresses a total of 1 MB from 00000h to FFFFFh. The 80386/80486/Pentium processors have a 32-bit address bus and can address from 00000000h to FFFFFFFFh.

A memory location is identified with a segment and an offset address and the standard notation is segment:offset. A segment address is a 4-digit hexadecimal address which points to the start of a 64 kB chunk of data. The offset is also a 4-digit hexadecimal address which defines the address offset from the segment base pointer. This is illustrated in Figure 8.1.

The segment:offset address is defined as the logical address, the actual physical address is calculated by shifting the segment address 4 bits to the left and adding the offset. The example given next shows that the actual address of 2F84:0532 is 2FD72h.

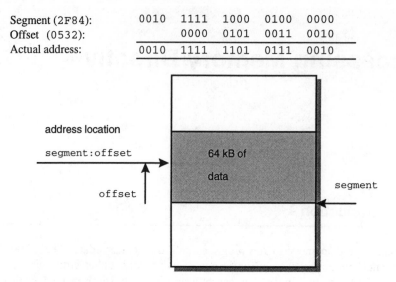

Segment (2F84):	0010	1111	1000	0100	0000
Offset (0532):		0000	0101	0011	0010
Actual address:	0010	1111	1101	0111	0010

Figure 8.1 Memory addressing.

8.2 Accessing memory using C and Pascal

In C the address `1234:9876h` is specified as `0x12349876`. Turbo Pascal accesses a memory location using the predefined array `mem[]` (to access a byte), `memw[]` (a word) or `memw[]` (a long integer). The general format is `mem[segment:offset]`.

8.3 Near and far pointers

A near pointer is a 16-bit pointer which can only be used to address up to 64 kB of data whereas a far pointer is a 20-bit pointer which can address up to 1 MB of data. A far pointer can be declared using the `far` data type modifier, as shown next.

```
char   far *ptr;      /* declare a far pointer          */

ptr=(char far *) 0x1234567;/*initialize far pointer      */
```

In the program shown in Figure 8.2 a near pointer `ptr1` and a far pointer `ptr2` have been declared. In the bottom part of the screen the actual addresses stored in these pointers is displayed. In this case `ptr1` is `DS:1234h` and `ptr2` is `0000:1234h`. Notice that the address notation of `ptr1` is limited to a 4-digit hexadecimal address, whereas `ptr2` has a `segment:offset` address. The address of `ptr1` is in the form `DS:XXXX` where DS (the data segment) is a fixed address in memory and XXXX is the offset.

```
                                        Edit
      Line 13    Col 9    Insert Indent Tab Fill Unindent * C:NEW.C
#include <stdio.h>

int      main(void)
{
int      *ptr1;
int      far *ptr2;

         ptr1=(int *)0x1234;
         ptr2=(int far *)0x1234;

         printf("Pointer 1 is %p\n",ptr1);
         printf("Pointer 2 is %p\n",ptr2);

         return(0);
}


                                ─── Watch ───
•ptr2: 0000:1234
 ptr1: DS:1234
```

Figure 8.2 Near and far pointers.

There are several modes in which the compiler operates. In the small model the compiler declares all memory addresses as near pointers and in the large model they are declared as far pointers. Figure 8.3 shows how the large memory model is selected in Borland C (Options→ Compiler→ Model→ Large). The large model allows a program to store up to 1 MB of data and code. Normally the small model is the default and only allows a maximum of 64 kB for data and 64 kB for code.

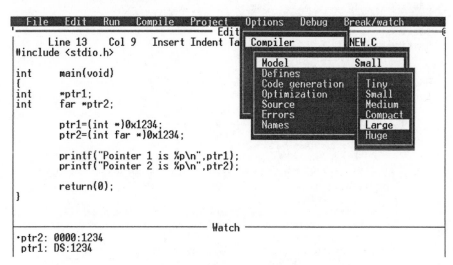

Figure 8.3 Compiling a program in the large model.

8.4 Memory viewer

Program 8.1 displays the contents of the memory while the program is being executed. Each address in memory contains one byte therefore a char pointer is set up to point to each location; the declaration char *ptr is used for this purpose. This pointer does not have a memory allocated to it when it is declared, thus at the start of the program it is set to the first memory location 0x00 (ptr=(char *)0x00).

After the content of each memory location has been read the pointer is incremented to the next address in the memory. As the declaration is a character pointer it will be incremented by a single address location.

The program reads 64 bytes from memory and displays these as ASCII characters. It then awaits the user to enter a character. If the entered character is an 'x' then the program quits. Any other character causes the program to continue displaying the memory contents. Some special control characters are non-printed, such as line-feeds, new-lines, form-feeds, and so on. For this purpose the program detects them and replaces then with a '?'. Macros such as CR (carriage return), VT (vertical tab) and BS (backspace), and so on are used to define these. Program 8.2 shows the equivalent Turbo Pascal program.

📄 Program 8.1

```
#include <stdio.h>
#define    BELL          7
#define    BS            8
#define    HT            9
#define    LF            10
#define    VT            11
#define    FF            12
#define    CR            13
int        main(void)
{
char       *ptr,ch=NULL;
int        i;
    puts("Memory viewer program Ver 1.00");
    puts("Enter an 'x' to exit the program");
    ptr=(char *)0x00;
    do
    {
        printf("%4p >> ",ptr); /* display memory pointer   */
        for (i=0;i<64;i++)
        {
            if ((*ptr!=BELL) && (*ptr!=CR) && (*ptr!=VT) &&
                    (*ptr!=BS) && (*ptr!=FF) && (*ptr!=LF))
                putchar(*ptr);
            else putchar('?');    /* display control character */
            ptr++;       /* move one byte in memory */
        }
        printf("\n");
        fflush(stdin);
```

```
        ch=getch();
    } while (ch!='x'); /* enter an 'x' to exit   */

    return(0);
}
```

📄 Program 8.2

```
uses      crt;

const     BELL=7;BS=8;HT=9;LF=10;VT=11;FF=12;CR=13;

var       ch:byte;
          inchar:char;
          i,offset:integer;
begin
    writeln('Memory viewer program Ver 1.00');
    writeln('Enter an "x" to exit the program');

    offset:=0;

    repeat
        write('0000:',offset:04,' ');
        for i:=1 to 64 do
        begin
            ch:=mem[0000:offset]; { memory location seg:off }
            if ((ch<>BELL) and (ch<>CR) and (ch<>VT) and(ch<>BS) and
                    (ch<>FF) and (ch<>LF)) then
                    write(chr(ch))
            else write('?'); { display control character   }
            offset:=offset+1;
        end;
        writeln;
        inchar:=readkey;
    until (inchar='x'); { enter an 'x' to exit   }
end.
```

Program 8.3 contains several enhancements. It displays 24 lines of memory contents before the user is prompted to continue. The number of rows is set up by the constant SCREEN_SIZE and the number of characters on a single row by COLUMN_SIZE.

📄 Program 8.3

```
#include <stdio.h>
#include <ctype.h> /* required for tolower() and isprint() */
#define    SCREEN_SIZE    24
#define    COLUMN_SIZE    64
int        main(void)
{
char       *ptr,ch=NULL; /* initialise ch as a NULL character*/
int        i,j;
    puts("Memory viewer program Ver 1.01");
    ptr=(char *) 0x00;
    do
    {
        for (j=0;j<SCREEN_SIZE;j++)
        {
            printf("%4p >> ",ptr);
            for (i=0;i<COLUMN_SIZE;i++)
            {
```

```
            if (isprint(*ptr))    putchar(*ptr);
            else                   putchar('?');
            ptr++;
        }
        printf("\n");
    }
    printf("Do you wish to continue (y/n) >> ");
    fflush(stdin);
    ch=tolower(getch());
} while (ch=='y');
return(0);
}
```

Figure 8.4 shows a sample run taken from an IBM compatible PC. Notice that the '?' character has replaced the special control characters, such as line-feed, horizontal tab, etc.

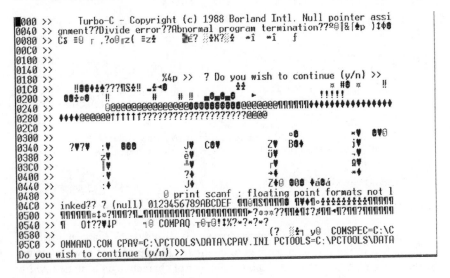

Figure 8.4   Test run for program 8.2.

8.5 DOS/ BIOS memory map

The memory of a PC splits into several function areas, as shown in Figure 8.5. The first 1024 bytes in memory (0000:0000h to 0040:0000h) contains a list of interrupt vectors. These give the memory addresses of where a calling program finds a program to service the interrupt. An interrupt occurs when a device requires the attention of the processor. This can occur when there is a key stroke, when outputting of graphics to a display, input data from a mouse, and so on.

The memory area from 0040:0000h to 0050:0000h contains information which BIOS and DOS programs use. A listing of some of the contents are given in Table 8.1. A byte is eight bits, a word is two bytes and a long word is four bytes.

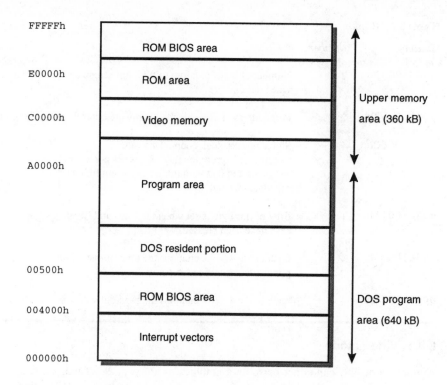

Figure 8.5 Memory usage in PCs.

Table 8.1 Sample memory ROM BIOS memory locations.

Starting address	Number of bytes	Function	Program reference
0040:0000h	8	Each word contains the base address of the serial ports (COM1: -COM4:).	Program 7.2
0040:0008h	8	Each word contains the base address of the parallel ports (LPT1: -LPT4:).	Program 8.6
0040:0010h	2	Equipment list data.	Exercise 8.4
0040:0013h	2	Amount of usable memory (in kB).	
0040:0017h	2	Keyboard status bits.	
0040:001Ch	2	Keyboard status bits.	
0040:0049h	1	Current video mode.	Program 8.4
0040:004Ah	2	Number of characters that can be displayed for each row of text.	Exercise 8.3

Table 8.1 (Cont.).

Starting address	Number of bytes	Function	Program reference
0040:004Ch	2	Number of bytes required to fill a full screen of video data.	Exercise 8.2
0040:0063h	2	Port address of video display hardware controller.	Program 8.5
0040:006Ch	4	Stores master clock count. This value is incremented approximately 18.2 times per second and is reset to 0 at midnight. The current time is calculated from it.	Program 8.7
0040:0071h	1	Bit 7 of this byte is set when the Cntrl and Break keys have been pressed.	
0040:0078h	4	Each of the 4 bytes contains the time-out value for printers connected to the parallel port.	
0040:007Ch	4	Each of the 4 bytes contains the time-out value for serial port.	

8.5.1 Video mode

A graphics display can either be set in a graphics or a text mode. Table 8.2 lists some typical modes. The display mode is stored as a byte at memory location 0040:0049h. A pointer which points to a single byte at this location is declared by:

```
char far     *ptr;
```

Program 8.4 is a program to display the current display mode.

Table 8.2 Video modes.

Mode	Description	Mode	Description
0 (00h)	Text:40×25 16-colour	17 (11)	Graphics:640×480 2-colour
1 (01h)	Text:40×25 16-colour	18 (12h)	Graphics:640×480 16-colour
2 (02h)	Text:80×25 16-colour	19 (13h)	Graphics:320×200 256-colour
3 (03h)	Text:80×25 16-colour	106 (6Ah)	Graphics:640×400 16-colour
4 (04h)	Graphics:320×200 4-colour	256 (100h)	Graphics:640×480 256-colour
5 (05h)	Graphics:320×200 16-colour	257 (101h)	Graphics:640×480 256-colour
6 (06h)	Graphics:640×480 2-colour	258 (102h)	Graphics:800×600 16-colour
7 (07h)	Text:80×25 2-colour	259 (103h)	Graphics:800×600 256-colour
13 (0Dh)	Graphics:320×200 16-colour	260 (104h)	Graphics:1280×768 16-colour
14 (0E)	Graphics:640×200 16-colour	261 (105h)	Graphics:1280×768 256-colour
15 (0F)	Graphics:640×350 2-colour	262 (106h)	Graphics:1280×1024 16-colour
16 (10h)	Graphics:640×350 16-colour	263 (107h)	Graphics:1280×1024 256-colour

📄 **Program 8.4**
```
#include <stdio.h>

int    main(void)
{
char far *ptr;
int    mode;

    ptr=(char far *)0x00400049;
          /* BIOS video mode is stored at 0040:0049h*/
    mode=*ptr;
    printf("Current display mode is %x\n",mode);

}
```

A sample run is given in test run 8.1. In this case the current mode is 80×25 16-colour text.

💻 **Test run 8.1**

```
Current display mode is 3
```

8.5.2 Display controller base address

As has been seen from previous chapters, I/O devices map into the I/O ports. Standard devices such as serial and parallel ports are located at a fixed location in the memory map. The EGA/VGA video card also contains registers which set the functionality of the graphics display. The base address of the EGA/VGA controller is stored at 0040:0063 and takes up two bytes. To declare a pointer which points to two bytes it must be initialized as an integer pointer, as given below.

```
    int far *ptr;
```

Program 8.5 displays the base address of the video controller and Test run 8.2 shows a sample run.

📄 **Program 8.5**
```
#include <stdio.h>
int    main(void)
{
int far *ptr;
unsigned int    address;

    ptr=(int far *)0x00400063;
        /* Address of display controller is stored at 0040:0063 */

    address=*ptr;

    printf("I/O port address of video is %x (hex)\n",address);
    return(0);
}
```

```
I/O port address of video is 3d4 (hex)
```

8.5.3 Parallel port address

A standard PC can support up to four serial and four parallel ports. Program 7.2 showed how the base address of the four serial ports can be displayed. The base address for COM1: is stored at 0040:0000h, COM2: at 0040:0002h, COM3: at 0040:0004h, COM4: at 0040:0006h. The parallel ports addresses are stored at eight memory locations above the serial ports. These are, LPT1: at 0040:0008h, LPT2: at 0040:000Ah, LPT3: at 0040:000Ch, LPT4: at 0040:000Eh. Program 8.6 displays the addresses of the primary and secondary parallel ports and Test run 8.3 shows a sample run.

📄 Program 8.6

```
#include <stdio.h>

int    main(void)
{
int    far *ptr;

    ptr=(int far *)0x00400008;
       /* Address of primary parallel port is at 0040:0008    */
       /* Address of secondary parallel port is at 0040:000A   */

    printf("Primary parallel port   is at %04x (hex)\n",*ptr);
    printf("Secondary parallel port is at %04x (hex)\n",*(ptr+1));

    return(0);
}
```

⌨ Test run 8.3

```
Primary parallel port   is at 0378 (hex)
Secondary parallel port is at 0278 (hex)
```

8.5.4 System timer

The PC keeps time by incrementing a 4-byte value 18.2 times each second. This value is stored at an address starting at 0040:004Ch. It is reset to 0 (zero) at midnight. From this the current system time is calculated. Program 8.7 interrogates the counter memory location and displays the number of seconds which have passed since midnight. As the counter value is 4 bytes a long int pointer is declared.

📄 Program 8.7

```
#include <stdio.h>
#include <conio.h>

int    main(void)
```

```
{
long int far    *ptr;
float     seconds;

    do
    {
        ptr=(long int far *)0x0040006c;
        seconds=(float)(*ptr)/18.2;
        printf("Seconds since midnight is %.0f\n",seconds);
    } while (!kbhit());
    return(0);
}
```

8.6 Exercises

8.1   The ROM BIOS date of a PC is stored at an address starting at F000:FFF5h (0xF000FFF5) and uses 8 bytes. Write a program that reads this date. A sample run is shown in Test run 8.4 (in this case the 8 characters read are 11/11/92).

Test run 8.4

```
BIOS RAM Date is 11/11/92
```

8.2   The PC stores a 2-byte value at a starting address of 0040:004Ch which gives the number of bytes that filsl a complete screen with video data. Write a program to display this value. A sample run is given in Test run 8.5.

Test run 8.5

```
Number of bytes to fill a whole screen of
video data is 4096
```

8.3   The PC stores a 2-byte value at a starting address of 0040:004Ah which gives the maximum number of characters in a row of text. Write a program which displays this value. A sample run is given in test run 8.6.

Test run 8.6

```
Number of characters in a row of text is 80
```

8.4   The PC stores a 2-byte value at a starting address of 0040:0010h which gives an indication of the PC's equipment list. Write a program that displays this value. Program 8.8 shows an outline of this program. The bit definitions of the word are given in Table 8.3.

Program 8.8

```c
#include <stdio.h>
int     main(void)
{
int     far     *ptr;
int     equip, printers;

    ptr=(int far *)0x00400010;
    equip=*ptr;
    printers=(equip & 0xB000)>> 13;
    if (equip & 0x01) printf("Floppy disk present\n");
    if (equip & 0x02) printf("Math coprocesser present\n");
        :::::::::::::::etc
    printf("No. of printers is %d\n",printers);
    return(0);
}
```

Table 8.3   Bit definitions for system equipment list word.

Bit(s)	Description
14,15	Number of printers installed
13	(Reserved)
12	Set to a '1' if there is a joy stick present
11,10,9	Number of RS-232 serial ports
8	(Reserved)
7,6	Number of floppy disks installed, 00 – 1 drive, 01 – 2 drives, 10 – 3 drives, 11 – 4 drives
5,4	Video mode: 00 – 40 column colour, 01 – 80 columns colour, 10 – 40 column B/W, 00 – other
3,2	(Not used)
1	Set to a '1' if there is a math co-processor present
0	Set to a '1' if there are floppy disk drives present

8.5   PCs with VGA monitors normally have a VGA BIOS copyright message at an address starting at C000:0000h and taking up 256 bytes. A sample run for a PC with a V7-MIRAGE SVGA card is shown in Test run 8.7. Write a program that displays the VGA BIOS copyright message and thus determine the version number of the video driver software.

🖳 Test run 8.7

```
Uª@ë 7400éö                        IB
M VGA Compatible BIOS.   »fG n ,
  ÿ  Quadtel S3 86C801 ISA Enhanc
ed VGA BIOS. Version 2.13.03F02


Copyright 1987-1992 Quadtel Cor
p., A Phoenix Technologies Ltd C
ompany.


       V7-MIRAGE BIOS version 3.05V
```

8.6   Modify Program 8.4 so that it displays the current display mode as
text. A sample outline is given in Program 8.9.

📄 Program 8.9

```c
#include <stdio.h>

char      *display_modes[19]=
              {  "40x25 16-colour","40x25 16-colour",
                 "80x25 16-colour",        ::: etc.

int   main(void)
{
char far *ptr;
int   mode;

  ptr=(char far *)0x00400049;
               /* BIOS video mode is stored at 0040:0049h*/

  mode=*ptr;

  printf("Current display mode is %s\n",
               display_mode[mode]);
}
```

8.7   Modify Program 8.7 so that it only prints to the display once every
second.

8.8   Modify Program 8.3 so that it uses far pointers. Notice that the
pointer is displayed with the format XXXX:YYYY (compile program
in the large memory model).

9
PC Video Text Memory

9.1 Accessing PC video text memory

A PC uses a specific area of memory to store the characters which appear on the
screen. For a colour monitor this starts at address B800:0000. Each character
has a text attribute associated with it. This attribute defines the text foreground
and background colour, and whether it is to blink or not (to flash on and off). A
typical monitor has 80 columns and 25 rows. Thus, a total of 4000 bytes are
used to store all the characters (80×25 characters and 80×25 attributes). Figure
9.1 shows how the characters and attributes are arranged in memory. Attribute
bit definitions are given in Figure 9.2.

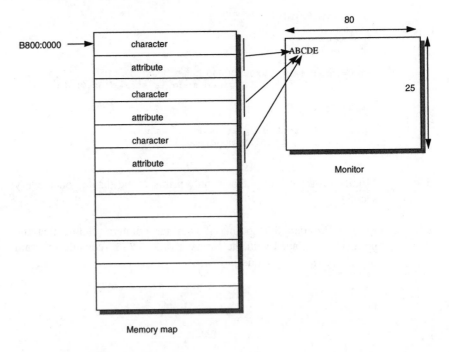

Figure 9.1   Video text memory map.

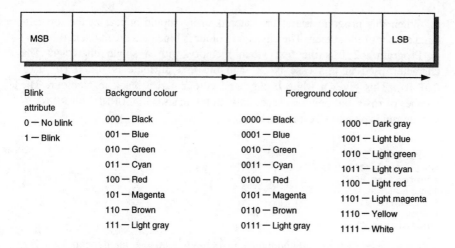

MSB							LSB

Blink attribute

Blink attribute	Background colour	Foreground colour	
0 — No blink	000 — Black	0000 — Black	1000 — Dark gray
1 — Blink	001 — Blue	0001 — Blue	1001 — Light blue
	010 — Green	0010 — Green	1010 — Light green
	011 — Cyan	0011 — Cyan	1011 — Light cyan
	100 — Red	0100 — Red	1100 — Light red
	101 — Magenta	0101 — Magenta	1101 — Light magenta
	110 — Brown	0110 — Brown	1110 — Yellow
	111 — Light gray	0111 — Light gray	1111 — White

Figure 9.2   Character attributes.

In Program 9.1 the user is prompted for a text string. The characters in this string are then written to display memory, starting at the top left position on the screen. The attribute for the characters is 0x21 (0 010 0001b). This gives a foreground colour of blue, a background colour of green and no blink. After each character and attribute has been written to memory the pointer is incremented by 2 to move onto the next character in memory. The strlen() function determines the number of characters in the string.

The PC defaults to a 16-bit address pointer (in most cases). In order to access the area of memory between 640 kB and 1 MB a far pointer is required. This is achieved by declaring it as char far *ptr.

▤ Program 9.1

```
#include <stdio.h>

int    main(void)
{
char    far    *ptr;
char           str[BUFSIZ];
int            i;
    ptr=(char far *) 0xb8000000; /* memory address B800:0000    */
    printf("\nEnter string for direct memory access >>");
    gets(str);
    for (i=0;i<strlen(str);i++)
    {
        *ptr=str[i];         /* write character                     */
        *(ptr+1)=0x21;     /* character attribute 0 010 0001       */
        /* B XXX YYYY B - Blink, XXX - B/G Colour YYYY - F/G Colour*/
        /* Colour 0-Black, 1 Blue, 2 Green, etc.                  */
        ptr+=2;
    }
    puts("");

    return(0);
}
```

When this program is run the entered string should appear at the top left-hand corner of the screen. The character colour is blue on a green background.

Program 9.2 fills the text video memory with a single character. The character used in this case is 'X' and the text attribute is 0x70 (0 111 0000b). This gives a white background colour and a black text colour. The number of rows and columns is set up with the macros COLUMNS and ROWS. A sample run is given in Test run 9.1.

📄 Program 9.2

```
#define     COLUMNS     80
#define     ROWS        25
#include <stdio.h>
int   main(void)
{
char  far *ptr;
int         i;
    ptr=(char far *) 0xb8000000; /* memory address B800:0000      */
    for (i=0;i<COLUMNS*ROWS;i++)
    {
        *ptr='X';               /* fill with an 'X'               */
        *(ptr+1)=0x70;          /* 0 111 0000                     */
        ptr+=2;                 /* move onto next character in memory */
    }
    getchar();
    puts("");
    return(0);
}
```

💻 Test run 9.1

```
XXXXXXXXXXXXXXXXXXX.....XXXXXXXXXXXXXXXXXXXXXXXXXXXXXX
XXXXXXXXXXXXXXXXXXX.....XXXXXXXXXXXXXXXXXXXXXXXXXXXXXX
   .  .  .
   .  .  .
   .  .  .
XXXXXXXXXXXXXXXXXXX.....XXXXXXXXXXXXXXXXXXXXXXXXXXXXXX
```

9.2 Exercises

9.1   Write a program that fills the text screen with a single character 'z', with a white background and a blue foreground colour, using direct video access.

9.2   Write a program that outputs a screen filled with a single character from 'A' to 'Z', that is, each screen should be filled with a single character. Determine the time to display all 26 screens.

9.3   Write a program that outputs a full screen filled with a single character 'A'. It should then cycle through the 16 available text colours.

9.4   Repeat Exercise 9.3, but cycle through the 8 available backgrounds.

9.5   Repeat Exercise 9.3, but cycle through the 8 available background and 16 text colours (that is, 256 different screens).

9.6   Write a program that fills a screen with an entered character, an entered background and an entered foreground colour. Test run 9.2 shows a sample run.

⌨ Test run 9.2

```
Enter a character to be displayed >> c
Select foreground colour
(0)- BLACK (1)- BLUE (2)- GREEN (3)- CYAN (4)- RED
>> 4
Select background colour
(0)- BLACK (1)- BLUE (2)- GREEN (3)- CYAN (4)- RED
>> 3
```

10
PC Graphics Using Turbo/ Borland C

10.1 Introduction

Displays can normally be used either in a text or a graphics mode. Programs which output to text displays are generally much faster than graphic displays because the characters displayed on a text display are preprogrammed into the hardware of the computer. Whereas, on graphics display the program must map each dot (pixel) onto the screen. A PC text display typically displays characters in an array of 80 columns by 25 rows, whereas in graphics mode the screen is made up of individual pixels, such as 640 pixels in the x-direction and 480 in the y-direction. Many currently available software packages display information in graphical form. If the basic interface is displayed in graphical form it is known as a graphical user interface (or GUI). Popular GUIs include Microsoft Windows and X-Windows. Typically, graphics are used in applications which require high-resolution images. These include schematic diagrams, circuit simulation graphs, animation, and so on.

Graphics are not an intrinsic part of most programming languages. They are normally found in a graphics library. These contain functions that can range from the generation of simple line drawings to 3D bit-mapped graphics manipulation. Many different libraries can be purchased but this chapter discusses Turbo/Borland C graphics. Note that ANSI-C does not include graphics functions so that the code produced will only work on DOS-based PC using Turbo/ Borland C.

To use the graphics routines the header file *graphics.h* should be included at the top of the file, as shown below. This helps the compiler check for incorrect usage of the functions. It also includes definitions that relate to colours, line styles, fill styles, and so forth.

```
#include <graphics.h>
```

The Turbo/Borland C libraries implement a complete library of more than 50 graphics routines. The main operations are as follows:

- Simple graphics operations, such as `putpixel`, `line` and `rectangle`;
- High-level calls, such as `setviewport`, `circle`, `bar3d`, and `drawpoly`;
- Several fill and line styles;
- Bit-oriented routines, like `getimage` and `putimage`;
- Several fonts that may be magnified, justified and oriented.

The basic graphics screen is made up of pixels, which are accessed using an x-y coordinate system. The x-direction is horizontally across the screen and the y-direction is vertically down the screen. The top left-hand corner is the (0,0) x-y point and the bottom of the screen is the (MaxX, MaxY) point. A diagram of this is shown in Figure 10.1.

A graphics display is interfaced to the PC system using a video driver card. The resolution and the number of displayable colours depends on the type of graphics driver and display used. A program can automatically detect the graphics driver and load the required file that contains information on how the program interfaces to the driver. This file is called a driver file. Table 10.1 shows typical graphics drivers and their associated driver files.

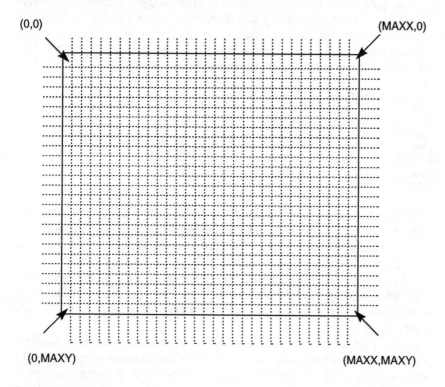

Figure 10.1 Screen resolution.

Table 10.1 Typical graphics drivers.

Graphics driver	Resolution	Colours	Driver file
CGA	320×200 (CGAC0)	4	CGA.BGI
	320×200 (CGAC1)	4	
	320×200 (CGAC2)	4	
	320×200 (CGAC3)	4	
	640×200 (CGAHI)	2	
EGA	640×200 (EGALO)	16 (BLACK...WHITE)	EGAVGA.BGI
	640×350 (EGAHI)	16	
VGA	640×200 (VGALO)	16	EGAVGA.BGI
	640×350 (VGAMED)	16	
	640×480 (VGAHI)	16	
SVGA	800×600	256	SVGA256.BGI
	1024×768	16	SVGA16.BGI

A program uses the graphics driver file when the program is run. This allows a single program to be used with several different types of graphics displays. Driver files are identified with a *BGI* filename extension (see Figure 10.2). It is advisable to copy the standard graphics drivers onto a disk or into the current working directory. A listing of these BGI files is shown below. Typically, these files will be found in the \TC or \BORLANDC\BGI directory.

```
C:\TC> dir *.bgi
  Directory of C:\TC
PC3270    BGI     6029 02/05/89    5:50
IBM8514   BGI     6665 02/05/89    5:50
HERC      BGI     6125 02/05/89    5:50
EGAVGA    BGI     5363 02/05/89    5:50
CGA       BGI     6253 20/04/90    9:23
ATT       BGI     6269 20/04/90    9:23
```

Other drivers are available such as *SVGA.BGI* (16-colour SVGA) and *SVGA256.BGI* (256-colour SVGA). EGA and VGA monitors can display at least 16 colours. Within a program these are accessed either as a numerical value or by a symbolic name, as given in Table 10.2.

The setcolor() function sets the current drawing colour. For example, to set the drawing colour to white the setcolor(WHITE); or setcolor(15); statement is used. The former is preferable as it is self-documenting.

Table 10.3 outlines the basic graphics functions. An on-line help facility is available by placing the cursor on the function name then pressing the CNTRL and function key F1 (CNTRL-F1) at the same time, or by pressing F1 for more general help. A sample help screen on initgraph() is given in Figure 10.3.

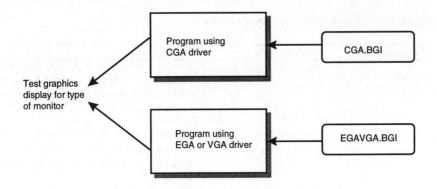

Figure 10.2   BGI files required for CGA/EGA and VGA graphics drivers.

Table 10.2   Displayable colours.

Numeric value	Symbolic name	Numeric value	Symbolic name
0	BLACK	8	DARKGRAY
1	BLUE	9	LIGHTBLUE
2	GREEN	10	LIGHTGREEN
3	CYAN	11	LIGHTCYAN
4	RED	12	LIGHTRED
5	MAGENTA	13	LIGHTMAGENTA
6	BROWN	14	YELLOW
7	LIGHTGRAY	15	WHITE

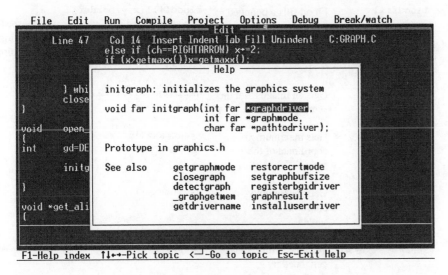

Figure 10.3   On-line help screen for `initgraph()`.

Table 10.3 Sample Borland graphics routines.

Graphic routine	Function	Description
arc	Draws a circular arc	arc(x,y,stangle,endangle,radius) draws an arc with centre point x,y at a start angle stangle, and end angle endangle and the radius is radius
bar	Draws a 2D bar	bar(left,top,right,bottom) draws a solid rectangular bar from (left,right) to (right,bottom) using current drawing colour
circle	Draws a circle of a given radius and centre	circle(x,y,radius)
cleardevice	Clears the graphic screen	cleardevice() erases the entire graphics screen
closegraph	Shuts down the graphics screen	closegraph() returns the screen to text mode
drawpoly	Draws the outline of a polygon	drawpoly(numpoints,polypoints) draws a polygon with numpoints using array polypoints. This array has consecutive x,y points. The number of values in the array will be twice the number of points to be displayed. For example, to display the polygon at the points (5,10), (50,100), (40,30) then an array needs to filled with the values 5, 10, 50, 100, 40, 30.
floodfill	Flood fills a bounded region	floodfill(x,y,border) fills an enclosed area where x,y is the seed point with the enclosed area to be filled. The floodfill continues outwards until the border colour is reached
getimage	Gets an image from the screen	getimage(x1,y1,x2,y2,ptr)
getmaxx	Gets maximum x-coordinate of the screen	x=getmaxx()
getmaxy	Gets maximum y-coordinate of the screen	y=getmaxy()
grapherrormsg	Displays error message generated by graphresult()	grapherrormsg(err)

Table 10.3 (Cont.).

Graphic routine	Function	Description
graphresult	Determines if the graphics screen has been initialized correctly	err=graphresult() Return codes include: grOk, grNoInitGraph, grNotDetected, grFileNotFound, grInvalidDriver, grFontNotFound, grInvalidMode, grError, grIOerror, grInvalidFont
imagesize	Determines the size of a graphics object	imagesize(ptr)
initgraph	Initializes graphics. It can determine the graphics driver and graphics mode to use by checking the hardware	initgraph(*gdriver,*gmode, pathtodriver) gmode returns the graphics driver, if gmode is set as DETECT then the graphics mode will be set to the highest possible resolution. Settings for gmode are DETECT, CGA, EGA, EGA64 and VGA. Typical settings for gdriver are given in Table 10.1. For example, VGALO(640×200, 16 colour), VGAMED (640×350, 16 colour), VGAHI (640×480, 16 colour)
line	Draws a line with the current drawing colour	line(x1,y1,x2,y2)
outtextxy	Displays a string of text to the graphics screen	outtextxy(x,y,str) displays the text str and coordinate x,y
putimage	Puts an image from memory onto the screen	putimage(x,y,ptr,mask)
putpixel	Puts a single pixel to the screen	putpixel(x,y,col) puts a pixel at (x,y) of colour col.
rectangle	Draws a rectangle of the current drawing colour	similar to bar() but no fill
setbkcolor	Sets the current background colour	setbkcolour(colour)
setcolor	Sets the current drawing colour	setcolor(colour) available colours on EGA/VGA are from BLACK to WHITE.

10.2 Basic graphics routines

There are two main display modes: text and graphics. The `initgraph()` function changes the mode from text to graphics and the `closegraph()` function changes it back into text mode.

10.2.1 Closing graphics

The `closegraph()` function shuts down the graphics system. The standard format is:

```
void    closegraph(void);
```

10.2.2 Initializing graphics

This function initializes the graphics system and puts the hardware into graphics mode. The standard format for the `initgraph()` routine is given next:

```
void    initgraph(int *graphdriver,
            int *graphmode,char *pathtodriver);
```

PCs can have different graphics drivers, for example:

- CGA (Colour Graphics Adaptor).
- EGA (Enhanced Graphics Adaptor).
- VGA (Video Graphics Adaptor).
- SVGA (Super Video Graphics Adaptor).
- IBM 8514.
- PC 3270.

It is possible for this function to automatically detect the graphics driver by setting the `graphdriver` parameter to `DETECT`. This has the advantage of setting the display to the maximum possible graphics range. The `pathtodriver` string informs the program as to where it will find the graphics driver file. This file is loaded when the program is run. If the string is a null (or empty) string `" "` then the program assumes that it will be found in the current working directory. Otherwise, if the driver file is to be found in the directory `\TC` on the `C:` drive then the string contains "`C:\\TC`" (a double slash indicates a sub-directory).

Program 10.1 displays a diagonal line from the top corner to the bottom corner of the screen. The graphics driver is initialized using `initgraph()`. After initialization the `graphresult()` routine determines if there were any errors in initializing the driver. A return of `grOk` indicates that there have been no problems and the graphics screen can now be used. If it does not return `grOk` then `grapherrormsg()` is used to display the error. Typical errors are "BGI

File not found" , "Graphics not initialised", "Invalid Font", and so on.

The getmaxx() and getmaxy() functions return the maximum screen size in the *x*- and *y*-directions, respectively. For a typical VGA display the maximum number of pixels in the *x*-direction will be 640 and in the *y*-direction 480.

📄 Program 10.1

```
#include <stdio.h>
#include <graphics.h>

int    main(void)
{
int    gdriver=DETECT,gmode,errorcode;

    initgraph(&gdriver,&gmode,"");

        /*    if driver file is not in the current working    */
        /*    directory then replace correct path name with    */
        /*    for example    "C:\\TC  " or "C:\\BORLANDC\\BGI"    */

    errorcode=graphresult();

    if (errorcode == grOk)
    {
        setcolor(WHITE);
        line(0,0,getmaxx(),getmaxy());
        closegraph();
    }
    else printf("Graphics error: %s\n",grapherrormsg(errorcode));

    return(0);
}
```

10.2.3 Drawing a pixel

The putpixel() function plots at pixel at a given position and colour. The standard format is:

```
void putpixel(int x,int y, int colour);
```

Program 10.2 displays pixels of a random colour at a random location. The function random(X) returns a random value from 0 to X-1. This random value is based upon the system timer. The initial value of the timer is set by calling randomize() at the start of the program.

The graphics display is initialized in open_graphics(). This function either returns GRAPHICS_ERROR on an error or NO_ERROR. The return value is then tested in main() and a decision is made as whether to quit the program. If there is no error the program continues to display pixels until the user presses a key on the keyboard. The function kbhit() is used for this purpose. It returns a TRUE value when a key is pressed, thus the loop do {..} while (!kbhit()) continues until the user presses a key.

📄 Program 10.2

```
#include <stdio.h>
#include <graphics.h>

#include <time.h>        /* required for randomize()     */
#include <stdlib.h>      /* required for random()        */
#include <conio.h>       /* required for kbhit()         */

enum      errors {NO_ERROR=0,GRAPHICS_ERROR};

int       open_graphics(void);

int       main(void)
{
int       x,y;

   if (open_graphics()==GRAPHICS_ERROR)   return(GRAPHICS_ERROR);

   randomize();   /* initialize random generator   */

   do
   {
      x=random(getmaxx());
      y=random(getmaxy());
      putpixel(x,y,random(15));
   } while (!kbhit()); /* do until a key is pressed */

   closegraph();

   return(NO_ERROR);
}

int       open_graphics(void)
{
int       gdriver=DETECT,gmode,errorcode;

   initgraph(&gdriver,&gmode,"");

   errorcode=graphresult();

   if (errorcode != grOk)
   {
      printf("Graphics error: %s\n",grapherrormsg(errorcode));
      return(GRAPHICS_ERROR);
   }

   return(NO_ERROR);
}
```

10.2.4 Drawing a line

The line() function draws a line of the current drawing colour from (*x1*, *y1*)
to (*x2*, *y2*). The standard format for line() is:

```
void line(int x1,int y1,int x2,int y2);
```

Program 10.3 draws many random lines of random colours.

Program 10.3

```
#include <stdio.h>
#include <graphics.h>
#include <time.h>          /* required for randomize()    */
#include <stdlib.h>        /* required for random()       */
#include <conio.h>         /* required for kbhit()        */

enum  errors {NO_ERROR=0,GRAPHICS_ERROR};
int   open_graphics(void);

int   main(void)
{
int   maxX,maxY;
   randomize();    /* initialize random generator   */
   if (open_graphics()==GRAPHICS_ERROR)   return(GRAPHICS_ERROR);
   maxX=getmaxx();
   maxY=getmaxy();
   do
   {
      setcolor(random(15));
      line(random(maxY),random(maxY),random(maxX),random(maxY));
   } while (!kbhit());
   closegraph();
   return(NO_ERROR);
}

int      open_graphics(void)
{
   see Program 10.2
}
```

10.2.5 Drawing a rectangle

The rectangle() function draws a rectangle using the current drawing colour. The standard format for the rectangle() routine is:

```
void rectangle(int x1,int y1,int x2,int y2);
```

Program 10.4 displays a single resistor on the screen. The draw_resistor(x,y) function draws this resistor at a point starting at (*x,y*). One problem in displaying graphics is that graphics displays can vary in the number of displayable pixels. If absolute coordinates are used then the object appears relatively small on a high-resolution display or relatively large on a low-resolution display. For this reason the resistor is scaled with respect to the maximum *x*- and *y*-coordinates, this makes its coordinates relative to the screen size. The scaling of the resistor is given in Figure 10.4.

Program 10.4

```
#include <stdio.h>
#include    <graphics.h>

enum      errors {NO_ERROR=0,GRAPHICS_ERROR};

int       open_graphics(void);
void      draw_resistor(int x,int y);
```

```
int        main(void)
{
    if (open_graphics()==GRAPHICS_ERROR)    return(GRAPHICS_ERROR);
    draw_resistor(100,200);
    getchar();
    closegraph();
    return(NO_ERROR);
}

int        open_graphics(void)
{
    see Program 10.2
}

void       draw_resistor(int x,int y)
{
int        maxx,maxy;
struct
{
    int length, width, connectline;
}    res;

    maxx=getmaxx();
    maxy=getmaxy();
    res.length=maxy/20;
    res.width=maxx/40;
    res.connectline=maxy/20;
    line(x,y,x,y+res.length);
    rectangle(x-res.width/2,y+res.connectline,
              x+res.width/2, y+res.connectline+res.length);
    line(x,y+res.connectline+res.length,
              x,y+res.length+2*res.connectline);
}
```

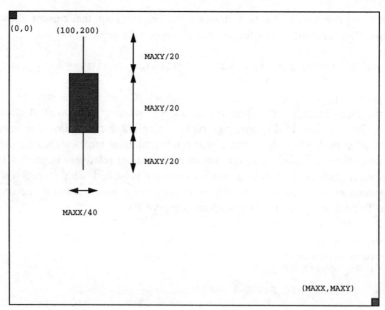

Figure 10.4 Layout of resistor graphic.

10.2.6 Displaying text

The outtextxy() function sends a string to the output device. Numerical values cannot be displayed to the screen directly and must be converted into a string before they are displayed. The standard format for the outtextxy() routine is:

```
void outtextxy(int x,int y,char *textstring);
```

Program 10.5 uses outtextxy() to display a resistor value string within the draw_resistor() function.

🖹 Program 10.5

```
#include <stdio.h>
#include    <graphics.h>

enum     errors {NO_ERROR=0,GRAPHICS_ERROR};

int      open_graphics(void);
void     draw_resistor(int x,int y, char str[]);

int      main(void)
{
   if (open_graphics()==GRAPHICS_ERROR)
      return(GRAPHICS_ERROR);

   draw_resistor(100,200,"100 K");
   draw_resistor(200,200,"200 K");

   getchar();
   closegraph();
   return(NO_ERROR);
}

int      open_graphics(void)
{
   see Program 10.2
}

void     draw_resistor(int x,int y, char str[])
{
int      maxx,maxy;
struct
{
   int length, width, connectline;
} res;

   maxx=getmaxx();
   maxy=getmaxy();

   res.length=maxy/20;
   res.width=maxx/40;
   res.connectline=maxy/20;

   line(x,y,x,y+res.length);
   rectangle(x-res.width/2,y+res.connectline,
           x+res.width/2, y+res.connectline+res.length);
   line(x,y+res.connectline+res.length,
```

```
                    x,y+res.length+2*res.connectline);
        outtextxy(x+res.width,y+res.length/2+res.connectline,str);
}
```

10.2.7 Drawing a circle

The circle() function draws a circle at a centre (*x,y*) of a given radius. The standard format for the circle() routine is:

```
    void circle(int x,int y,int radius);
```

Program 10.6 uses circle() to display a voltage source.

📄 Program 10.6
```
#include <stdio.h>
#include     <graphics.h>

enum       errors {NO_ERROR=0,GRAPHICS_ERROR};

int        open_graphics(void);
void       draw_resistor(int x,int y, char str[]);
void       draw_voltage_source(int x,int y, char str[]);

int        main(void)
{
    if (open_graphics()==GRAPHICS_ERROR)        return(GRAPHICS_ERROR);

    draw_resistor(200,200,"100 K");
    draw_resistor(300,200,"200 K");
    draw_voltage_source(100,200,"5 V");

    getchar();
    closegraph();
    return(NO_ERROR);
}


int        open_graphics(void)
{
    see program 10.2
}

void       draw_resistor(int x,int y, char str[])
{
    see Program 10.5
}

void       draw_voltage_source(int x,int y, char str[])
{
int        maxy;
struct
{
    int radius, connectline;
} volt;

    maxy=getmaxy();
    volt.radius=maxy/40;
    volt.connectline=maxy/20;
```

```
line(x,y,x,y+volt.connectline);
circle(x,y+volt.connectline+volt.radius,volt.radius);
line(x,y+volt.connectline+2*volt.radius,
          x,y+2*volt.radius+2*volt.connectline);
outtextxy(x+volt.connectline+volt.radius,
          y+volt.radius+volt.connectline,str);
}
```

10.2.8 Bit-mapped graphics

Program 10.7 displays a face which can be moved around the screen using the arrowkeys. Figure 10.5 shows a sample screen.

The getch() function gets a single keystroke from the keyboard. If the return value is a 0 then the keystroke is an extended character, such as a function key (F1...F12), page up, page down, arrowkeys, and so on. The extended character can be determined by calling getch() again. Sample return values are given in Table 10.4.

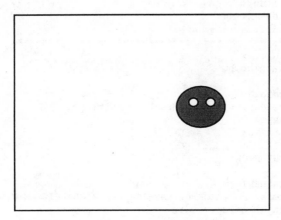

Figure 10.5   Face to be displayed.

Table 10.4   Sample returns for extended characters.

Return value	Key
Up arrow	72
Down arrow	80
Left arrow	75
Right arrow	77
Escape key	27

The following code determines whether a function key has been pressed.

```
ch=getch(); if (ch==0) ch=getch();
```

For example, if the Escape key is pressed then ch stores the value 27.

The getimage(x1,y1,x2,y2) function captures the image from the

Basic graphics routines   **187**

coordinates (x1,y1) to (x2,y2) into memory and putimage(x,y, BITMASK) is used to display the image and to clear it from the screen. The quickest way of erasing a graphics object is to exclusive-OR all the bits in the object bit map with itself. The putimage(x,y,BITMASK) function allows a bitmask to be applied to the image. An exclusive-OR function is defined with XOR_PUT. For example, if the bits on a section of the screen are 11001010, then when this is exclusive-ORed with itself the result will be 00000000.

📄 Program 10.7

```
/*******************************************************/
/* FACE.C                                            */
/* Title: Shape moving program                       */
/* Function: Program to display a shape which        */
/* can be moved using the arrow-keys                 */
/* Author(s): Bill Buchanan                          */
/* Version: 1.00                                     */
/* Created: 07-MAR-94                                */
/* Recent Modifications: NONE                        */
/*******************************************************/
#include <conio.h>
#include <graphics.h>
#include <alloc.h>
#include <stdio.h>
#include <process.h> /* required for exit() */
#define   UPARROW        72
#define   DOWNARROW      80
#define   LEFTARROW      75
#define   RIGHTARROW     77
#define   ESC            27
#define   INCREMENT       4
enum      errors {NO_ERROR=0,GRAPHICS_ERROR,GRAPHICS_MEM_ERROR};
int       open_graphics(void);
void      *get_shape(void);
int       main(void)
{
void      *shape;
int       x,y,ch;
   if (open_graphics()==GRAPHICS_ERROR)      return(GRAPHICS_ERROR);
   shape=get_shape();
   if (shape==NULL)
   {
      puts("Cannot allocate enough graphics memory");
      return(GRAPHICS_MEM_ERROR);
   }
   x=getmaxx()/2; y=getmaxy()/2;              /* start co-ordinates  */
   do
   {
      putimage(x, y, shape, XOR_PUT);    /*    draw image        */
      ch=getch(); if (ch==0) ch=getch(); /*    get extended key  */
      putimage(x, y, shape, XOR_PUT);    /*    erase image       */
      if      (ch==UPARROW)       y-=INCREMENT;
      else if (ch==DOWNARROW)     y+=INCREMENT;
      else if (ch==LEFTARROW)     x-=INCREMENT;
```

```
        else if (ch==RIGHTARROW)        x+=INCREMENT;
            /* test if shape is off the screen */
        if (x>0.9*getmaxx())x=0.9*getmaxx();
        if (x<0) x=0;
        if (y>0.9*getmaxy())y=0.9*getmaxy();
        if (y<0) y=0;

    } while (ch!=ESC);
    closegraph();

    return(NO_ERROR);
}

int      open_graphics(void)
{
    see Program 10.2
}

void  *get_shape(void)
{
int       startx,starty ;
void      *al;
int       ulx, uly, lrx, lry, size, buffsize;
    /* Draw shape */
    setfillstyle( SOLID_FILL,WHITE );

    startx=getmaxx()/2; starty=getmaxy()/2;
    size=getmaxx()/20;

    /* draw face outline */
    circle(startx,starty,size);
    floodfill(startx,starty,WHITE);

    /* draw eyes         */
    setcolor(RED);
    circle(startx+size/3,starty,size/3);
    floodfill(startx+size/3,starty,WHITE);
    circle(startx-size/3,starty,size/3);
    floodfill(startx+size/3,starty,WHITE);

    /* get size of face */
    ulx = startx-size;
    uly = starty-size;
    lrx = startx+size;
    lry = starty+size;

    buffsize = imagesize(ulx, uly, lrx, lry);
    al = malloc( buffsize );
    getimage(ulx, uly, lrx, lry, al);
    putimage(ulx, uly, al, XOR_PUT);
    return(al);
}
```

10.3 Exercises

10.1   Draw a cross which touches each corner of the screen.

10.2   Draw a triangle with its base on the bottom of the screen and an apex
which reaches the centre of the top of the screen.

10.3 Write a program that draws circles of radius 1, 2, 4, 8, 16, 32, 64... units. Each of the circles should be drawn one at a time with a delay of one second between updates. The function delay(milliseconds) delays the program for a number of milliseconds; for example, delay(1000) delays for one second.

10.4 Write a program that covers the screen with random blue pixels.

10.5 Write a program that moves a red rectangle across the screen from left to right. Use the delay() function to animate it. The rectangle should physically move. A possible method could be:

(a) display the rectangle in red at *x,y* coordinates;
(b) delay for a small time period;
(c) display the rectangle in black (which erases the red rectangle);
(d) increment the *x*- coordinate and go back to (a).

10.6 Write a program in which the user enters the values of the resistor colour bands and the program displays the resistor with the correct colour bands.

10.7 Write a program that displays the schematic given in Figure 10.6.

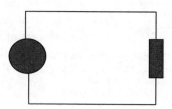

Figure 10.6 Schematic.

10.8 Write a program that draws a graph axis for *x* and *y* with a given maximum *x* and *y*. For example,

```
void drawaxis(int maxx,int maxy);
```

10.9 Change the program in Exercise 10.8 so that it draws text to the graph (for example, with maximum *x* and *y* values).

11
Interrupts

11.1 Introduction

A computer system may perform many tasks and have many different types of equipment connected, such as disk drives, printers, monitors and keyboards. There are two main methods that the processor can use if it wishes to communicate with devices. One method is to poll the external devices and determine if they are ready to communicate with the processor or if they wish to receive or give data. The programs in Chapter 6 used this technique to communicate with an ADC and in Chapter 7 to communicate with the serial port. This is known as device polling. In Chapter 6 the $\overline{\text{EOC}}$ line was tested to determine if data had been sent. In Chapter 7 the get_character() function, in the RS-232 programs, tested the S_6 bit of the LSR to determine if a character had been recevied. The main disadvantage of this method is that it is wasteful in processor time especially when communicating with relatively slow devices.

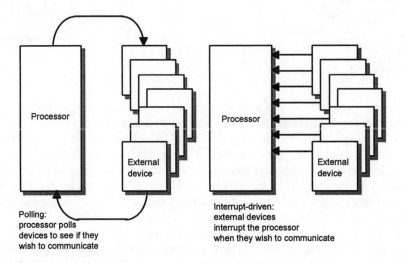

Figure 11.1   Polling or interrupt-driven communications.

An improved method is to allow devices to interrupt the processor when they require attention. Depending on the type of interrupt the processor leaves the current program and goes to a special program called an interrupt service routine (ISR). This program knows how to communicate with the device and how to process or give data. After it has completed its task, program execution returns to the program that was running before the interrupt occurred. Examples of interrupts include the processing of keys from a keyboard and data from a sound card. Figure 11.1 illustrates the two main methods.

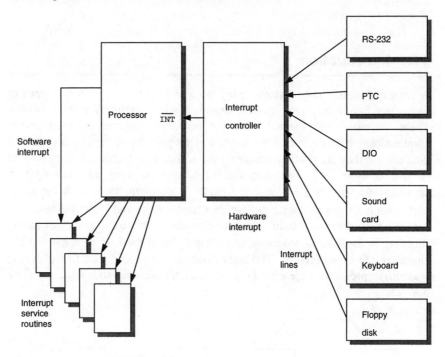

Figure 11.2   Interrupt handling.

The generation of an interrupt can occur by hardware or software, as illustrated in Figure 11.2. If a device wishes to interrupt the processor it informs the programmable interrupt controller (PIC). The PIC then decides whether it should interrupt the processor. If there is a processor interrupt then the processor reads the PIC to determine which device caused the interrupt. Then, depending on the device that caused the interrupt, a call to an ISR is made. The ISR then communicates with the device and processes any data. When it has finished the program execution returns to the original program.

A software interrupt causes the program to interrupt its execution and goes to an interrupt service routine. Typical software interrupts include reading a key from the keyboard, outputting text to the screen and reading the current date and time.

11.2 BIOS and the operating system

The Basic Input/ Output System (BIOS) communicates directly with the hardware of the computer. It consists of a set of programs which interface with devices such as keyboards, displays, printers, serial ports and disk drives. These programs allow the user to write application programs that contain calls to these functions, without having to worry about controlling them or which type of equipment is being used. Without BIOS the computer system would simply consist of a bundle of wires and electronic devices.

There are two main parts to BIOS. The first is the part permanently stored in a ROM (the ROM BIOS). It is this part that starts the computer (or boots it) and contains programs which communicate with resident devices. The second stage is loaded when the operating system is started. This part is non-permanent.

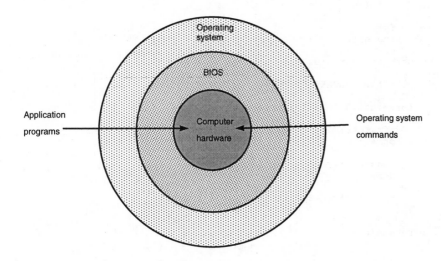

Figure 11.3 Interface between the user and computer hardware.

An operating system allows the user to access the hardware in an easy-to-use manner. It accepts commands from the keyboard and displays them to the monitor. The Disk Operating System, or DOS, gained its name from its original purpose of providing a controller for the computer to access its disk drives. The language of DOS consists of a set of commands which are entered directly by the user and are interpreted to perform file management tasks, program execution and system configuration. It makes calls to BIOS to execute these. The main functions of DOS are to run programs, copy and remove files, create directories, move within a directory structure and to list files. The relationship between the computer's hardware, BIOS, DOS and application programs is illustrated in Figure 11.3. Microsoft Windows 95 calls BIOS programs directly.

11.3 Interrupt vectors

Interrupt vectors are addresses which inform the interrupt handler as to where to find the ISR. All interrupts are assigned a number from 0 to 255. The interrupt vectors associated with each interrupt number are stored in the lower 1024 bytes of PC memory. For example, interrupt 0 is stored from 0000:0000 to 0000:0003, interrupt 1 from 0000:0004 to 0000:0007, and so on. The first two bytes store the offset and the next two store the segment address. Program 11.1 can be used to determine the addresses of the ISRs. Test run 11.1 shows an example run. In this case, the address of the ISR for interrupt 0 is 0EE5:0158, for interrupt 1 it is 0070:06F4.

📖 Program 11.1
```c
#include <stdio.h>

int    main(void)
{
int    far    *ptr;
int    seg,off,intr;

    ptr=(int far *)0x00;

    puts("INT ADDRESS");

    for (intr=0;intr<16;intr++)
    {
        off=*ptr;
        ptr++;

        seg=*ptr;
        ptr++;

        printf("%02d %04x:%04x\n",intr,seg,off);
    }

    return(0);
}
```

Each interrupt number is assigned a predetermined task, as outlined in Table 11.1. An interrupt can be generated either by external hardware, software, or by the processor. Interrupts 0, 1, 3, 4, 6 and 7 are generated by the processor. Interrupts from 8 to 15 and interrupt 2 are generated by external hardware. These get the attention of the processor by activating a interrupt request (IRQ) line. The IRQ0 line connects to the system timer, the keyboard to IRQ1, and so on. Most other interrupts are generated by software.

🖥 Test run 11.1
```
INT ADDRESS
00 0ee5:0158
01 0070:06f4
02 0707:0016
03 0070:06f4
```

```
04  0070:06f4
05  f000:ff54
06  f000:50b2
07  f000:3509
08  0955:0000
09  ca51:1923
10  f000:3509
11  d101:02cd
12  f000:3509
13  f000:3509
14  0705:00b7
15  0070:06f4
```

Table 11.1 Interrupt handling.

Interrupt	Name	Generated by
00 (00h)	Divide error	processor
01 (00h)	Single step	processor
02 (02h)	Non-maskable interrupt	external equipment
03 (03h)	Breakpoint	processor
04 (04h)	Overflow	processor
05 (05h)	Print screen	Shift-Print screen key stroke
06 (06h)	Reserved	processor
07 (07h)	Reserved	processor
08 (08h)	System timer	hardware via IRQ0
09 (09h)	Keyboard	hardware via IRQ1
10 (0Ah)	Reserved	hardware via IRQ2
11 (0Bh)	Serial communications (COM2)	hardware via IRQ3
12 (0Ch)	Serial communications (COM1)	hardware via IRQ4
13 (0Dh)	Reserved	hardware via IRQ5
14 (0Eh)	Floppy disk controller	hardware via IRQ6
15 (0Fh)	Parallel printer	hardware via IRQ7
16 (10h)	BIOS – Video access	software
17 (11h)	BIOS – Equipment check	software
18 (12h)	BIOS – Memory size	software
19 (13h)	BIOS – Disk operations	software
20 (14h)	BIOS – Serial communications	software
22 (16h)	BIOS – Keyboard	software
23 (17h)	BIOS – Printer	software
25 (19h)	BIOS – Reboot	software
26 (1Ah)	BIOS – Time of day	software
28 (1Ch)	BIOS – Ticker timer	software
33 (21h)	DOS – DOS services	software
39 (27h)	DOS – Terminate and stay resident	software

11.4 Processor interrupts

The processor-generated interrupts normally occur either when a program causes a certain type of error or if it is being used in a debug mode. In the debug mode the program can be made to break from its execution when a break-point occurs. This allows the user to test the current status of the computer. It can also be forced to step through a program one operation at a time (single step mode).

11.4.1 Interrupt 00h: Divide error

If the divisor of a divide operation is zero, or if the quotient overflows, then the processor generates an interrupt 00h. Many compilers use their own ISR for this interrupt as this allows the program to handle the error without crashing it.

11.4.2 Interrupt 02h: Non-maskable interrupt

This interrupt is used by external equipment to flag that a serious fault has occurred. Typical non-maskable interrupts (NMIs) are:

- For power-failure procedures;
- Memory parity error;
- Breakout switch on hardware debuggers;
- Co-processor interrupt;
- I/O channel check;
- Disk-controller power-on request.

12
Software Interrupts

12.1 Generating software interrupts

In Turbo/Borland C there are four main functions to interrupt the processor:
int86x(), intdos(), intr() and int86(). These functions are
prototyped in the header file dos.h. This header file also contains a structure
definition that allows a C program to gain access to the processor's registers.
Parameters are passed into and out of the interrupt sevice routines via these
registers. The format of the structure is:

```
struct   WORDREGS
{
   unsigned int ax;
   unsigned int bx;
   unsigned int cx;
   unsigned int dx;
   unsigned int si;
   unsigned int di;
   unsigned int cflag;
}
struct   BYTEREGS
{
   unsigned char al,ah;
   unsigned char bl,bh;
   unsigned char cl,ch;
   unsigned char dl,dh;
}

union REGS
{
   struct   WORDREGS x;
   struct   BYTEREGS h;
}
```

Registers are accessed either as 8-bit registers (such as AL, AH) or 16-bit
registers (such as AX, BX). If a structure name regs is declared, then:

regs.h.al   accesses the 8-bit AL register
regs.x.ax   accesses the 16-bit AX register.

The syntax of the function int86() is given in Figure 12.1. This shows that the interrupt number is the first argument of the parameter list, the input registers are passed as the second argument and the output registers the third. Parameters are passed to the interrupt routine by setting certain input registers and parameters are passed back from the interrupt in the output registers.

In a similiar way Turbo Pascal provides access throught the routine named Intr(). To gain access to this procedure the *uses dos;* statement is placed near the top of the program. A data type named Registers has also been predefined, as shown below. Note that it is possible to use either the 16-bit registers (such as AX, BX) or 8-bit (such as AL, AH):

```
type
    Registers = record
                    case Integer of
                        0:  (AX,BX,CX,DX,BP,SI,DI,DS,ES,Flags: Word);
                        1:  (AL,AH,BL,BH,CL,CH,DL,DH: Byte);
    end;
```

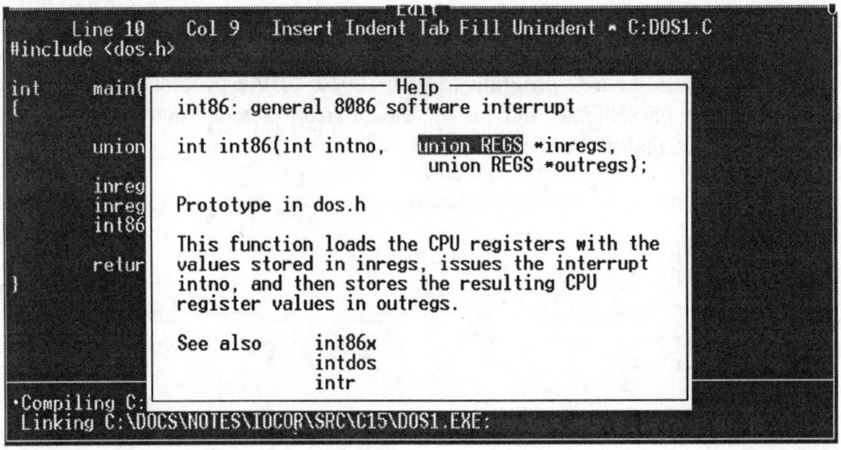

```
        Line 10    Col 9    Insert Indent Tab Fill Unindent ▪ C:DOS1.C
#include <dos.h>

int     main(┌─────────────────── Help ────────────────────┐
{            │ int86: general 8086 software interrupt       │
             │                                              │
    union    │ int int86(int intno,  union REGS *inregs,    │
             │                       union REGS *outregs);  │
    inreg    │                                              │
    inreg    │ Prototype in dos.h                           │
    int86    │                                              │
             │ This function loads the CPU registers with the│
    retur    │ values stored in inregs, issues the interrupt │
             │ intno, and then stores the resulting CPU     │
}            │ register values in outregs.                  │
             │                                              │
             │ See also      int86x                         │
             │               intdos                         │
             │               intr                           │
•Compiling C:└──────────────────────────────────────────────┘
 Linking C:\DOCS\NOTES\IOCOR\SRC\C15\DOS1.EXE:
```

Figure 12.1 Help screen for int86().

12.1.1 Interrupt 10h: BIOS video mode

Interrupt 10h allows access to the video display. Table 12.1 outlines typical interrupt calls. Program 12.1 uses the BIOS video interrupt to display a border around the screen which changes colour each second from black to light blue. These colours are set-up with an enum data type definition. In this case, BLACK is defined as 0, BLUE as 1, and so on.

To display a border the AH register is loaded with 0Bh, BH with 00h and BL with the border colour. Next, the interrupt 10h is called with these parameters. Typical Turbo/Borland C functions which use this interrupt are textcolor(), textbackground(), textattr(), gotoxy(), wherex(), wherey(), textmode() and gettextinfo(). Figure 12.2 shows the bit definition for the colours.

Table 12.1 BIOS video interrupt.

Description	Input registers	Output registers
Set video mode	AH=00h	AL = video mode flag
		0 (Text:40×25 B/W)
		1 (Text:40×25 B/W)
		2 (Text:80×25 Colour)
		3 (Text:60×25 Colour)
		4 (Graphics:320×200 Colour)
		5 (Graphics:320×200 B/W)
		6 (Graphics: 640×200 Colour)
Set cursor position	AH = 02h	
	BH = 00h	
	DH = row (00h is top)	
	DL = column (00h is left)	
Read cursor position	AH = 02h	DH = row (00h is top)
	BH = 00h	DL = column (00h is left)
Write character and attribute at cursor position	AH = 09h	
	AL = character to display	
	BH = 00h	
	BL = attribute (text mode) or colour (graphics mode) if bit 7 set in graphics mode, character is Exclusive-ORed on the screen	
	CX = number of times to write characters	
Read character and attribute at cursor position	AH = 08h	AH = attribute (see Figure 12.2)
	BH = 00h	AL = character
Set background/ border colour	AH = 0Bh	
	BH = 00h	
	BL = background/border colour (border only in text modes)	

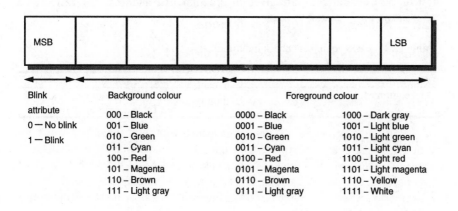

Figure 12.2 Character attribute.

📄 Program 12.1

```c
#include <stdio.h>
#include <dos.h>

void    setborder(int colour);

int     main(void)
{

enum border_cols {   BLACK,BLUE,GREEN,CYAN,RED,
                     MAGENTA,BROWN,LIGHTGRAY,DARKGRAY,LIGHTBLUE} colour;

    puts("Program to display borders from black to light blue");

    for (colour=BLACK;colour<=LIGHTBLUE;colour++)
    {
        setborder(colour);
        sleep(1);
    }

    return(0);
}

void    setborder(int col)
{
union REGS inregs,outregs;

    inregs.h.ah=0x0b;
    inregs.h.bh=0x00;
    inregs.h.bl=col;

    int86(0x10,&inregs,&outregs);
}
```

12.1.2 Interrupt 11h: BIOS equipment check

Interrupt 11h returns a word which gives a basic indication of the types of equipment connected. It is useful in determining if there is a math co-processor present and the number of parallel and serial ports connected. A program and test run use this interrupt are given in Program 12.2 and Test run 12.1. Table 12.2 shows the format of the call.

Table 12.2   BIOS equipment check interrupt.

Description	Input registers	Output registers
Get equipment list		AX = BIOS equipment list word see Table 8.3 for bit definitions

📄 Program 12.2

```c
#include <stdio.h>
#include <dos.h>

int    main(void)
{
union REGS inregs,outregs;
unsigned int ax,printers,vmode,nfloppies;
```

```
    int86(0x11,&inregs,&outregs);

    ax=outregs.x.ax;

    printers=(ax & 0xB000)>> 13;

    vmode=((ax & 0x0030)>> 4)+1;

    nfloppies=((ax & 0x00C0)>>6)+1;

    if (ax & 0x01) printf("Floppy disk present\n");

    if (ax & 0x02) printf("Math coprocesser present\n");

    printf("No. of printers is %d\n",printers);

    printf("Video mode %d\n",vmode);

    printf("No. of floppies is(are) %d\n",nfloppies);

    return(0);
}
```

🖳 Test run 12.1

```
Floppy disk present
Math coprocesser present
No. of printers is 4
Video mode 3
No. of floppies is(are) 1
```

12.1.3 Interrupt 13h: BIOS disk access

Interrupt 13h allows access to many disk operations. Table 12.3 lists two typical interrupt calls.

Table 12.3 BIOS disk access interrupt.

Description	Input registers	Output registers
Reset disk system	AH = 00h DL = drive (if bit 7 is set both hard disks and floppy disks are reset)	Return: AH = status
Get status of last operation	AH = 01h DL = drive (bit 7 set for hard disk)	Return: AH = status

12.1.4 Interrupt 14h: BIOS serial communications

In Chapter 8 serial communications were discussed in some detail. BIOS interrupt 14h can be used to transmit and receive characters and also to determine the status of the serial port. Table 12.4 lists the main interrupt calls. Program 12.3 initializes COM2: with 4800 baud, even parity, 1 stop bit and 7 data bits.

Table 12.4 BIOS serial communications interrupts.

Description	Input registers	Output registers
Initialize serial port	AH = 00h AL = port parameters (see Figure 12.3) DX = port number (00h–03h)	AH = line status (see get status) AL = modem status (see get status)
Write character to port	AH = 01h AL = character to write DX = port number (00h–03h)	AH bit 7 clear if successful AH bit 7 set on error AH bits 6–0 = port status (see get st
Read character from port	AH = 02h DX = port number (00h–03h)	Return: AH = line status (see get sta AL = received character if AH bit 7
Get port status	AH = 03h DX = port number (00h–03h)	AH = line status bit 7: timeout 6: transmit shift register empty 5: transmit holding register empty 4: break detected 3: framing error 2: parity error 1: overrun error 0: receive data ready

📄 **Program 12.3**

```
#include <stdio.h>
#include <dos.h>

int    main(void)
{
union REGS inregs,outregs;

    inregs.h.ah=0x00;

    inregs.h.al=0xD2;     /*    1101 0010                       */
                          /*    110 - 4800 bps, 10 - even parity,*/
                          /*    0 - 1 stop bit, 10 - 7 data bits */
    inregs.x.dx=0x01;     /* COM2:                             */

    int86(0x14,&inregs,&outregs);

    return(0);
}
```

12.1.5 Interrupt 16h: BIOS keyboard

Interrupt 16h allows access to the keyboard, Table 12.5 shows typical interrupt calls. Program 12.4 uses the BIOS keyboard interrupt to display characters, entered from the keyboard, to the screen. A function khit() determines if there is a character in the keyboard buffer. If there is then it returns a 1, otherwise it returns a 0. The check for keystroke interrupt call sets the zero flag (ZF) if there are no characters in the buffer, otherwise it will be a 0.

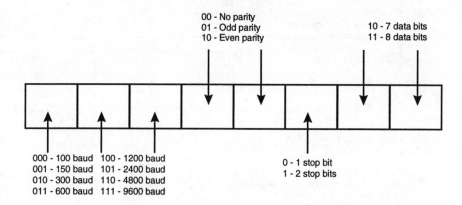

Figure 12.3 Bit definitions for serial port initialization.

Table 12.5 BIOS keyboard interrupt.

Description	Input registers	Output registers
Get keystroke	AH = 00h	AH = scan code AL = ASCII character
Check for keystroke	AH = 01h	Return: ZF set if no keystroke available ZF clear if keystroke available AH = scan code AL = ASCII character
Get shift flags	AH = 02h	AL = shift flags bit 7: Insert active 6: CapsLock active 5: NumLock active 4: ScrollLock active 3: Alt key pressed 2: Ctrl key pressed 1: left shift key pressed 0: right shift key pressed

📄 Program 12.4

```
#include <stdio.h>
#include <dos.h>

void    show_keys(void);
int     khit(void);

int     main(void)
{
int     ch;
    puts("Enter 'x' to exit");
    do
    {
        if (khit())
```

```
        {
            ch=get_character();
            printf("%c",ch);
        }
    } while (ch!='x');

    return(0);
}

int khit(void)
{
union REGS inregs,outregs;
unsigned int zf;

    inregs.h.ah=1;
    int86(0x16,&inregs,&outregs);
    zf=outregs.x.flags & 0x40;
    if (zf) return(0);
    else return(1);
}

int    get_character(void)
{
union REGS inregs,outregs;
int    ch;

    inregs.h.ah=0;
    int86(0x16,&inregs,&outregs);
    ch=outregs.h.al;
    return(ch);
}
```

12.1.6 Interrupt 17h: BIOS printer

The BIOS printer interrupts allow a program either to get the status the printer or to write a character to it. Table 12.6 outlines the interrupt calls.

Table 12.6   BIOS printer interrupt.

Description	Input registers	Output registers
Initialize printer port	AH = 01h DX = printer number (00h-02h)	AH = printer status bit 7: not busy 6: acknowledge 5: out of paper 4: selected 3: I/O error 2: unused 1: unused 0: timeout
Write character to printer	AH = 00h AL = character to write DX = printer number (00h-02h)	AH = printer status
Get printer status	AH = 02h DX = printer number (00h-02h)	AH = printer status

12.1.7 Interrupt 21h - DOS services

Programs access DOS functions using interrupt 21h. The functionality of the call is set by the contents of the AH register. Other registers are used either to pass extra information to the function or to return values back. For example, to determine the system time the AH is loaded with the value 2AH. Next, the processor is interrupted with interrupt 21H. Finally, when the program returns from this interrupt the CX register will contain the year, DH the month, DL the day and AL the day of the week.

Table 12.7 DOS interrupts.

Description	Input registers	Output registers
Read character from keyboard with echo	AH=01h	AL=character returned
Write character to output	AH=02h DL=character to write	
Write character to printer	AH=05h DL=character to print	
Read character with no echo	AH=07h	AL=character read from keyboard
Get k/b status	AH=0Bh	AL=0 no characters AL=FFh characters
Get system date	AH=2Ah	CX=year, DH=month DL=day, AL=day of week (0–Sunday, and so on)
Set system date	AH=2Bh, CX=year, DH-month, DL=day	
Get system time	AH=2Ch	CL=hour CL=minute DH=second DL=1/100 seconds
Set system time	AH=2Dh, CH=hour CL=minute, DH=second DL=1/100 second	
Get DOS version	AH=30h	AL=major version number AH=minor version number
Terminate and stay resident	AH=32h DL=driver (0–default, 1– A:,and so on)	

Table 12.7 (Cont.).

Description	Input registers	Output registers
Get boot drive	AX=3305h	DL=boot drive (1=A, and so on)
Get free disk space	AL=36h DL=drive number (0=A, etc.)	AX=sectors per cluster BX=number of free clusters CX=bytes per sector DX=total clusters on driver
DOS exit	AH=4ch	

Table 12.7 is only a small section of all the DOS related interrupts. For example, function 2Fh contains many functions that control the printer. Note that for the *Get free disk space* function the total free space on a drive is AX×BX×CX and total space on disk, in bytes, is AX×CX×DX.

In Program 12.5, function 02h (write character to the output) is used to display the character 'A'. In this case, the function number 02h is loaded into AH and the character to be displayed is loaded into DL. The equivalent Turbo Pascal program is given in program 12.6.

🗎 **Program 12.5**
```
#include <dos.h>

int    main(void)
{
union REGS inregs,outregs;

    inregs.h.ah=0x02;
    inregs.h.dl='A';

    int86(0x21,&inregs,&outregs);

    return(0);
}
```

🗎 **Program 12.6**
```
program DOS1;
{         Program to display 'A' using DOS interrupt         }

uses dos;

var REGS:registers;

begin
    regs.ah:=$02;
    regs.dl:=65;

    intr($21,regs);

end.
```

Program 12.7 uses the function 01h to get a character from the keyboard.

📄 Program 12.7

```
/* Program using DOS interrupt to get a character from the    */
/* keyboard.    Interrupt 21h is used and AH=02h              */

#include <stdio.h>
#include <dos.h>

int    main(void)
{
char   ch;
union     REGS inregs,outregs;

    inregs.h.ah=0x01;
    printf("Enter character >> ");
    int86(0x21,&inregs,&outregs);
    ch=outregs.h.al;
    printf(" Character entered was %c\n",ch);
    return(0);
}
```

Program 12.8 uses 01h and 02h function to read and write a character from/to the input/output.

📄 Program 12.8

```
/* Program using DOS interrupt to get a character from the */
/* the keyboard and display it.  Interrupt 21h is          */
/* used and AH=01 (read)and AH=02h (display)               */

#include <stdio.h>
#include <dos.h>

int    main(void)
{
union REGS inregs,outregs;

    inregs.h.ah=0x01;
    printf("Enter character >> ");
    int86(0x21,&inregs,&outregs);

        /* Display character */
    inregs.h.ah=0x02;
    inregs.h.dl=outregs.h.al;
    int86(0x21,&inregs,&outregs);
    return(0);
}
```

Programs 12.9 and 12.10 show how a program can gain access to the system date. The function used in this example is 2Ah.

📄 Program 12.9

```
#include <stdio.h>
#include <dos.h>

int    main(void)
{
int    day,month,year,day_of_week;

union REGS inregs,outregs;
```

```
    inregs.h.ah=0x2A;
    int86(0x21,&inregs,&outregs);
    day=outregs.h.dl;
    month=outregs.h.dh;
    year=outregs.x.cx;
    day_of_week=outregs.h.al;
    printf("\nDate is %d/%d/%d day of week %d\n",
                                    day,month,year,day_of_week);
    return(0);
}
```

📄 **Program 12.10**

```
program DOS2;
uses dos;

var REGS:registers;
    day,month,year,day_of_week:integer;

begin
    regs.ah:=$2a;
    intr($21,regs);
    day:=regs.dl;
    month:=regs.dh;
    year:=regs.cx;
    day_of_week:=regs.al;
    writeln('Date is ',day,'/',month,'/',year);
    writeln('Day of week is ',day_of_week);
end.
```

Test run 12.2 gives a sample run.

💻 **Test run 12.2**

```
Date is 8/9/1993
Day of week is 3
```

Program 12.11 displays the default boot drive. Test run 12.3 shows, in this case, it is the C: drive.

📄 **Program 12.11**

```
#include <stdio.h>
#include <dos.h>

int    main(void)
{
union REGS inregs,outregs;
char   *drive[5]={NULL,"A:","B:","C:","D:"};
    inregs.x.ax=0x3305;
    int86(0x21,&inregs,&outregs);
    printf("Boot drive is %s\n",drive[outregs.h.dl]);
    return(0);
}
```

💻 **Test run 12.3**

```
Boot drive is C:
```

12.1.8 Interrupt 19: BIOS reboot

Interrupt 19h reboots the system without clearing memory or restoring interrupt vectors. For a warm boot, equivalent to Ctrl-Alt-Del, then 1234h should be stored at 0040h:0072h. For a cold boot, equivalent to a reset, then 0000h is stored at 0040h:0072h. Care should be taken with this interrupt as it may cause the PC to 'hang'.

12.1.9 Interrupt 1Bh: BIOS control-break handler

This interrupt invokes the interrupt handling routine for the Cntrl-C keystroke. Turbo/ Borland C makes use of this for the function ctrlbrk().

12.1.10 Interrupt 1Ch: BIOS system timer tick

The PC system clock is updated 18.2 times every second. This clock update is automatically generated by the system timer tick interrupt. It is possible to use it to create a multi-tasking system. To achieve this the timer ISR is redirected from the system time update to a user-defined routine. This is achieved using the function setvect(intr,handler), where intr is the interrupt number and handler is the name of the new ISR for this interrupt.

In Program 12.12, the function my_interrupt() is called 18.2 times every second. Each time it is called a variable named count is incremented by one (notice in the main program there are no calls to this function). The main program tests the variable count and if it is divisible by 18 then the program displays a new count value.

In order to leave the system in the way in which it was started then the old ISR address must be restored. To achieve this the getvect() function is used to get the address of the interrupt routine at the start of the program. This is then restored with setvect() at the end. A test run is shown in Test run 12.4.

📄 Program 12.12
```
#include <stdio.h>
#include <dos.h>
#include <conio.h>
void interrupt (*oldvect)(void);
void interrupt my_interrupt();

long count=0;

int main(void)
{
long  oldcount=0,newcount=0;
   puts("Press any key to exit");
   oldvect= getvect(0x1C); /* save the old interrupt vector    */
   setvect(0x1C,my_interrupt);/* install the new interrupt handler */
   do
   {
      if (!(count % 18))
      {
         newcount=count;
```

```
            if (oldcount!=newcount) printf("%ld\n",count);
            oldcount=count;
        }
    } while (!kbhit());
    /* set the old interrupt handler back */
    setvect(0x1c, oldvect);
    return 0;
}

void interrupt my_interrupt(void)
{
    count++;
    oldvect(); /* call the old routine */
}
```

🖥 Test run 12.4

```
Press any key to exit
18
36
54
72
90
108
126
144
162
180
198
216
```

12.1.11 Interrupt 1Ah: BIOS system time

The BIOS system time interrupt allows a program to get access to the system timer. Table 12.8 outlines the interrupt calls.

Table 12.8   BIOS system time interrupt.

Description	Input registers	Output registers
Get system time	AH = 00h	CX:DX = number of clock ticks since midnight AL = midnight flag, non-zero if midnight passed since time last read
Set system time	AH = 01h	CX:DX = number of clock ticks since midnight
Set real-time clock time	AH = 03h CH = hour (BCD) CL = minutes (BCD) DH = seconds (BCD) DL = daylight savings flag (00h standard time, 01h daylight time)	

Table 12.8 (Cont.).

Get real-time clock time	AH = 02h	Return: CF clear if successful CH = hour (BCD) CL = minutes (BCD) DH = seconds (BCD) DL = daylight savings flag (00h standard time, 01h daylight time) CF set on error

12.2 Exercises

12.1   Using BIOS interrupt 10h, write a program that contains the following functions.

Function	Description
ch=read_character(x,y)	read character from screen position (x,y) and put the result into ch.
moveto(x,y)	move the screen cursor to position (x,y)
get_cursor(&x,&y)	get the current cursor postion and return it in x and y.

12.2   Using DOS interrupt (21h) write a program that determines the DOS version. Note that DOS uses a major and minor number for version control. The general format is VER MAJOR.MINOR. For example,

🖥 Test run 12.5

```
DOS Ver 3.01 is major 3 and minor 1.
```

Check the version number using the DOS command *VER*.

12.3   Using DOS interrupt (21h) write a program that determines the amount of free and total disk space on the default disk drive.

12.4   Using DOS interrupts, write a program that determines the system time.

12.5   Modify the DOS interrupt program that displays the date so that it will display the actual day (e.g. SUNDAY, etc.) and not the day of the week. For example,

12.6 Using DOS interrupts write a program that displays if a key has been pressed.

12.7 Program 12.13 uses a DOS interrupt. When it is run it prints the text PROGRAM START but does not print the text PROGRAM END. Explain why?

📄 Program 12.13
```c
#include <stdio.h>
#include <dos.h>

int    main(void)
{
union REGS inregs,outregs;
  puts("PROGRAM STARTED");

  inregs.h.ah=0x4c;
  int86(0x21,&inregs,&outregs);
  puts("PROGRAM END");

  return(0);
}
```

12.8 Using BIOS video interrupt 10h write programs which perform the following:

(a) fill a complete screen with the character 'A' of a text colour of red with a background of blue;

(b) repeat (a), but the character displayed should cycle from 'A' to 'Z' with a one-second delay between outputs;

(c) repeat (a), but the foreground colour should cycle through all available colours with a one-second delay between outputs;

(d) repeat (a) so that the background colour cycles through all available colours with a one-second delay between outputs.

12.9 Using BIOS keyboard interrupt 16h write a program that displays the status of the Shift, Caps lock, Cntrl, Scroll and Num keys.

12.10 Repeat some of the Exercises from Chapter 7 using the BIOS serial communications interrupt (14h).

12.11 If there is a line printer connected to the parallel port then write a program which sends text entered from a keyboard to the printer. The message should be entered followed by a CNTRL-D (4 ASCII). Use BIOS printer interrupt 17h.

The program should also contain error checking of each character sent. Errors should include printer out-of-paper, printer time-out and printer I/O error. If possible, test the program by switching the printer off while it is printing.

13
Hardware Interrupts

13.1 Introduction

Hardware interrupts allow external devices to gain the attention of the processor. Depending on the type of interrupt the processor leaves the current program and goes to a special program called an interrupt service routine (ISR). This program communicates with the device and processes any data. After it has completed its task then program execution returns to the program that was running before the interrupt occurred. Examples of interrupts include the processing of keys from a keyboard and data from a sound card.

If a device wishes to interrupt the processor it must inform the programmable interrupt controller (PIC). The PIC then decides if it should interrupt the processor. If it does then the processor reads the PIC to determine which device caused the interrupt. Then, depending on the device that caused the interrupt, a call to an ISR is made. Each PIC allow access to eight interrupt request lines. Most PCs use two PICs which gives access to 16 interrupt lines.

13.2 Interrupt vectors

Each device that requires to be 'interrupt-driven' is assigned an IRQ (interrupt request) line. Each IRQ is active high. The first eight (IRQ0–IRQ7) map into interrupts 8 to 15 (08h–0Fh) and the next eight (IRQ8–IRQ15) into interrupts 112 to 119 (70h–77h). Table 13.1 outlines the usage of each of these interrupts. When IRQ0 is made active the ISR corresponds to interrupt vector 8. IRQ0 normally connects to the system timer, the keyboard to IRQ1, and so on. The standard set-up of these interrupts is illustrated in Figure 13.1. The system timer interrupts the processor 18.2 times per second and is used to update the system time. When the keyboard has data it interrupts the processor with the IRQ1 line.

Data received from serial ports interrupts the processor with IRQ3 and IRQ4 and the parallel ports use IRQ5 and IRQ7. If one of the parallel, or serial ports does not exist then the IRQ line normally assigned to it can be used by another device. It is typical for interrupt-driven I/O cards, such as a sound card, to have a programmable IRQ line which is mapped to an IRQ line that is not being used.

Table 13.1 Interrupt handling.

Interrupt	Name	Generated by
08 (08h)	System timer	IRQ0
09 (09h)	Keyboard	IRQ1
10 (0Ah)	Reserved	IRQ2
11 (0Bh)	Serial communications (COM2:)	IRQ3
12 (0Ch)	Serial communications (COM1:)	IRQ4
13 (0Dh)	Parallel port (LPT2:)	IRQ5
14 (0Eh)	Floppy disk controller	IRQ6
15 (0Fh)	Parallel printer (LPT1:)	IRQ7
112 (70h)	Real-time clock	IRQ8
113 (71h)	Redirection of IRQ2	IRQ9
114 (72h)	Reserved	IRQ10
115 (73h)	Reserved	IRQ11
116 (74h)	Reserved	IRQ12
117 (75h)	Math co-processor	IRQ13
118 (76h)	Hard disk controller	IRQ14
119 (77h)	Reserved	IRQ15

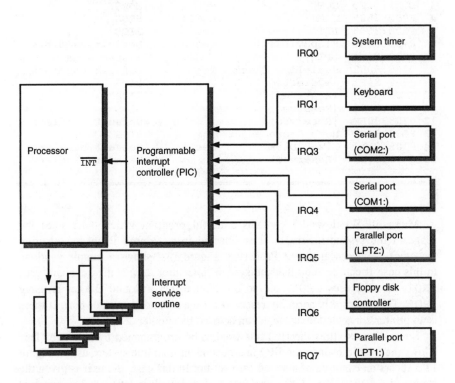

Figure 13.1 Standard usage of IRQ lines.

Note that several devices can use the same interrupt line. A typical example is COM1: and COM3: sharing IRQ4 and COM2: and COM4: sharing IRQ3. If they do share then the ISR must be able to poll the shared devices to determine which of them caused the interrupt. If two different types of device (such as a sound card and a serial port) use the same IRQ line then there may be a contention problem as the ISR may not be able to communicate with different types of interfaces.

The Microsoft program MSD.EXE and similar utilities can be used to display the current usage of the IRQ lines. A sample run of MSD is given in Test run 13.1.

⌨ Test run 13.1

```
IRQ  Address  Description       Detected      Handled By
---  -------  -----------       --------      ----------
0    0955:0000  Timer Click       Yes           win386.exe
1    CA51:1923  Keyboard          Yes           Block Device
2    F000:3509  Second 8259A      Yes           BIOS
3    D101:02CD  COM2: COM4:       COM2:         MOUSE
4    F000:3509  COM1: COM3:       COM1:         BIOS
5    F000:3509  LPT2:             Yes           BIOS
6    0705:00B7  Floppy Disk       Yes           Default Handlers
7    0070:06F4  LPT1:             Yes           System Area
8    0705:0052  Real-Time Clock   Yes           Default Handlers
9    F000:34F1  Redirected IRQ2   Yes           BIOS
10   F000:3509  (Reserved)                      BIOS
11   F000:3509  (Reserved)                      BIOS
12   0705:00FF  (Reserved)                      Default Handlers
13   F000:34FA  Math Coprocessor  Yes           BIOS
14   0705:0117  Fixed Disk        Yes           Default Handlers
15   0705:012F  (Reserved)                      Default Handlers
```

Microsoft Windows 95 contains a useful program which determines the usage of the system interrupts. It is selected from Control Panel by selecting System→ Device Manager→ Properties. Figure 13.2 shows a sample window. In this case it can be seen that the system timer uses IRQ0, the keyboard uses IRQ1, the PIC uses IRQ2, and so on. Notice that a Sound Blaster is using IRQ5. This interupt is normally reserved for the secondary printer port. If there is no printer connected then IRQ5 can be used by another device.

Some devices allow the IRQ line used to be programmed by software. This allows the user to change the IRQ line dependent upon the system usage. Figure 13.3 shows an example of a sound card set-up. In this case, the user is given the choice of IRQ2, IRQ5, IRQ7 or IRQ10. The default is set to IRQ5, which is the interrupt normally used by a secondary parallel port. Notice also that the Sound Blaster allows the base I/O address to be programmed.

Figure 13.2 Standard usage of IRQ lines.

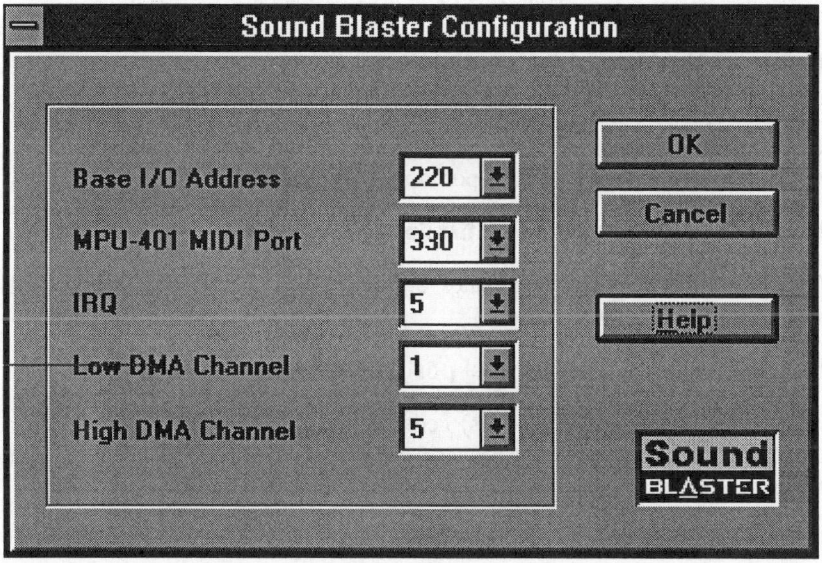

Figure 13.3 Sound Blaster configuration.

13.2.1 IRQ0: System timer

The system timer uses IRQ0 to interrupt the processor 18.2 times per second and is used to keep the time-of-day clock updated.

13.2.2 IRQ1: Keyboard data ready

The keyboard uses IRQ1 to signal to the processor that data is ready to be received from the keyboard. This data is normally a scan code, but the interrupt handler performs differently for the following special keystrokes:

- *Ctrl-Break* invokes interrupt 1Bh;
- *SysRq* invokes interrupt 15h/AH=85h;
- *Ctrl-Alt-Del* performs hard or soft reboot;
- *Shift-PrtSc* invokes interrupt 05h.

13.2.3 IRQ2: Redirection of IRQ9

The BIOS redirects the interrupt for IRQ9 back here.

13.2.4 IRQ3: Secondary serial port (COM2:)

The secondary serial port (COM2:) uses IRQ3 to interrupt the processor. Typically, COM3: to COM8: also use it, although COM3: may use IRQ4.

13.2.5 IRQ4: Primary serial port (COM1:)

The primary serial port (COM1:) uses IRQ4 to interrupt the processor. Typically, COM3: also uses it.

13.2.6 IRQ5: Secondary parallel port (LPT2:)

On older PCs the IRQ5 line was used by the fixed disk. On new systems the secondary parallel port uses it. Typically, it is used by a sound card on PCs which have no secondary parallel port connected.

13.2.7 IRQ6: Floppy disk controller

The floppy disk controller activates the IRQ6 line on completion of a disk operation.

13.2.8 IRQ7 - Primary parallel port (LPT1:)

Printers (or other parallel devices) activate the IRQ7 line when they become active. As with IRQ5 it may be used by another device, if there is no other devices connected to this line.

13.2.9 IRQ9

Redirected to IRQ2 service routine.

13.3 Programmable interrupt controller (PIC)

The PC uses the 8259 IC to control hardware-generated interrupts. It is known as a programmable interrupt controller and has eight input interrupt request lines and an output line to interrupt the processor. Originally, PCs only had one PIC and eight IRQ lines (IRQ0-IRQ7). Modern PCs can use up to 15 IRQ lines which are set up by connecting a secondary PIC interrupt request output line to the IRQ2 line of the primary PIC. The interrupt lines on the secondary PIC are then assigned IRQ lines of IRQ8 to IRQ15. This set-up is shown in Figure 13.4. When an interrupt occurs on any of these lines it is sensed by the processor on the IRQ2 line. The processor then interrogrates the primary and secondary PIC for the interrupt line which caused the interrupt.

The primary and secondary PICs are programmed via port addresses 20h and 21h, as given in Table 13.2.

Table 13.2 Interrupt port addresses.

Port address	Name	Description
20h	Interrupt control port (ICR)	Controls interrupts and signifies the end of an interrupt
21h	Interrupt mask register (IMR)	Used to enable and disable interrupt lines

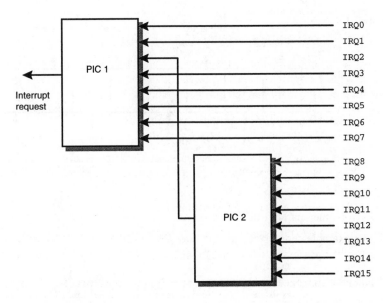

Figure 13.4 PC PIC connections.

The operation of the PIC is programmed using registers. The IRQ input lines are either configured as level-sensitive or edge-triggered interrupt. With edge-triggered interrupts a change from a low to a high on the IRQ line causes the interrupt. A level-sensitive interrupt occurs when the IRQ line is high. Most devices generate edge-triggered interrupts.

The PIC controllers can be set up in many different modes using ICW (initialization command words); refer to an Intel data book for more information on these modes. The following code initializes the PICs with edge-triggered interrupts and interrupt lines IRQ8–IRQ15 enabled.

```
#define    ICR   0x20  /* Interrupt control port              */
#define    IMR   0x21  /* Interrupt mask register port        */

outportb(ICR,0x13);  /* edge triggered, one 8259, ICW4 required  */
outportb(IMR,8);     /* use interrupt vectors 08h-0Fh for IRQ0-IRQ7 */
outportb(IMR,9);     /* ICW4: buffered mode, normal EOI, 8088     */
```

Note that this initialization is normally carried out when the system is rebooted and there is thus no need to reinitialize it in a user program (unless any of the initialization parameters requires to be changed). After initialization these ports are used either to enable or disable an interrupt lines using the IMR or to control the interrupts with the ICR.

In the IMR an interrupt line is enabled by setting the assigned bit to a 0 (zero). This allows the interrupt line to interrupt the processor. Figure 13.5 shows the bit definitions of the IMR. For example, if bit 0 is set to a 0 then the system timer on IRQ0 is enabled.

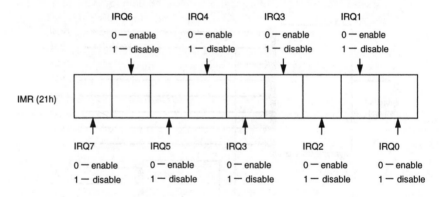

Figure 13.5 Interrupt mask register bit definitions.

In the example code given next the lines IRQ0, IRQ1 and IRQ6 are allowed to interrupt the processor, whereas, IRQ2, IRQ3, IRQ4 and IRQ7 are disabled.

```
outportb(IMR,0xBC);  /* 1011 1100 enable disk (bit 6),
                        keyboard (1) and timer (0) interrupts */
```

When an interrupt occurs all other interrupts are disabled and no other device can interrupt the processor. Interrupts are enabled again by setting the EOI bit on the interrupt control port, as shown in Figure 13.6.

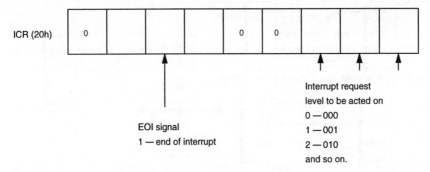

Figure 13.6 Interrupt control register bit definitions.

The following code enables interrupts.:

```
#define    EOI    0x20
           outportb(ICR,EOI);    /* EOI command */
```

13.4 Interrupt-driven RS-232

Interrupt-driven devices are efficient on the processor time as they allow the processor to run a program without having to poll the devices. This allows fast devices almost instant access to the processor and stops slow devices from 'hogging' the processor. For example, a line printer tends to be slow in printing characters. If the printer only interrupted the processor when it was ready for data then the processor can do other things while the printer is printing the character. Another example can be found in serial communications. Characters sent over an RS-232 link are transmitted and received relatively slowly. In a non interrupt-driven system the computer must poll the status register to determine if a character has been received, which is inefficient in processor time. But, if the amount of time spent polling the status register is reduced, there is a possibility of the computer missing the received character as another could be sent before the first is read from the receiver buffer. If the serial communications port was set up to interrupt the processor when a new character arrived then it is guaranteed that the processor will always process the receiver buffer.

A major disadvantage with non interrupt-driven software is when the processor is involved in a 'heavy processing' task such as graphics or mathematical calculations. This can have the effect of reducing the amount of time that can be spent polling and/or reading data.

Program 13.4 is a simple interrupt driven RS-232 program. If possible connect two PCs together with a cable which swaps the TX and RX lines, as shown in Figure 13.7. Each of the computers should be able to transmit and receive concurrently. A description of this program is given in the next section. The header file associated with this program is **serial.h**.

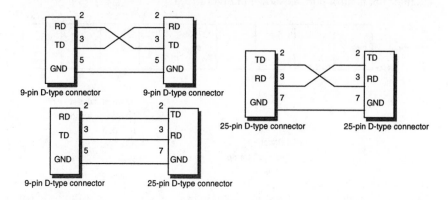

Figure 13.7 Connection from one PC to another.

13.4.1 Program listing

📄 Program 13.1

```
#include <dos.h>
#include <conio.h>
#include <stdio.h>
#include <bios.h>
#include "serial.h"

void    interrupt rs_interrupt(void);
void    setup_serial(void);
void    send_character(int ch);
int     get_character(void);
int     get_buffer(void);
void    set_vectors(void);
void    reset_vectors(void);
void    enable_interrupts(void);
void    disable_interrupts(void);

void    interrupt(*oldvect)();

char    buffer[RSBUFSIZE];

unsigned int    startbuf=0,endbuf = 0;

int     main(void)
{
int     ch, done  = FALSE;

    setup_serial();
    set_vectors(); /* set new interrupt vectors and store old ones */
    enable_interrupts();
    printf("Terminal emulator, press [ESC] to quit\n");
    do
    {
        if (kbhit())
        {
            ch=getche();
```

```
              if (ch==ESC) break;
              send_character(ch);
          }
          /* empty RS232 buffer    */
          do
          {
              if ((ch=get_buffer()) != -1) putch(ch);
          } while (ch!=-1);
      } while (!done);
      disable_interrupts();
      reset_vectors();
      return(0);
}

void  interrupt rs_interrupt(void)
{
      disable();
      if ((inportb(IIR) & RX_MASK) == RX_ID)
      {
          buffer[endbuf] = inportb(RXR);
          endbuf++;
          if (endbuf == RSBUFSIZE) endbuf=0;
      }
      /* Set end of interrupt flag */
      outportb(ICR, EOI);
      enable();
}

void      setup_serial(void)
{
int       RS232_setting;

      RS232_setting=BAUD1200 | STOPBIT1 | NOPARITY | DATABITS7;
      bioscom(0,RS232_setting,COM1);
}

void  send_character(int ch)
{
char  status;
      do
      {
          status = inportb(LSR) & 0x40;
      } while (status!=0x40);
      /*repeat until Tx buffer empty ie bit 6 set*/
      outportb(TXDATA,(char) ch);
}

int   get_character(void)
{
int   status;
      do
      {
          status = inportb(LSR) & 0x01;
      } while (status!=0x01);
      /* Repeat until bit 1 in LSR is set */
      return( (int)inportb(TXDATA));
}

int   get_buffer(void)
{
int   ch;

      if (startbuf == endbuf) return (-1);
```

```
        ch = (int) buffer[startbuf];
        startbuf++;
        if (startbuf == RSBUFSIZE) startbuf = 0;
        return (ch);
}

void    set_vectors(void)
{
        oldvect = getvect(0x0C);
        setvect(0x0C, rs_interrupt);
}

/* Uninstall interrupt vectors before exiting the program */
void    reset_vectors(void)
{
        setvect(0x0C, oldvect);
}

void        disable_interrupts(void)
{
int         ch;

        disable();
        ch = inportb(IMR) | ~IRQ4; /* disable IRQ4 interrupt */
        outportb(IMR, ch);
        outportb(IER, 0);
        enable();
}

void        enable_interrupts(void)
{
int     ch;

        disable();
        /* initialize rs232 port   */
        ch = inportb(MCR) | MC_INT;
        outportb(MCR, ch);
        /* enable interrupts for IRQ4 */
        outportb(IER, 0x01);
        ch = inportb(IMR) & IRQ4;
        outportb(IMR, ch);
        enable();
}
```

Header 13.1 lists the associated header file.

📖 Header file 13.1: serial.h

```
#define  FALSE            0
/* RS232 set up parameters */
#define COM1              0
#define COM2              1

#define DATABITS7         0x02
#define DATABITS8         0x03

#define STOPBIT1          0x00
#define STOPBIT2          0x04

#define NOPARITY          0x00
#define ODDPARITY         0x08
#define EVENPARITY        0x18
```

```
#define BAUD110        0x00
#define BAUD150        0x20
#define BAUD300        0x40
#define BAUD600        0x60
#define BAUD1200       0x80
#define BAUD2400       0xA0
#define BAUD4800       0xC0
#define BAUD9600       0xE0

#define ESC            0x1B        /* ASCII Escape character  */
#define RSBUFSIZE      10000       /* RS232 buffer size       */

#define COM1BASE       0x3F8       /* Base port address for COM1 */

#define TXDATA         COM1BASE    /* Transmit register       */
#define RXR            COM1BASE    /* Receive register        */
#define IER            (COM1BASE+1) /* Interrupt Enable       */
#define IIR            (COM1BASE+2) /* Interrupt ID           */
#define LCR            (COM1BASE+3) /* Line control           */
#define MCR            (COM1BASE+4) /* Line control           */
#define LSR            (COM1BASE+5) /* Line Status            */

#define RX_ID          0x04
#define RX_MASK        0x07
#define MC_INT         0x08

/* Addresses of the 8259 Programmable Interrupt Controller (PIC).*/

#define IMR            0x21   /* Interrupt Mask Register port  */
#define ICR            0x20   /* Interrupt Control Port        */

/* An end of interrupt needs to be sent to the Control Port of  */
/* the 8259 when a hardware interrupt ends.                     */
#define EOI            0x20   /* End Of Interrupt              */

#define IRQ4           0xEF  /* COM1 */
```

13.4.2 Description of program

The initial part of the program sets up the required RS-232 parameters. It uses `bioscom()` to set `COM1:` with the parameters of 1200 bps, 1 stop bit, no parity and 7 databits.

```
void      setup_serial(void)
{
int       RS232_setting;

   RS232_setting=BAUD1200 | STOPBIT1 |
                                  NOPARITY | DATABITS7;
   bioscom(0,RS232_setting,COM1);
}
```

After the serial port has been initialized the interrupt service routine for the IRQ4 line is set to point to a new 'user-defined' service routine. The primary serial port COM1: sets the IRQ4 line active when it receives a character. The interrupt associated with IRQ4 is 0Ch (12). The getvect() function gets the ISR address for this interrupt, which is then stored in the variable oldvect so that at the end of the program it can be restored. Finally, in the set_vectors() function, the interrupt assigns a new 'user-defined' ISR (in this case it is the function rs_interrupt()).

```
void      set_vectors(void)
{
    oldvect = getvect(0x0C);
          /* store IRQ4 interrupt vector      */
    setvect(0x0C, rs_interrupt);
          /* set ISR to rs_interrupt()        */
}
```

At the end of the program the ISR is restored with the following code.

```
void     reset_vectors(void)
{
    setvect(0x0C, oldvect);
      /* reset IRQ4 interrupt vector    */
}
```

The COM1: port is initialized for interrupts with the code given next. The statement

```
ch = inportb ( MCR )  |  0x08;
```

resets the RS-232 port by setting bit 3 for the modem control register (MCR) to a 1. Some RS-232 ports require this bit to be set. The interrupt enable register (IER) enables interrupts on a port. Its address is offset by 1 from the base address of the port (that is, 0x3F9 for COM1:). If the least significant bit of this register is set to a 1 then interrupts are enabled, else they are disabled.

To enable the IRQ4 line on the PIC, bit 5 of the IMR (interrupt mask register) is to be set to a 0 (zero). The statement

```
ch = inportb(IMR) & 0xEF;
```

achieves this as it bitwise ANDs all the bits, except for bit 4, with a 1. This is because any bit which is ANDed with a 0 results in a 0. The bit mask 0xEF has been defined with the macro IRQ4.

```
void      enable_interrupts(void)
{
int    ch;

    disable();
    /* initialize rs232 port    */
    ch = inportb(MCR)  |  MC_INT;
    outportb(MCR, ch);
    /* enable interrupts for IRQ4 */
    outportb(IER, 0x01);
    ch = inportb(IMR) & IRQ4;
    outportb(IMR, ch);
    enable();
}
```

At the end of the program the function `disable_interrupts()` sets IER register to all 0s. This disables interrupts on the COM1: port. Bit 4 of the IMR is also set to a 1 which disables IRQ4 interrupts.

```
void      disable_interrupts(void)
{
int       ch;

    disable();
    ch = inportb(IMR) | ~IRQ4;
                /* disable IRQ4 interrupt */
    outportb(IMR, ch);
    outportb(IER, 0);
    enable();
}
```

The ISR for the IRQ4 function is set to `rs_interrupt()`. When it is called, the Interrupt Status Register (this is named IIR to avoid confusion with the interrupt service routine) is tested to determine if a character has been received. Its address is offset by 2 from the base address of the port (that is, 0x3FA for COM1:). The first three bits give the status of the interrupt. A 000b indicates that there are no interrupts pending, a 100b that data has been received, or a 111b that an error or break has occurred. The statement `if ((inportb(IIR) & 0x7) == 0x4)` tests if data has been received. If this statement is true then data has been received and the character is then read from the receiver buffer array with the statement `buffer[endbuf] = inportb(RXR);`. The end of the buffer variable (endbuf) is then incremented by 1.

At the end of this ISR the end of interrupt flag is set in the interrupt control register with the statement `outportb(ICR, 0x20);`. The startbuf and endbuf variables are global, thus all parts of the program have access to them.

Turbo/Borland functions `enable()` and `disable()` in `rs_interrupt()` are used to enable and disable interrupts, respectively.

```
void interrupt rs_interrupt(void)
{
    disable();
    if ((inportb(IIR) & RX_MASK) == RX_ID)
    {
        buffer[endbuf] = inportb(RXR);
        endbuf++;
        if (endbuf == RSBUFSIZE) endbuf=0;
    }
    /* Set end of interrupt flag */
    outportb(ICR, EOI);
    enable();
}
```

The `get_buffer()` function is given next. It is called from the main program and it tests the variables startbuf and endbuf. If they are equal then it returns −1 to the main(). This indicates that there are no characters in the buffer. If there are characters in the buffer then the function returns the character pointed to by the startbuf variable. This variable is then incremented. The difference between startbuf and endbuf gives the number of characters in the buffer. Note that when startbuf or endbuf reach the end of the buffer (RSBUFSIZE) they are set back to the first character, that is, element 0.

```
int    get_buffer(void)
{
int    ch;

    if (startbuf == endbuf) return (-1);
    ch = (int) buffer[startbuf];
    startbuf++;
    if (startbuf == RSBUFSIZE) startbuf = 0;
    return (ch);
}
```

The get_character() and send_character() functions are similar to those developed in Chapter 7. For completeness these are listed next.

```
void   send_character(int ch)
{
char   status;
    do
    {
        status = inportb(LSR) & 0x40;
    } while (status!=0x40);

    /*repeat until Tx buffer empty ie bit 6 set*/
    outportb(TXDATA,(char) ch);
}

int        get_character(void)
{
int        status;
    do
    {
        status = inportb(LSR) & 0x01;
    } while (status!=0x01);

    /* Repeat until bit 1 in LSR is set */
    return( (int)inportb(TXDATA));

}
```

The main() function calls the initialization and the de-initialization functions. It also contains a loop which continues until the Esc key is pressed. Within this loop the keyboard is tested to determine if a key has been pressed. If it has then the getche() function is called. This function returns a key from the keyboard and displays it to the screen. Once read into the variable ch it is tested to determine if it is the Esc key. If it is then the program exits the loop, else it transmits the entered character using the send_character() function. Next the get_buffer() function is called. If there are no characters in the buffer then a −1 value is returned, else the character at the start of the buffer is returned and displayed to the screen using putch().

```
int      main(void)
{
int      ch, done  = FALSE;

   setup_serial();
   /* set new interrupt vectors and store old ones */
   set_vectors();
   enable_interrupts();

   printf("Terminal emulator, press [ESC] to quit\n");
   do
   {
      if (kbhit())
      {
         ch=getche();
         if (ch==ESC) break;
         send_character(ch);
      }
      /* empty RS232 buffer   */
      do
      {
         if ((ch=get_buffer()) != -1) putch(ch);
      } while (ch!=-1);
   } while (!done);

   disable_interrupts();

   reset_vectors();
   return(0);
}
```

13.5 Exercices

13.1   Determine which interrupts are enabled and which are disabled on a
PC. This can be achieved by reading from the interrupt mask register
(IMR). A sample run is shown in Test run 13.2 and an outline of a
possible program is given in Program 13.2.

⌨ Test run 13.2

```
IRQ0 enabled
IRQ1 enabled
IRQ2 enabled
IRQ3 enabled
IRQ4 disabled
IRQ5 disabled
IRQ6 enabled
IRQ7 disabled
```

📄 Program 13.2
```
#include <stdio.h>
#include <dos.h>

enum  ints {      IRQ0=0x01,IRQ1=0x02,IRQ2=0x04,IRQ3=0x08,
                  IRQ4=0x10,IRQ5=0x20,IRQ6=0x40,IRQ7=0x80};

#define  IMR    0x21
```

```
int    main(void)
{
int    ch;

    ch = inportb(IMR);

    if (ch & IRQ0) printf("IRQ0 disabled\n");
    else printf("IRQ0 enabled\n");
    if (ch & IRQ1) printf("IRQ1 disabled\n");
    else printf("IRQ1 enabled\n");
        :::::: etc

    return(0);
}
```

13.2   Modify the program in Exercise 13.1 so that it uses a for() loop to test the interrupt status bits. A sample outline is given in Program 13.3.

📄 **Program 13.3**
```
#include <stdio.h>
#include <dos.h>

#define  IMR    0x21

int       main(void)
{
int       ch, bitmask;
    for (bitmask=0x01;bitmask<=0x80;bitmask<<=1)
    {
        ch = inportb(IMR);
        if (ch & bitmask)
            ::: etc
    }
    return(0);
}
```

13.3   Determine, if possible, the devices which use the interrupt lines on various PCs.

13.4   Modify Program 13.1 so that a new-line character is displayed properly.

13.5   Prove that Program 13.1 is a true multi-tasking system by inserting a delay in the main loop, as shown next. The program should be able to buffer all received characters and display them to the screen when the sleep delay is over.

```
do
{
    sleep(10);
        /*go to sleep for 10 seconds, real-time system */
    /* will  buffer all received characters          */
    if (kbhit())
```

```
    {
        ch=getche();
        if (ch==ESC) break;
        send_character(ch);
    }
    /* empty RS232 buffer   */
    do
    {
        if ((ch=get_buffer()) != -1) putch(ch);
    } while (ch!=-1);
} while (!done);
```

13.6   Modify Program 13.1 so that the transmitted characters are displayed in the top half of the screen and then received in the bottom half of the screen.

13.7   Modify Program 13.1 so that it communicates via COM2 : (if the PC has one).

14
Mouse Interfacing

14.1 Introduction

No modern PC would be complete without a mouse. It is an extremely simple device with two or three buttons and a roller ball. Most users prefer to use a mouse rather than typing commands from a keyboard. Many packages are now WIMPs (windows, icons, menus and pointers) based and use a mouse to guide the user in a selection of options. The movement of a mouse guides a pointer (or cursor) on the screen. Pressing one of the mouse buttons selects an object or item. Typically objects are dragged or scaled by keeping a mouse button pressed down and moving the mouse cursor.

14.2 Mouse interrupts

BIOS interrupt 33h provides a whole host of mouse functions. These range from mouse initialization to the definition of the cursor. Table 14.1 lists some of these. Program 14.1 displays the mouse driver version number, the mouse interface type and the interrupt line it uses. There are five main types of interface, these are: serial port (COM1: or COM2:), bus type, inport, PS/2 and HP. The interrupts line ranges from IRQ2 to IRQ7. Normally, a serial mouse uses either IRQ4 for COM1: (or COM3:) or IRQ3 for COM2: (or COM4:).

Table 14.1 BIOS mouse interrupt.

Description	Input registers	Output registers
Reset mouse driver and read status	AX = 0000h	AX = status
		0000h hardware/driver not installed
		FFFFh hardware/driver installed
		BX = number of buttons
		FFFFh two buttons
		0000h other than two
		0003h Mouse Systems/Logitech mouse

Table 14.1   (Cont.).

Description	Input registers	Output registers
Show mouse cursor	AX = 0001h	
Hide mouse cursor	AX = 0002h	
Return position and button status	AX = 0003h	Return: BX = button status bit 0 left button pressed if 1 bit 1 right button pressed if 1 bit 2 middle button pressed if 1 CX = column DX = row
Position mouse cursor	AX = 0004h CX = column DX = row	
Return button press data	AX = 0005h BX = button 0000h left 0001h right 0002h middle	AX = button states bit 0 left button pressed if 1 bit 1 right button pressed if 1 bit 2 middle button pressed if 1 BX = number of times specified button has been pressed since last call CX = column at time specified button was last pressed DX = row at time specified button was last pressed
Define horizontal cursor range	AX = 0007h CX = minimum column DX = maximum column	
Define vertical cursor range	AX = 0008h CX = minimum row DX = maximum row	
Get software version and mouse type	AX = 0024h	Return: AX = FFFFh on error else, BH = major version BL = minor version CH = type 1=Bus, 2=Serial, 3=InPort, 4=PS/2, 5=HP CL = interrupt 0=PS/2, 2=IRQ2, =IRQ3,...,7=IRQ7)

📄 **Program 14.1**

```c
#include <stdio.h>
#include <dos.h>

int    main(void)
{
union REGS inregs,outregs;
char    *mtypes[5]={"Bus","Serial","InPort","PS/2","HP"};
char    *int_type[8]={"PS/2","IRQ2","IRQ3","IRQ4","IRQ5","IRQ6","IRQ7"};

    inregs.x.ax=0x0024;
    int86(0x33,&inregs,&outregs);
    if (outregs.x.ax==0xFFFF)
    {
        puts("No mouse driver found");
        return(1);
    }
    printf("Mouse driver version is %x.%x\n",outregs.h.bh,outregs.h.bl);
    printf("Mouse type: %s\n",mtypes[outregs.h.ch-1]);
    printf("Interrupt:  %s\n",int_type[outregs.h.cl-1]);
    return(0);
}
```

Test run 14.1 shows a sample run of a mouse connected to serial port COM2 : (which uses IRQ3). The mouse driver version is 8.20.

🖥 **Test run 14.1**

```
Mouse driver version is 8.20
Mouse type: Serial
Interrupt:   IRQ3
```

14.3 Text-mode cursor

Program 14.2 uses interrupt 33h to display a text based cursor and its current x, y coordinates. It has three main functions: mouse_init(), mouse_show() and mouse_read(). The mouse_show() function displays the mouse cursor by loading AX with 0001h and using interrupt 33h.

📄 **Program 14.2**

```c
#include <stdio.h>
#include <dos.h>
#include <conio.h>
int      mouse_init(void);
void     mouse_show(void);
void     mouse_read(int *col, int *row, int *but);
int      main(void)
{
int      x,y,button;
    mouse_init();
    mouse_show();
    clrscr();
    do
    {
```

```
        gotoxy(1,1);
        mouse_read(&x,&y,&button);
        cprintf("%4d,%4d Button:%d (Press any key to ESC)",
                            x,y,button);
    } while (!kbhit());
    return(0);
}

int      mouse_init(void)
{
union REGS inregs,outregs;
        inregs.x.ax = 0;
        int86(0x33, &inregs, &outregs);
        return(outregs.x.ax);
}

void      mouse_show(void)
{
union REGS inregs,outregs;
        inregs.x.ax = 1;
        int86(0x33, &inregs, &outregs);
}

void      mouse_read(int *col, int *row, int *but)
{
union REGS inregs,outregs;
        inregs.x.ax = 3;
        int86(0x33, &inregs, &outregs);
        *but = outregs.x.bx;
        *col = outregs.x.cx;
        *row = outregs.x.dx;
}
```

In text mode the top left-hand side of the screen is the (0,0) position. Test run 14.2 shows a sample run with the mouse cursor at the top left-hand side of the screen.

⌨ Test run 14.2

```
    0,    0 Button: 0 (Press any key to ESC)
```

Test run 14.3 shows a sample run with the mouse cursor at the bottom left-hand side of the screen.

⌨ Test run 14.3

```
  612,    0 Button: 0 (Press any key to ESC)
```

Test run 14.4 shows a sample run with the mouse cursor at the top right-hand side of the screen.

⌨ Test run 14.4

```
    0, 192 Button: 1 (Press any key to ESC)
```

Test run 14.5 shows a sample run with the mouse cursor at the bottom right-hand side of the screen.

⌨ Test run 14.5

```
612, 192 Button: 2 (Press any key to ESC)
```

14.4 Mouse coordinates

The mouse operates on a set of x, y coordinates. Table 14.2 outlines the coordinates from differing screen modes. In a basic text mode the maximum screen coordinate in the x-direction is 640, whereas in the y-direction it is 200. In 640×480 graphics mode this changes to 640×480.

Table 14.2 Mouse resolution for differing video modes.

Video mode	Video adapter	Display type	Screen resolution	Mouse resolution
00h	CGA/EGA/VGA	Text	80×25	640×200
0Dh	EGA/VGA	Graphics	320×200	640×200
12h	VGA	Graphics	640×480	640×480
25h	SVGA	Graphics	1024×768	1024×768

14.5 Selecting a menu option using a mouse

In Table 14.2 it can be seen that the mouse resolution in text mode is 640×200 and the screen resolution is 80 characters in 25 rows. Thus, the mouse cursor coordinate must be converted into a row and column coordinate by mouse_x*80/640 and mouse_y*25/200 (where mouse_x is the returned x mouse coordinate and mouse_y the y coordinate). Program 14.3 uses this conversion to select from a menu of three options.

📄 Program 14.3

```
#include <stdio.h>
#include <dos.h>
#include <conio.h>

#define   MAXMOUSE_Y  200/* mouse resolution in text mode is 640x200    *
#define   N_TEXT_ROWS 25 /* 25 lines of text                            *

int       mouse_init(void);
void      mouse_show(void);
void      mouse_read(int *col, int *row, int *but);

int       main(void)
{
int       x,y,button;
```

```c
    clrscr();

    puts("Program to select a menu option");
    puts("Use mouse button to select");
    puts("Press any key to continue >>");

    getch();
    mouse_init();
    mouse_show();

    clrscr();

    do
    {
        gotoxy(1,1);
        puts("Option 1");
        puts("Option 2");
        puts("Program exit");

        do
        {
            mouse_read(&x,&y,&button);
        } while (button==0);
        if (button==1)
        {
            if (y<MAXMOUSE_Y/N_TEXT_ROWS)
                puts("Option 1 selected");
            else if (y<2*(MAXMOUSE_Y/N_TEXT_ROWS))
                puts("Option 2 selected");
            else if (y<3*(MAXMOUSE_Y/N_TEXT_ROWS)) break;
        }
    } while (!kbhit());
    return(0);
}

int     mouse_init(void)
{
union REGS inregs,outregs;

    inregs.x.ax = 0;
    int86(0x33, &inregs, &outregs);
    return(outregs.x.ax);
}

void    mouse_show(void)
{
union REGS inregs,outregs;

    inregs.x.ax = 1;
    int86(0x33, &inregs, &outregs);
}

void    mouse_read(int *col, int *row, int *but)
{
union REGS inregs,outregs;

    inregs.x.ax = 3;
    int86(0x33, &inregs, &outregs);
    *but = outregs.x.bx;
    *col = outregs.x.cx;
    *row = outregs.x.dx;
}
```

14.6 Graphics mode cursor

The cursor in graphics mode differs to the text mode cursor. Figure 14.1 shows a typical shape. If the display is in graphics mode then this cursor is shown when the show mouse cursor interrupt is called. Program 14.4 displays the mouse cursor in graphics mode. Interrupt 10h and AX=0011h sets up the 640×480 graphics mode. Loading AX with 0003h and using interrupt 10h restores text mode.

Figure 14.1   Graphics mode cursor.

📄 **Program 14.4**

```
#include <stdio.h>
#include <dos.h>
#include <conio.h>

int      mouse_init(void);
void     mouse_show(void);
void     graphics(void);
void     text(void);

int      main(void)
{
   graphics();
   mouse_init();
   mouse_show();
   do { } while (!kbhit());
   text();
   return(0);
}

void     graphics(void)
{
union REGS inregs,outregs;
   inregs.x.ax=0x0011;
   int86(0x10,&inregs,&outregs); /* 640 x 480 graphics */
}
```

```
void       text(void)
{
union REGS inregs,outregs;
    inregs.x.ax=0x0003;
    int86(0x10,&inregs,&outregs);  /* text mode */
}

int        mouse_init(void)
{
union REGS inregs,outregs;
    inregs.x.ax = 0;
    int86(0x33, &inregs, &outregs);
    return(outregs.x.ax);
}

void       mouse_show(void)
{
union REGS inregs,outregs;

    inregs.x.ax = 1;
    int86(0x33, &inregs, &outregs);
}
```

14.7 Exercises

14.1   Determine the maximum x and y coordinates for the mouse in text mode and also in graphics mode.

14.2   Write a program that automatically moves a text-mode mouse cursor from the top left-hand corner of the screen to the bottom right-hand side of the screen. Each increment of movement should take one second.

14.3   Repeat Exercise 14.2, but make the cursor move along the outside of the screen, that is, along the top of the screen, then down one of the sides, then along the bottom and up the other side, and so on.

14.4   Write a program in which the text-mode mouse cursor is toggled on and off using the first mouse key.

14.5   Repeat Exercise 14.4, but use the second mouse key.

14.6   Write a program that limits the mouse cursor to the top half of the screen.

14.7   Write a program that limits the mouse cursor to the bottom half of the screen.

14.8   Write a program that splits the screen into four quadrants. When the first mouse key is pressed in one of these quadrants then a message is displayed to inform the user as to the current quadrant.

14.9   Repeat Exercises 14.2 to 14.8 but use a graphics mode cursor.

14.10   Write a text mode program that displays the following menu options:

```
OPTION 1
OPTION 2
OPTION 3
OPTION 4
OPTION 5
EXIT
```

If the mouse cursor is placed over the Option 1 option and the first mouse button is pressed then a message OPTION 1 HAS BEEN SELECTED is displayed, and so on.

14.11   Write a program, in graphics mode, that draws a rectangle on the screen using the mouse cursor. The start and end points of the rectangle are defined by positioning the mouse cursor and then pressing the first mouse button.

14.12   Revise programs from previous chapters so that they contain mouse-driven menus.

15
Reading Keys from the Keyboard

15.1 Introduction

The original PC keyboard contains 83 keys. It can be identified by the function keys (F1–F10) down the left-hand side of it. It has a standard typewriter layout for the letters and numeric keys and also includes other keys such as function keys (F1–F10), page up, page down, and so on. A modern enhanced keyboard contains 101/102 keys. This chapter discusses how a program can access to function keys, arrow keys and other keys such as Home, Insert, Page Up, Page Down, and so on.

15.2 Interrupt 16h: BIOS keyboard

Interrupt 16h allows access to the keyboard. Table 15.1 shows typical interrupt calls. Refer to Program 12.4 for an example usage of the BIOS keyboard interrupt.

Table 15.1 BIOS keyboard interrupt.

Description	Input registers	Output registers
Get keystroke	AH = 00h	AH = scan code
		AL = ASCII character
Check for keystroke	AH = 01h	Return: ZF set if no keystroke available
		ZF clear if keystroke available
		AH = scan code
		AL = ASCII character

15.3 Scan codes and ASCII characters

A modern enhanced keyboard contains 101/102 keys; a typical keyboard is shown in Figure 15.1. Most keys on the keyboard return a scan code. This is returned in the AH register when the interrupts in Table 15.1 are called. For example, if the F1 function key is pressed then the return scan code is 59. If the Enter key is pressed it returns a 28. Program 15.1 displays the scan code for

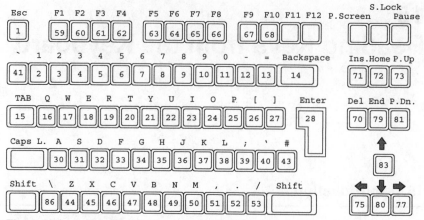

Figure 15.1 Scan codes for a typical enhanced keyboard.

📄 Program 15.1

```c
#include <stdio.h>
#include <dos.h>
void      show_keys(void);
int       get_scan_code(void);
int       main(void)
{
int       ch;
   puts("Program to display scan code");
   puts("Press F10 to exit");
   do
   {
      ch=get_scan_code();
      printf("Scan code: %02X (%d decimal)\n",ch,ch);
   } while (ch!=68);
   return(0);
}
int       get_scan_code(void)
{
union REGS inregs,outregs;
int       scan_code;
   inregs.h.ah=0;
   int86(0x16,&inregs,&outregs);
   scan_code=outregs.h.ah; /* get scan code */
   return(scan_code) ;
}
```

each key pressed. Test run 15.1 shows a sample run. In this case the '1' key (scan code 2) is pressed, then the '2' key, '3' key, '4' key, '5' key, '6' key, '7' key, F1 key, ... F10 key.

Over the years various keys have been moved around the keyboard. This is the reason why some keys return a scan code which is out of sequence with its neighbours. For example, the Esc key on the original PC keyboard was located to the left of the '1' key.

```
Program to display scan code
Press F10 to exit
Scan code: 02 (2 decimal)
Scan code: 03 (3 decimal)
Scan code: 04 (4 decimal)
Scan code: 05 (5 decimal)
Scan code: 06 (6 decimal)
Scan code: 07 (7 decimal)
Scan code: 08 (8 decimal)
Scan code: 3B (59 decimal)
Scan code: 3C (60 decimal)
Scan code: 3D (61 decimal)
Scan code: 3E (62 decimal)
Scan code: 3F (63 decimal)
Scan code: 40 (64 decimal)
Scan code: 41 (65 decimal)
Scan code: 42 (66 decimal)
Scan code: 43 (67 decimal)
Scan code: 44 (68 decimal)
```

Table 15.2 shows the scan code and the ASCII key returned for each of the keys. For example, when the 'X' key is pressed a scan code of 2Dh and an ASCII value of 78h are returned. If the Shift key is pressed with the 'X' then the scan code is still 2Dh, but the returned ASCII value is 58h. Also, if the Cntrl key is pressed with the 'X' the ASCII value returned is 18h.

Table 15.2   Scan and ASCII codes.

Key	Scan code	ASCII code	ASCII code with Shift key	ASCII code with Cntrl key
Esc	1 (01h)	1Bh	1Bh	1Bh
1 !	2 (02h)	31h	21h	
2 @	3 (03h)	32h	40h	00h
3 #	4 (04h)	33h	23h	
4 $	5 (05h)	34h	24h	
5 %	6 (06h)	35h	25h	
6 ^	7 (07h)	36h	5Eh	1Eh
7 &	8 (08h)	37h	26h	
8 *	9 (09h)	38h	2Ah	
9 (	10 (0Ah)	39h	28h	
0)	11 (0Bh)	30h	29h	
- _	12 (0Ch)	2Dh	5Fh	1Fh
= +	13 (0Dh)	3Dh	2Bh	
Backspace	14 (0Eh)	08h	08h	7Fh
Tab	15 (0Fh)	09h	00h	00h
Q	16 (10h)	71h	51h	11h
W	17 (11h)	77h	57h	17h
E	18 (12h)	65h	45h	05h
R	19 (13h)	72h	52h	12h
T	20 (14h)	74h	54h	14h
Y	21 (15h)	79h	59h	19h

Table 15.2   (Cont.).

Key	Scan code	ASCII code	ASCII code with Shift key	ASCII code with Cntrl key
U	22 (16h)	75h	55h	15h
I	23 (17h)	69h	49h	09h
O	24 (18h)	6Fh	4Fh	0Fh
P	25 (19h)	70h	50h	10h
[{	26 (1Ah)	5Bh	7Bh	1Bh
] }	27 (1Bh)	5Dh	7Dh	1Dh
Enter	28 (1Ch)	0Dh	0Dh	0Ah
A	30 (1Eh)	61h	41h	01h
S	31 (1Fh)	73h	53h	13h
D	32 (20h)	64h	44h	04h
F	33 (21h)	66h	46h	06h
G	34 (22h)	67h	47h	07h
H	35 (23h)	68h	48h	08h
J	36 (24h)	6Ah	4Ah	0Ah
K	37 (25h)	6Bh	4Bh	0Bh
L	38 (26h)	6Ch	4Ch	0Ch
; :	39 (27h)	3Bh	3Ah	
` "	40 (28h)	27h	22h	
\ |	43 (2Bh)	5Ch	7Ch	1Ch
Z	44 (2Ch)	7Ah	5Ah	1Ah
X	45 (2Dh)	78h	58h	18h
C	46 (2Eh)	63h	43h	03h
V	47 (2Fh)	76h	56h	16h
B	48 (30h)	62h	42h	02h
N	49 (31h)	6Eh	4Eh	0Eh
M	50 (32h)	6Dh	4Dh	0Dh
, <	51 (33h)	2Ch	3Ch	
. >	52 (34h)	2EH	3EH	
/ ?	53 (35h)	2Fh	3Fh	
Space	57 (39h)	20h	20h	20h
F1	59 (3Bh)	00h	00h	00h
F2	60 (3Ch)	00h	00h	00h
F3	61 (3Dh)	00h	00h	00h
F4	62 (3Eh)	00h	00h	00h
F5	63 (3Fh)	00h	00h	00h
F6	64 (40h)	00h	00h	00h
F7	65 (41h)	00h	00h	00h
F8	66 (42h)	00h	00h	00h
F9	67 (43h)	00h	00h	00h
F10	68 (44h)	00h	00h	00h
Home	71 (47h)	00h	37H	00h
Up arrow	72 (48h)	00h	38h	00h
Page Up	73 (49h)	00h	39h	00h
-	74 (4Ah)	2DH	2DH	00h
Left arrow	75 (4Bh)	00h	34h	00h
Right arrow	78 (4Dh)	00h	36h	00h
+	79 (4Eh)	2BH	2BH	00h
End	80 (4Fh)	00h	31h	00h
Down arrow	81 (50h)	00h	32h	00h
Page Down	82 (51h)	00h	33h	00h
Insert	83 (52h)	00h	30h	00h
Delete	84 (53h)	00h	2Eh	00h

Many special keys such as function keys, page up, page down and the arrow keys do not return an ASCII value. These keys can be mapped to a character value by assigning them a value which is greater than 255 (the extended ASCII character set ranges from 0 to 255). This is achieved by testing if the returned ASCII value is 0. If it is then 256 is added to the scan code, that is:

```
if (ascii_char==0)   ch_value=scan_code + 256;
else                     ch_value=ascii_char;
```

where `ascii_char` is the returned ASCII value and `scan_code` the returned scan code. Thus, the function key F1 is assigned a value of 59+256, which is 315. A header file with the special key assignments is given in header file 15.1. This header file is used in Program 15.2 to define F10. The program displays the value assigned for each of the keys on the keyboard. When the function key F1 is pressed it should display a character code of 315, F2 should display 316 and so on.

📖 Header file 15.1

```
/*      defkey.h                                                  */
/*      Function keys                                             */
#define F1                   315     /* scan code + 256           */
#define F2                   316
#define F3                   317
#define F4                   318
#define F5                   319
#define F6                   320
#define F7                   321
#define F8                   322
#define F9                   323
#define F10                  324

/* Special keys                          */

#define        HOMEKEY       327
#define        UPKEY         328
#define        PGUPKEY       329
#define        LEFTKEY       331
#define        RIGHTKEY      333
#define        ENDKEY        335
#define        DOWNKEY       336
#define        PGDNKEY       337
#define        INSKEY        338
#define        DELKEY        339
```

📄 Program 15.2

```
/*      Program to display character values    */
#include "defkey.h"
#include <stdio.h>
#include <dos.h>

void      show_keys(void);
int       get_extended_character(void);

int       main(void)
{
int       ch;
```

```
    puts("Program to display chararacter code");
    puts("Press F10 to exit");
    do
    {
        ch=get_extended_character();
        printf("Character code: %d\n",ch);
    } while (ch!=F10);
    return(0);
}

int     get_extended_character(void)
{
union REGS inregs,outregs;
int   ascii_char,scan_code;
    inregs.h.ah=0;
    int86(0x16,&inregs,&outregs);
    scan_code=outregs.h.ah; /* get scan code */
    ascii_char=outregs.h.al; /* get ascii code */

    if (ascii_char==0) return(scan_code + 256);
                               /* if extended key add 255 */
    else return(ascii_char);

}
```

15.4 Exercises

15.1   Write a program that displays which of the following keys have been pressed: F1, F2, F3, F4, F5, F6, F7, F8, F9, F10, Page Up, Page Down, Home, End, Insert or Delete. Test run 15.2 shows a sample run.

⌨ Test run 15.2

```
Key pressed:
F1
F1
F4
Page Up
Page Down
Delete
F10
```

15.2   Write a program that displays which control key has been pressed, that is, when the Cntrl key and a letter are pressed at the same time. Test run 15.3 shows a sample run. A Cntrl-D should exit the program.

⌨ Test run 15.3

```
Cntrl-A
Cntrl-B
Cntrl-Z
Cntrl-Q
```

15.3   Write a program that uses the arrow keys to move a character around the screen. One possible method is to clear the screen each time an arrow key is pressed then update the character with a new screen coordinate.

15.4   Write a program that contains the menus and sub-menus in Table 15.3. The menu options are selected using the function keys. The main menu should contain four options, that is, File, Edit, Run and Exit. Pressing F1 should call up the File sub-menu (New, Open, Close and Return to main), F2 the Edit menu (Copy, Paste, Undo and Return to main), and so on. When a sub-menu option is selected a message should display the main menu option and the sub-menu option, for example File>Open selected. After the sub-menu message has been displayed the program should return back to the sub-menu.

Table 15.3   Main and sub-menus.

Main menu	Sub menu
F1 – File	F1 – New
	F2 – Open
	F3 – Close
	F4 – Return to main
F2 – Edit	F1 – Copy
	F2 – Paste
	F3 – Undo
	F4 – Return to main
F3 – Run	F1 – Step
	F2 – Go
	F3 – Return to main
F4 – Exit	F1 – Don't quit
	F2 – Quit

The user can quit from a sub-menu by selecting the Return to main menu option. A program exit is selected by the Exit main menu option. The user is then given the opportunity to quit or not. If the user does not want to quit then the program returns to the main menu, else it quits.

15.5   Modify programs from previous chapters so that they contain menu options with function keys. For example, modify an RS-232 program so that the baud rate, parity, and so on, are selected by function keys.

16

Modems

16.1 Introduction

The word 'modem' is a contraction of MOdulator/DEModulator. A modem connects digital equipment to a speech bandwidth-limited communications channel. Typically, they are used on telephone lines which have a bandwidth of between 400 Hz and 3.4 kHz. If digital pulses were applied directly to these lines they would end up severely distorted.

If the modem connects to the public telephone line it should normally be able to do the following:

- Automatically dial another modem using either touch-tone or pulse dialling;
- Automatically answer calls and make a connection with another modem;
- Disconnect a phone connection when data transfer has completed or if an error occurs;
- Convert bits into a form suitable for the line (modulator);
- Convert received signals back into bits (demodulator);
- Software or hardware handshaking of data or no handshaking.

Figure 16.1 shows how two computers connect to each other using RS-232 converters and modems. The RS-232 converter is normally an integral part of the computer, while the modem can either be external or internal to the computer. If it is externally connected then it is normally connected by a cable with a 25-pin male D-type connector on either end.

There are two types of circuits available from the public telephone network:

- Direct distance dialling (DDD).
- Private line.

The DDD is a dial-up network where the link is established in the same manner as normal voice calls with a standard telephone or some kind of an automatic dial/answer machine. They can use either touch-tones or pulses to make the connection. With private line circuits, the subscriber has a permanent dedicated communication link.

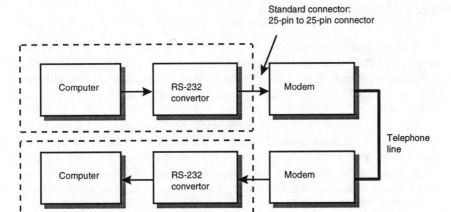

Standard connector:
25-pin to 25-pin connector

Telephone line

Figure 16.1 Computer communications using a modem.

Modems are either synchronous or asynchronous. A synchronous modem recovers the clock at the receiver. There is no need for start and stop bits in a synchronous modem. Asynchronous modems are by far the most popular types. A measure of the speed of the modem is the baud rate or bps (bits per second).

16.2 Modem standards

The CCITT (now known as the ITU) have defined standards which relate to RS-232 and modem communications. Each uses a V. number to define their type, as given in Table 16.1.

Most currently available modems use V.21, V.22, V.22bis, V.23 and V.32 line speeds and are Hayes compatible. Hayes was the company that pioneered modems and defined a standard method of programming the mode of the modem with the AT command language.

Table 16.1 CCITT V. series standards.

CCITT	Description
V.21	Full-duplex modem transmission at 300 bps.
V.22	Half-duplex modem transmission at 600 bps and 1200 bps.
V.22bis	Full-duplex modem transmission at 1200 bps and 2400 bps.
V.23	Full-duplex modem transmission at 1200 bps and receive at 75 bps.
V.24	The CCITT standard for the RS-232 interface.
V.32	Full-duplex modem transmission at 4800 and 9600 bps.
V.25bis	Modem command language.
V.32bis	Full-duplex modem transmission at 7200, 12000 and 14400 bps.
V.42	Error control protocol.

16.3 Modem commands

A computer gets the attention of the modem by sending an 'AT' command. For example, 'ATDT' is the dial command. Initially, a modem is in command mode and accepts commands from the computer. These commands are sent at either 300 bps or 1200 bps (the modem automatically detects which of the speeds is being used).

Most commands are sent with the AT prefix. Each command is followed by a carriage return character (ASCII character 13 decimal); a command without a carriage return character is ignored. More than one command can be placed on a single line and, if necessary, spaces can be entered to improve readability. Commands can be sent either in upper or lower case. Example AT commands are listed in Table 16.2.

Table 16.2 Example AT modem commands.

Command	Description
ATDT12345	Automatically phone number 12345 using touch-tone dialling.
ATPT12345	Automatically phone number 12345 using pulse dialling.
AT S0=2	Automatically answer a call. The S0 register contains the number of rings the modem uses before it answers the call. In this case there will be two rings before it is answered. If S0 is zero then the modem will not answer a call.
ATH	Hang-up telephone line connection.
+++	Disconnect line and return to on-line command mode.

The modem can enter into one of two states: the normal state and the command state. In the normal state the modem transmits and/or receives characters from the computer. In the command state, characters sent to the modem are interpreted as commands. Once a command is interpreted the modem goes into the normal mode. Any characters sent to the modem are then sent along the line. To interrupt the modem so that it goes back into command mode, three consecutive '+' characters are sent, that is, '+++'.

The modem contains various status registers called the S-registers which store modem settings. For example the S0 register stores the number of rings that the modem receives before it answers a call. Table 16.3 lists some of these registers.

Most modems have an area of non-volatile random access memory (NVRAM) which can be programmed electronically. This allows the modem to automatically power up in a pre-programmed mode.

Table 16.3 Modem registers.

Register	Function	Range [typical default]
S0	Rings to Auto–answer	0–255 rings [0 rings]
S1	Ring counter	0–255 rings [0 rings]
S2	Escape character	[43]
S3	Carriage return character	[13]
S6	Wait time for dial tone	2–255 s [2 s]
S7	Wait time for carrier	1–255 s [50 s]
S8	Pause time for automatic dialing	0–255 [2 s]
S32	XON character	0–255 [11h]
S33	XOFF character	0–255 [13h]

After the modem has received an AT command it responds with a return code. Example return codes are given in Table 16.4. For example if a modem calls another which is busy then the return code is 7. A modem dialling another modem returns the codes for OK (when the ATDT command is received), CONNECT (when it connects to the remote modem) and CONNECT 1200 (when it detects the speed of the remote modem). Note that the return code from the modem can be suppressed by sending the AT command 'ATQ1'. The AT code for it to return the code is 'ATQ0', normally this is the default condition.

16.4 Modem connections

RS-232C is a standard that defines the signal functions and their electrical characteristics for connecting a DTE (data terminal equipment, such as, a computer) and a DCE (data circuit termination equipment, such as, a modem). CCITT has adopted the RS-232C standard as V.24 for the signal functions and V.28 as the electrical characteristics. The most common connector on the cable for this type of communication is a 25-pin D-type male connector.

The computer sends data to the modem via the TX data line and receives it from the RX data line. A ground line is also required, see Figure 16.2.

Table 16.4 Example return codes.

Message	Digit	Description
OK	0	Command executed without errors
CONNECT	1	A connection has been made
RING	2	A incoming call has been detected
NO CARRIER	3	No carrier detected
ERROR	4	Invalid command
CONNECT 1200	5	Connected to a 1200 bps modem
NO DIALTONE	6	Dial tone not detected
BUSY	7	Remote line is busy
NO ANSWER	8	No answer from remote line
CONNECT 600	9	Connected to a 600 bps modem
CONNECT 2400	10	Connected to a 2400 bps modem
CONNECT 4800	11	Connected to a 4800 bps modem

The modem can either use no handshaking, flow control handshaking or hardware handshaking. With hardware handshaking the sending computer sets the Read To Send (RTS) signal on the modem. It then replies, when ready, with a Clear To Send (CTS). Data Set Ready (DSR) from the modem and Data Terminal Ready (DTR), from the computer, work in the same way but for received data.

With no handshaking or flow control handshaking, the RTS and DTR signals are normally set active by the computer to inform the modem that it is ready to transmit and/or receive data continuously.

The Ring Indicator (RI) line is active when the modem detects an incoming call. The Data Carrier Detect (DCD) line is active when a connection has been established. DTR is used to control most modems for auto-answer dialling and hang-up circuits; it must be active to auto-answer and if it is inactive then the modem hangs up.

Figure 16.3 shows a sample window from the Microsoft Windows Terminal program. It shows the Modem commands window. In this case, it can be seen that when the modem dials a number the prefix to the number dialled is 'ATDT'. The hang-up command sequence is '+++ ATH'. A sample dialling window is shown in Figure 16.4. In this case the number dialled is 9,4567890. A ',' character represent a delay. The actual delay is determined by the value in the S8 register (see Table 16.3). Typically, this value is about two seconds.

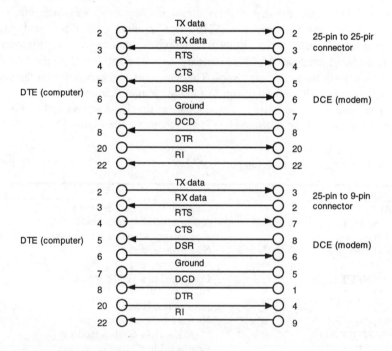

Figure 16.2 Modem line connections.

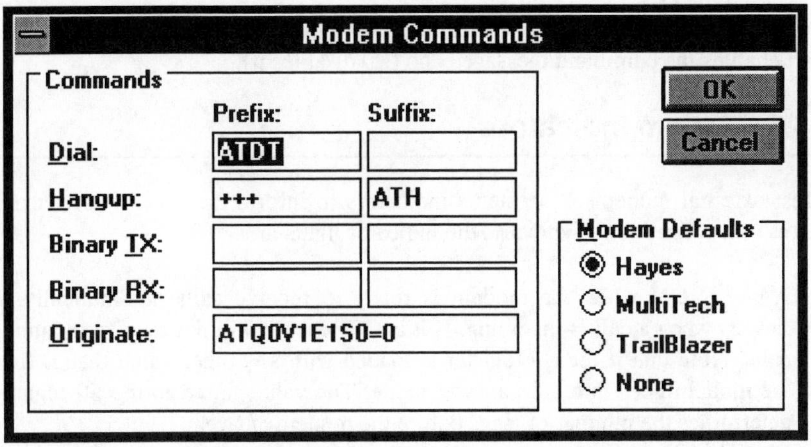

Figure 16.3 Modem commands.

On many private switched telephone exchanges a 9 must prefix the number if an outside line is required. A delay is normally required after the 9 prefix before dialling the actual number. To modify the delay to 5 seconds, dial the number 9 0112432 and to wait 30 seconds for the carrier, then the following command line can be used:

```
ATDT 9,0112432 S8=5 S7=30
```

It can be seen in Figure 16.3 that a prefix and a suffix is sent to the modem. This is to ensure that there is a time delay between the transmission prefix and the suffix string. For example when the modem is to hang up the connection, the '+++' is sent followed by a delay then the 'ATH'.

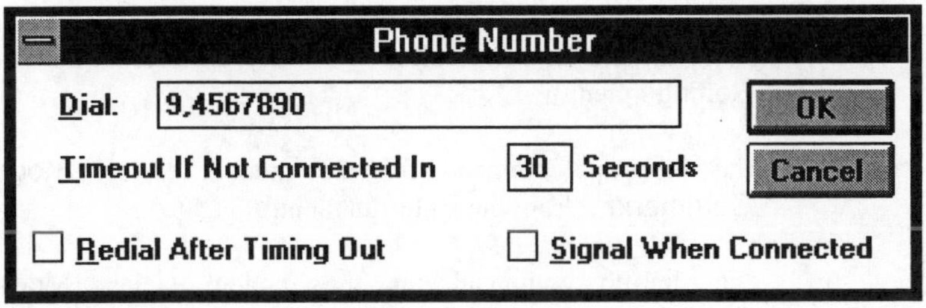

Figure 16.4 Dialling a remote modem.

In Figure 16.3 there is an option for the Originator. This is the string that is sent initially to the modem to set it up. In this case the string is 'ATQ0V1E1S0=0'. The Q0 part informs the modem to return a send status code. The V1 part informs the modem that the return code message is to be displayed rather than just the value of the return code; for example, it displays

CONNECT 1200 rather than the code 5 (V0 displays the status code). The E1 part enables the command message echo (E0 disables it).

16.5 Modem indicators

Most external modems have status indicators to inform the user of the current status of a connection. Typically, the indicator lights are:

- AA – is ON when the modem is ready to receive calls automatically. It flashes when a call is incoming. If it is OFF then it will not receive incoming calls. Note that if the S0 register is loaded with any other value than 0 then the modem goes into auto-answer mode. The value stored in the S0 register determines the number of rings before the modem answers.
- CD – is ON when the modem detects the remote modem's carrier, else it is OFF.
- OH – is ON when the modem is on-hook, else it is OFF.
- RD – flashes when the modem is receiving data or is getting a command from the computer.
- SD – flashes when the modem is sending data.
- TR – shows that the DTR line is active (that is, the computer is ready to transmit or receive data).
- MR – shows that the modem is powered on.

16.6 Exercises

16.1   Find a PC with Microsoft Windows and run the Terminal program (normally found in the Accessories group). Determine the following:

(a)   the default RS-232 settings, such as baud rate, the parity, flow control, and so on (select Communications... from the Settings menu);

(b)   the hang-up command for the modem (select Modem Command... from the Settings menu);

(c)   the dial-up command for the modem (select Modem Command... from the Settings menu).

16.2   Explain how a DTE (a computer) gets the attention of the modem. Also, explain how the DTE gets the modem to go into the command mode once it is in normal mode.

16.3   Which modem indicators would be ON when a modem has made a connection and is receiving data? Which indicators will be flashing?

16.4   Which modem indicators would be ON when a modem has made a connection and is sending data? Which indicators will be flashing?

16.5   Investigate the complete set of AT commands by referring to a modem manual or reference book.

16.6   Investigate the complete set of S-registers by referring to a modem manual or reference book.

16.7   Determine the location of modems on a network or in a works building. If possible, determine the type of data being transferred and its speed.

16.8   If possible, connect a modem to a computer and dial a remote modem.

16.9   If possible connect two modems together and, using a program such as Terminal, transfer text from one computer to the another.

17
Disk Input/Output

17.1 Introduction

This chapter discusses disk drives and how software interfaces with them. In Chapter 12 it was seen that a software interrupt can be used to interface to disk drives. In ANSI-C there is a standard set of functions which use these interrupts and can be used to read and write information to the disk.

Disks are used to store data reliably in the long term. Typical disk drives either store binary information as magnetic fields on a fixed disk (as in a hard disk drive), a plastic disk (as in a floppy disk), or as optical representation (on optical disks).

17.2 Tracks and sectors

A disk must be formatted before it is used, which allows data to be stored in a logical manner. The format of the disk is defined by a series of tracks and sectors on either one or two sides. A track is a concentric circle around the disk where the outermost track is track 0. The next track is track 1 and so on, as shown in Figure 17.1. Each of these tracks is divided into a number of sectors. The first sector is named sector 1, the second is sector 2, and so on. Most disks also have two sides: the first side of the disk is called side 0 and the other is side 1.

Figure 17.1 also shows how each track is split into a number of sectors, in this case there are eight sectors per track. Typically each sector stores 512 bytes. The total disk space, in bytes, will thus be given by:

Disk Space = No. of sides × tracks × sectors per track × bytes per sector

For example, a typical floppy disk has 2 sides, 80 tracks per side, 18 sectors per track and 512 bytes per sector, so:

$$
\begin{aligned}
\text{Disk capacity} &= 2 \times 80 \times 18 \times 512 &&= 1\ 474\ 560\ \text{B} \\
&= 1474\ 560/\ 1\ 024\ \text{KB} &&= 1\ 440\ \text{KB} \\
&= 1440/1024\ \text{MB} &&= 1.4\ \text{MB}
\end{aligned}
$$

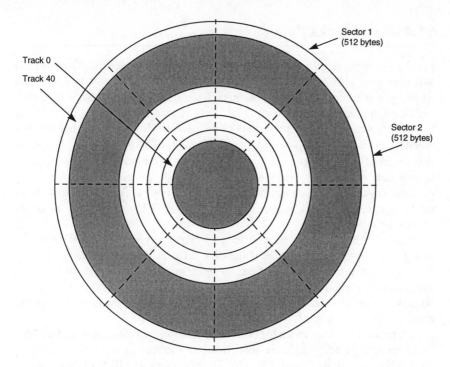

Figure 17.1 Tracks and sectors on a disk.

17.3 Floppy disks

A 5¼ inch DD (double density) disk can be formatted with 2 sides, 9 sectors per disk with either 40 or 80 tracks per side. The maximum capacity of these formats is 360 KB (40 tracks) or 720 KB (80 tracks). A 5¼ inch HD (high density) disk can be formatted with 15 sectors per track which gives a total capacity of 1.2 MB. When reading data the disks rotate at 300 rpm.

A 3½ inch DD disk can be formatted with 2 sides, 9 sectors per track and 40 tracks per side. This gives a total capacity of 720 KB. A 3.5" HD disk has a maximum capacity when formatted with 80 tracks per side. Table 17.1 outlines the differing formats.

Table 17.1 Capacity of different disk types.

Size	Tracks per side	Sectors per track	Capacity
5¼ "	40	9	360K
5¼ "	80	15	1.2M
3½ "	40	9	720K
3½ "	80	18	1.44M

17.4 Fixed disks

Fixed disks store large amounts of data and vary in their capacity, from several MB to several GB. A fixed disk (or hard disk) consists of one or more platters which spin at around 3 000 rpm (ten times faster than a floppy disk). A hard disk with 4 platters is shown in Figure 17.2. Data is read from the disk by a flying head which sits just above the surface of the platter. This head does not actually touch the surface as the disk is spinning so fast. The distance between the platter and the head is only about 10 μin (which is no larger than the thickness of a human hair or a smoke particle). It must thus be protected from any outer particles by sealing it in an airtight container. A floppy disk is prone to wear as the head touches the disk as it reads but a fixed disk has no wear as its heads never touch the disk.

One problem with a fixed disk is head crashes, typically caused when the power is abruptly interrupted or if the disk drive is jolted. This can cause the head to crash into the disk surface. In most modern disk drives the head is automatically parked when the power is taken away. Older disk drives which do not have automatic head parking require a program to park the heads before the drive is powered down.

There are two sides to each platter and, like floppy disks, each side divides into a number a tracks which are subdivided into sectors. A number of tracks on fixed disks are usually named cylinders. For example a 40 MB hard disk has two platters with 306 cylinders, 4 tracks per cylinder, 17 sectors per track and 512 bytes per sector, thus each side of a platter stores:

$$
\begin{aligned}
306{\times}4{\times}17{\times}512 \text{ B} \quad &= \quad 10\,653\,696 \text{ B} \\
&= \quad 10\,653\,696/\,1\,048\,576 \text{ MB} \\
&= \quad 10.2 \text{ MB}
\end{aligned}
$$

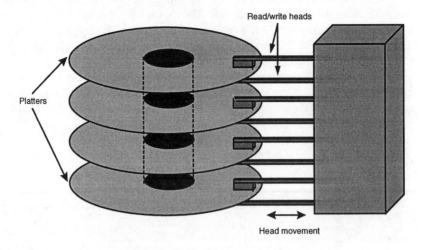

Figure 17.2 Hard disk with four platters.

17.5 Hard disk interfaces

There are two main interfaces involved with a hard disk. One connects the disk controller to the system (system/ controller interface) and the other connects the disk controller to the disk drive (disk/controller interface), as shown in Figure 17.3.

The controller can be interfaced by standards such as ISA, EISA, MCA, VL-Local Bus or PCI Bus (see Chapter 2). For the interface between the disk drive and the controller then standards such as ST-506, ESDI, SCSI or IDE can be used. ST-506 was developed by Seagate Technologies and is used in many older machines with hard disks of a capacity less than 40 MB. The enhanced small disk interface (ESDI) is capable of transferring data between itself and the processor at rates approaching 10 MB/s.

The small computer system interface (SCSI) allows up to seven different disk drives or other interfaces to be connected to the system through the same interface controller. SCSI is a common interface for large capacity disk drives and is illustrated in Figure 17.4.

The most popular type of PC disk interface is the integrated drive electronics (IDE) standard. It has the advantage of incorporating the disk controller in the disk drive, and attaches directly to the motherboard through an interface cable. This cable allows many disk drives to be connected to a system without worrying about bus or controller conflicts. The IDE interface is also capable of driving other I/O devices besides a hard disk. It also normally contains at least 32K of disk cache memory. Common access times for an IDE are often less than 16 ms, where access time for a floppy disk is about 200 ms. With a good disk cache system the access time can reduce to less than 1 ms. A comparison of the maximum data rates is given in Table 17.2.

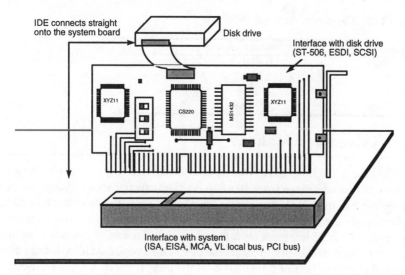

Figure 17.3 Disk drive interfaces.

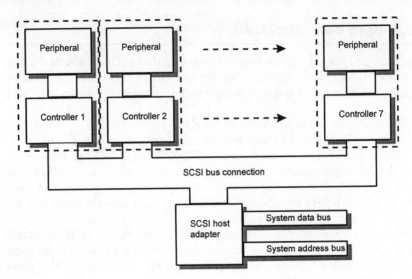

Figure 17.4 SCSI interface.

A typical modern PC contain two IDE connections on the motherboard, named IDE0 and IDE1. The IDE0 connection connects to the master drive (C:) and IDE1 to the slave drive (D:). These could connect either to two hard disks or, possibility, to one hard disk and a CD-ROM drive (or even a tape backup system). Unfortunately the IDE standard only allows disk access up to 520 MB. A new standard called Enhanced-IDE (E-IDE) allows for disk capacities of over this limit. The connector used is the same as IDE but the computers' BIOS must be able to recognize the new standard. Most computers manufactured since 1993 are able to fully access E-IDE disk drives.

Table 17.2 Capacity of different disk types.

Interface	Maximum data rate
ST-506	0.6 MB/s
ESDI	1.25 MB/s
SCSI	4 MB/s
SCSI-II	10 MB/s

17.6 Drive specifications

Access time is the time taken for a disk to locate data. Typical access times for modern disk drives range from 10 to 30 ms. The average access time is the time for the head to travel half way across the platters. Once the head has located the correct sector then there may be another wait until it locates the start of the data within the sector. If it is positioned at a point after the start of the data it requires another rotation of the disk to locate the data. This average wait, or latency time, is usually taken as half of a revolution of the disk. If the disk spins at 3600rpm then the latency is 8.33 ms.

The main parameters which affect the drive specification are the data transfer rate and the average access time. The transfer rate is dependent upon the interface for the controller/disk drive and system/controller and the access time is dependent upon the disk design.

17.7 File storage

Files store data in a permanent form. They normally have a name followed by a filename extension which identifies the type of file.

There are two types of files that can be operated on, these are binary and text. A text file uses ASCII characters when reading from and writing to a file, whereas a binary file uses the binary digits which the computer uses to store values. It is not normally possible to view a binary file without a special program, but a text file can be viewed with a text editor. Text files use the functions fscanf() and fprintf() to read and write, whereas binary files use fread() and fwrite().

Figure 17.5 shows an example of two files which contain four integer values. The binary file stores integers using two bytes in 2s complement signed notation, whereas the text file uses ASCII characters to represent the values. For example, the value of −1 is represented as 11111111 11111111 in 2s complement. This binary pattern is stored to the binary file. The text file uses ASCII characters to represent −1 (these will be '−' and '1'), and the bit pattern stored for the text file will thus be 0010 1101 (ASCII '−') and 0011 0001 (ASCII '1'). If a new line is required after each number then a new-line character is inserted after it. Note, there is no new-line character in ASCII and it is typical to represent a new-line with two characters, a carriage return (CR) and a line feed (LF). In ANSI-C the new-line character is denoted by '\n'.

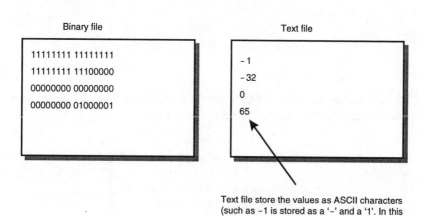

Text file store the values as ASCII characters (such as −1 is stored as a '−' and a '1'. In this example there is a new line character at the end of each line.

Figure 17.5   Binary and text files.

The number of bytes used to store each of the elements depends on the data type of the variable. For example, a long int will be stored as four bytes, whereas a floating-point value can be stored as four bytes (on some systems). The floating-point format differs from an integer format; the standard floating-point format uses a sign-bit, a significant and an exponent. The end of the file is signified by an EOF character.

There are 11 main functions used in file input/output (I/O), as listed below. The fprint() and fscanf() functions are similar to printf() and scanf(), but their output goes to a file.

- `file_ptr=fopen(filename,"attributes");`
- `fclose(file_ptr);`
- `fprintf(file_ptr,"format",arg1,arg2,..);`
- `fscanf(file_ptr,"format",arg1,arg2...);`
- `fgets(str,n,file_ptr);`
- `fputs(str,file_ptr);`
- `fputc(ch,file_ptr);`
- `ch=fgetc(file_ptr);`
- `fwrite(ptr,size,n,file_ptr);`
- `fread(ptr,size,n,file_ptr);`
- `feof(file_ptr);`

A file pointer stores the current position of a read or write within a file. All operations within the file are made with reference to the pointer. The data type of this pointer is defined in *stdio.h* and is named FILE.

```
#include <stdio.h>

int     main(void)
{
FILE    *fileptr;


}
```

The file pointer moves as each element is read/written. Figure 17.6 shows a file pointer pointing to the current position within the file.

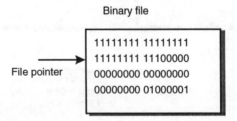

Figure 17.6 File pointer.

17.7.1 Opening a file (`fopen()`)

A file pointer is assigned using `fopen()`. The first argument is the file name and the second a string which defines the attributes of the file; these are listed in Table 17.3.

Table 17.3 File attributes.

Attribute	Function
`"r"`	Open for reading only
`"w"`	Create for writing
`"a"`	Append; open for writing at the end-of-file or create for writing if the file does not exist
`"r+"`	Open an existing file for update (read and write)
`"w+"`	Create a new file for update
`"a+"`	Open for append: open (or create if the file does not exist) for update at the end of the file)

The default mode for opening files is text, but a `t` attribute can be appended onto the attribute string to specify a text file. For example, the attribute `"wt"` opens a text file for writing. A binary file is specified by appending a `b` onto the attribute string. For example, `"rb"` opens a binary file for reading.

The format of the `fopen()` function is:

```
file_ptr=fopen("Filename","attrib");
```

If `fopen()` is completed successfully a file pointer will be returned, and this is initialized to the start of the file. If it was not able to open the file then a NULL will be returned. There can be many reasons why a file cannot be opened, such as:

* The file does not exist;
* The file is protected from reading from and/or writing to;
* The file is a directory.

It is important that a program does not read from a file that cannot be opened as it may cause the program to act unpredictably. A test for this condition is as follows:

```
int     main(void)
{
FILE    *in;

   if ((in=fopen("in.dat","r"))==NULL)
   {
      printf("File IN.DAT could not be opened");
   }
   ::::::::::::::::::::::::::::
   return(0);
}
```

17.7.2 Closing a file (`fclose()`)

Once a file has been used it must be closed before the program is terminated. A file which is not closed properly can cause problems in the file system. The standard format is given below; the return value (`rtn`) returns a 0 (a zero) on success, otherwise EOF if any errors occur. The macro EOF is defined in *stdio.h*.

```
rtn=fclose(file_ptr)
```

17.7.3 Printing text to a file (`fprintf()`)

The `fprintf()` function is used with text files and has a similar format to `printf()` but the output goes to a file. An example of the `fprintf()` function is given below. The return value (`rtn`) returns the number of bytes sent to the file; in the event of an error it returns EOF.

```
rtn=fprintf(file_ptr,"%s %d",str1,value1);
```

17.7.4 Reading text from a file (`fscanf()`)

The `fscanf()` function is used with text files and has a similar format to `scanf()` but the input is read from a file. An example of the `fscanf()` function is:

```
rtn=fscanf(file_ptr,"%s %d %d",str1,&val1,&val2);
```
This function returns the number of fields successfully scanned (`rtn`) or, if there was an attempt to read from the end-of-file, an EOF value is returned.

17.7.5 Finding the end of a file (`feof()`)

The `feof()` function detects the end-of-file character. It returns a non-zero value (that is, a TRUE) if the file pointer is at the end of a file, else a 0 is returned. The function shown next uses the `feof()` function to detect the end of the file and also tests the return from the `fscanf()` so that an unsuccessful reading from the file is disregarded.

```
int     get_values(int maxval, char fname[],int *n,float arr[])
{
FILE    *in;
int     i=0,rtn;

   if ((in=fopen(fname,"r"))==NULL)
   {
      printf("Cannot open %s\n",fname);
      return(NOFILE);
   }

   while (!(feof(in)))
   {
      rtn=fscanf(in,"%f",&arr[i]);
      if (rtn!=EOF) i++;
```

```
        if (i==maxval) break;
    }
    fclose(in);

    *n=i;
    return(!NOFILE);
}
```

17.7.6 Getting a string of text from a file (`fgets()`)

The `fgets()` function is similar to `gets()` and is used to get a string of text
from a file up to a new-line character. The standard format is given next.

```
rtn=fgets(str,n,file_ptr)
```

It reads from the file specified by `file_ptr` into `str` with a maximum of `n`
characters. The return (`rtn`) points to a string pointed to by `str` or will return a
`NULL` if the end-of-file (or an error) is encountered.

17.7.7 Putting a string of text to a file (`fputs()`)

The `fputs()` function is similar to `puts()` and is used to write a string of
text to a file. It does not append the output with a new line. The standard format
is:

```
rtn=fputs(str,file_ptr)
```

This outputs `str` to the file specifed by `file_ptr`. The return (`rtn`) returns
the last character written; if there is an error it returns EOF.

17.7.8 Putting a character to a file (`fputc()`)

The `fputc()` function is similar to `putchar()` and is used to write a single
character to a file. The standard format is:

```
rtn=fputc(ch,file_ptr)
```

This writes `ch` to the file specifed by `file_ptr`. The return (`rtn`) returns the
last character written; if there is an error it returns EOF.

17.7.9 Getting a character from a file (`fgetc()`)

The `fgetc()` function is similar to `getchar()` and is used to read a single
character from a file. The standard format is:

```
ch=fgetc(file_ptr)
```

This reads `ch` from the file specified by `file_ptr`. If there is an error in
getting the character an EOF will be returned.

17.8 Binary files

17.8.1 Reading binary data from a file (`fread()`)

The `fread()` function reads data in a binary format. The standard format is:

```
rtn=fread(ptr,size,n,file_ptr)
```

This reads n items of data into the data block specified by `ptr`, each of length `size` bytes, from the input file specified by `file_ptr`. The value returned `rtn` specifies the number of blocks (or items) which have been successfully read. If no error occurs in the reading then the number of items specified (n) will be the same as the return value (`rtn`). If they differ, an error or end of file has occurred.

The `fread()` function is used in the function given next. In this case, one floating-point value is read from the file and the return value is tested to see if it has been read properly. The `sizeof()` function is used to determine the number of bytes used to store a `float`.

```
int      read_data(char fname[],float arr[],int *nov)
{
FILE     *in;
int      i;

    *nov=0; /* number of values in the array */

    if ((in=fopen(fname,"rb"))==NULL)
    {
       printf("Cannot open %s\n",fname);
       return(NOFILE);
    }

    while (!feof(in))
    {
       if (fread(&arr[i],sizeof (float),1,in)==1)  /*read 1 value*/
          (*nov)++;
    }

    fclose(in);
    return(!NOFILE);
}
```

17.8.2 Writing binary data to a file (`fwrite()`)

The `fwrite()` function writes data in binary format. The standard format is:

```
rtn=fwrite(ptr,size,n,file_ptr)
```

This writes n items of data from the data block specified by `ptr`, each of length `size` bytes, to the output file specified by `file_ptr`. The value returned `rtn` specifies the number of blocks which have been successfully written. The `fwrite()` function is used in the function given below:

```
int      dump_data(char fname[],float arr[],int nov)
{
FILE     *out;
int      i;

   if ((out=fopen(fname,"wb"))==NULL)
   {
      printf("Cannot open %s\n",fname);
      return(NOFILE);
   }
   for (i=0;i<nov;i++)
      fwrite(&arr[i],sizeof (float),1,out);
   fclose(out);
   return(!NOFILE);
}
```

17.9 Examples

17.9.1 Averages program

Program 17.1 uses text files to determine the average value of a number of floating-point values contained in a file. The get_values() function is used to read the values from a file – in this case, *IN.DAT*. This file can be created using a text editor.

📖 Program 17.1

```
/* prog17_1.c                                           */
/* Program to determine the average of a file           */
/* containing a number of floating point values         */

#include <stdio.h>

#define    NOVALUES 100 /* max. number of entered values   */
#define    NOFILE       0

int      get_values(int maxvals, char fname[],int *n,float arr[]);
float    calc_average(int nval,float arr[]);
void     display_average(int nval,float arr[],float aver);

int      main(void)
{
float    values[NOVALUES],average;
int      nvalues;

   if (get_values(NOVALUES,"IN.DAT",&nvalues,values)==NOFILE)
         return(1);
   average=calc_average(nvalues,values);
   display_average(nvalues,values,average);
   return(0);
}

int      get_values(int maxvals, char fname[],int *n,float arr[])
{
FILE     *in;
```

```
int        i=0,rtn;

    if ((in=fopen(fname,"r"))==NULL)
    {
        printf("Cannot open %s\n",fname);
        return(NOFILE);
    }

    while (!feof(in))
    {
        rtn=fscanf(in,"%f",&arr[i]);
        if (rtn!=EOF) i++;
        if (i==maxvals) break;
    }
    fclose(in);
    *n=i;
    return(!NOFILE);
}

float calc_average(int nval,float arr[])
{
int        i;
float running_total=0;

    for (i=0;i<nval;i++)
        running_total+=arr[i];
    /* note there is no test for a divide by zero */
    return(running_total/nval);
}

void       display_average(int nval,float arr[],float aver)
{
int        i;

    puts("INPUT VALUES ARE:");
    for (i=0;i<nval;i++)
        printf("%8.3f\n",arr[i]);
    printf("Average is %8.3f\n",aver);
}
```

An example of the contents of the *IN.DAT* file is:

```
3.240
1.232
6.543
-1.432
```

A sample run using this file is given in Test run 17.1.

🖥 Test run 17.1

```
INPUT VALUES ARE:
    3.240
    1.232
    6.543
   -1.432
Average is      2.396
```

17.9.2 Binary read/write

Program 17.2 is an example of how an array of floating-point values is written to a binary file using `fwrite()` and then read back using `fread()`. Note that the `NOFILE` flags returned from `dump_data()` and `read_data()` are ignored by `main()`.

📄 **Program 17.2**

```
/* prog17_2.c                                */
/* Writes and reads an array of floats       */
/* to and from a binary file                 */
#include <stdio.h>
#define     NOFILE        0     /* error flag is file does not exist */
#define     MAXSTRING     100   /* max. number of char's in filename */
#define     MAXVALUES     100   /* max. number of floats in array    */

void        get_filename(char fname[]);
void        get_values(int maxvals, float vals[],int *nov);
int         dump_data(char fname[],float arr[],int nov);
int         read_data(char fname[],float arr[],int *nov);
void        print_values(float arr[],int nov);

int         main(void)
{
char        fname[MAXSTRING];
float       values[MAXVALUES];
int         no_values;  /* number of values in the array */

    get_filename(fname);
    get_values(MAXVALUES,values,&no_values);
    dump_data(fname,values,no_values);
    read_data(fname,values,&no_values);
    print_values(values,no_values);
    return(0);
}

void        get_filename(char fname[])
{
    printf("Enter file name >>");
    scanf("%s",fname);
}

void        get_values(int maxvals, float vals[],int *nov)
{
int         i;

    do
    {
        printf("Number of values to be entered >>");
        scanf("%d",nov);
        if (*nov>maxvals)
            printf("Too many values: MAX: %d\n",MAXVALUES);
    } while (*nov>MAXVALUES);

    for (i=0;i<*nov;i++)
    {
        printf("Enter value %d >>",i);
        scanf("%f",&vals[i]);
    }
}
```

```
int     dump_data(char fname[],float arr[],int nov)
{
FILE    *out;
int     i;
        /* open for binary write */
   if ((out=fopen(fname,"wb"))==NULL)
   {
      printf("Cannot open %s\n",fname);
      return(NOFILE); /* unsuccessful file open */
   }
   for (i=0;i<nov;i++)
      fwrite(&arr[i],sizeof (float),1,out);

   fclose(out);

   return(!NOFILE);
}

int     read_data(char fname[],float arr[],int *nov)
{
FILE    *in;

   *nov=0;      /* number of values in the array */
      /* open for binary read */
   if ((in=fopen(fname,"rb"))==NULL)
   {
      printf("Cannot open %s\n",fname);

      return(NOFILE); /* unsuccessful file open */
   }

   while (!feof(in))
   {
      if (fread(&arr[*nov],sizeof (float),1,in)==1)
         (*nov)++;
   }

   fclose(in);

   return(!NOFILE);
}

void    print_values(float arr[],int nov)
{
int     i;

   printf("Values are:\n");

   for (i=0;i<nov;i++)
      printf("%d %8.3f\n",i,arr[i]);
}
```

A sample test run is given in test run 17.2.

⌨ Test run 17.2

```
Enter file name >>number.dat
Number of values to be entered >>5
Enter value 0 >>1.435
Enter value 1 >>0.432
```

```
Enter value 2 >>-54.32
Enter value 3 >>-1.543
Enter value 4 >>100.01
Values are:
0      1.435
1      0.432
2    -54.320
3    -1.543
4   100.010
```

17.10 Exercises

17.1   Write a program that determines the average, the largest and the smallest values of a text file containing floating-point values.

17.2   Write a program that counts the number of characters in a text file.

17.3   Write a program that counts the occurrences of the letter 'a' in a text file. Use either `ch=fgetc()` or `fscanf(in,"%c",&ch)` to read individual characters in the file.

17.4   Write a program in which the user enters any character and the program determines the number of occurrences of that character in a specified file. Test run 17.3 shows a sample test run.

■ Test run 17.3

```
Enter filename: fred.dat
Enter character to search for: i
There are 14 occurrences of the character i in the file
fred.dat.
```

17.5   Write a program that determines the number of words in a file.

17.6   Write a program that determines the number of lines in a file. A possible method is to count the new-line characters, as follows:

```
ch=getc(in);
if (ch=='\n') no_lines++;
```

17.7   Write a program that reads a text file containing ASCII characters that represent binary digits (that is, the characters '0' and '1'). Each line of the file contains five digits. The program should read all sequences and display them in binary format. A sample run is given in Test run 17.4.

⌨ Test run 17.4

```
Input file name > BINARY.DAT
Scanning file .....
Binary sequences
1   10010
2   00011
3   10111
4   11111
5   10010
Program end.  BYE
```

The contents of text file *BINARY.DAT* is:

```
1 0  0  1  0
0 0  0  1  1
1 0  1  1  1
1 1  1  1  1
1 0  0  1  0
```

17.8   Modify Exercise 17.7 so that it reads in binary sequences of variable lengths. A sample run is given in Test run 17.5.

⌨ Test run 17.5

```
Input file name > BINARY.DAT
Scanning file .....
Binary sequences
1  100101010001
2  00
3  101110101
4  111110001000
5  1001011
Program end.  BYE
```

The contents of text file *BINARY.DAT* is:

```
1 0 0 1 0 1 0 1 0 0 0 1
0 0
1 0 1 1 1 0 1 0 1
1 1 1 1 1 0 0 0 1 0 0 0
1 0 0 1 0 1 1
```

17.9   Modify the program in Exercise 17.7 so that only the characters '0' and '1' are displayed for a file which contains other characters.

⌨ Test run 17.6

```
Input file name > BINARY.DAT
Scanning file .....
Binary sequences
1  100101010001
2  00
3  101110101
```

```
4  111110001000
5  1001011
Program end. BYE
```

The contents of *BINARY.DAT* is:

```
1 X 0 0 1 0 1 C 0 1 0 0 0 1
0 P 0
1 0 1 1 1 0 1 0 1
1 1 Q 1 1 1 0 0 0 1 0 0 0
1 0 0 ! 1 0 1 1
```

18
Parallel Printer Interface

18.1 Introduction

Chapter 7 discussed serial communications. This chapter discusses parallel communications. The Centronics printer interface transmits 8 bits of data at a time to an external device, normally a printer. A 25-pin D-type connector is used to connect to the PC and a 36-pin Centronics interface connector normally connects to the printer. This interface is not normally used for other types of interfacing as the standard interface only transmits data over the data lines in one direction, that is, from the PC to the external device. Some interface devices overcome this problem by using four of the input handshaking lines to input data and then mulitplexing using an output handshaking line to multiplex them to produce eight output bits.

18.2 PC connections

Figure 18.1 shows the pin connections on the PC connector. The data lines (D0-D7) output data from the PC and each of the data lines has an associated ground line (GND).

18.3 Data handshaking

The main handshaking lines are $\overline{\text{ACK}}$, BUSY and $\overline{\text{STROBE}}$. Initially the computer places the data on the data bus, then it sets the $\overline{\text{STROBE}}$ line low to inform the external device that the data on the data bus is valid. When the external device has read the data it sets the $\overline{\text{ACK}}$ lines low to acknowledge that it has read the data. The PC then waits for the printer to set the BUSY line inactive, that is, low. Figure 18.2.3 shows a typical handshaking operation.

The parallel interface can be accessed either by direct reads to and writes from the I/O memory addresses or from a program which uses the BIOS printer interrupt. This interrupt allows a program either to get the status of the printer or to write a character to it. Table 18.1 outlines the interrupt calls.

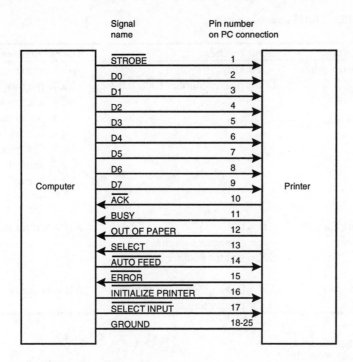

Figure 18.1 Centronics parallel interface showing pin numbers on PC connector.

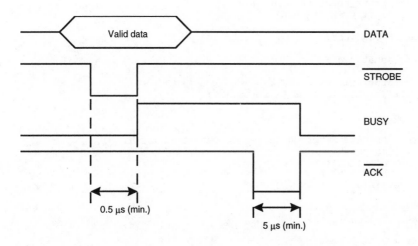

Figure 18.2 Data handshaking with the Centronics parallel printer interface.

Program 18.1 uses the BIOS printer interrupt to test the status of the printer and output characters to the printer.

Table 18.1 BIOS printer interrupt.

Description	Input registers	Output registers

Initialize printer port	AH = 01h
	DX = printer number (00h-02h)
		AH = printer status
		  bit 7: not busy
		  bit 6: acknowledge
		  bit 5: out of paper
		  bit 4: selected
		  bit 3: I/O error
		  bit 2: unused
		  bit 1: unused
		  bit 0: timeout

Write character to printer	AH = 00h AL = character to write DX = printer number (00h-02h)	AH = printer status
Get printer status	AH = 02h DX = printer number (00h-02h)	AH = printer status

▤ Program 18.1

```
#include <dos.h>
#include <stdio.h>
#include <conio.h>

#define  PRINTERR -1

void  print_character(int ch);
int   init_printer(void);

int   main(void)
{
int   status,ch;

    status=init_printer();
    if (status==PRINTERR) return(1);

    do
    {
       printf("Enter character to output to printer");
       ch=getch();
       print_character(ch);
    } while (ch!=4);
    return(0);
}

int   init_printer(void)
{
union REGS inregs,outregs;

    inregs.h.ah=0x01; /* initialize printer */
    inregs.x.dx=0; /* LPT1: */
    int86(0x17,&inregs,&outregs);
    if (inregs.h.ah & 0x20)
```

```
    { puts("Out of paper"); return(PRINTERR); }
    else if (inregs.h.ah & 0x08)
    { puts("I/O error"); return(PRINTERR); }
    else if (inregs.h.ah & 0x01)
    { puts("Printer timeout"); return(PRINTERR); }

    return(0);
}

void print_character(int ch)
{
union REGS inregs,outregs;

    inregs.h.ah=0x00; /* print character */
    inregs.x.dx=0; /* LPT1: */
    inregs.h.al=ch;

    int86(0x17,&inregs,&outregs);
}
```

18.4 Exercises

18.1   Write a printer status program and simulate printer faults and test the program without no printer paper, connecting cable disconnected, and so on.

18.2   If a line printer (and not a network printer) is being used, determine the maximum rate at which characters can be sent to the printer.

18.3   Write a program that counts the occurrences of the letter 'a' in a text file. Use either `ch=fgetc()` or `fscanf(in,"%c",&ch)` to read individual characters in the file.

19

Processor and IC Interface Connections

19.1 Introduction

In previous chapters many different types of interface ICs were introduced. This chapter discusses the signals that control them. Normally these devices are connected into a system and the control signals, data and the addressing of them is invisible to the software. A knowledge of how they interface to the processor is useful in understanding system timings and can help when interfacing problems occur.

19.2 80386/ 80486 microprocessor

Figure 19.1 shows the main 80386/80486 processor connections. The Pentium processor connections are similar but it has a 64-bit data bus. There are three main interface connections: the memory/IO interface, interrupt interface and DMA interface.

The write/read ($W/\overline{R}$) line determines whether data is written to (W) or read from ($\overline{R}$) memory. PCs can interface directly with memory or can interface

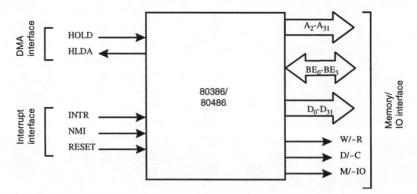

Figure 19.1   Some of the 80386/80486 signal connections.

to isolated memory. Signal line M/$\overline{\text{IO}}$ differentiates between the two types.If it is high then the direct memory is addressed, else if it is low then the isolated memory is accessed.

The 80386DX and 80486 have an external 32-bit data bus (D_0-D_{31}) and a 32-bit address bus ranging from A_2 to A_{31}. The two lower address lines, A_0 and A_1, are decoded to produce the byte enable signals $\overline{\text{BE0}}$, $\overline{\text{BE1}}$, $\overline{\text{BE2}}$ and $\overline{\text{BE3}}$. The $\overline{\text{BE0}}$ line activates when A_1A_0 is 00, $\overline{\text{BE1}}$ activates when A_1A_0 is 01, $\overline{\text{BE2}}$ activates when A_1A_0, $\overline{\text{BE3}}$ actives when A_1A_0 is 11. Figure 19.2 illustrates this addressing.

The byte enable lines are also used to access either 8, 16, 24 or 32 bits of data at a time. When addressing a single byte, only the $\overline{\text{BE0}}$ line will be active (D_0-D_7), if 16 bits of data are to be accessed then $\overline{\text{BE0}}$ and $\overline{\text{BE1}}$ will be active (D_0-D_{15}), if 32 bits are to be accessed then $\overline{\text{BE0}}$, $\overline{\text{BE1}}$, $\overline{\text{BE2}}$ and $\overline{\text{BE3}}$ are active (D_0-D_{31}).

The D/$\overline{\text{C}}$ line differentiates between data and control signals. When it is high then data is read from or written to memory, else if it is low then a control operation is indicated, such as a shutdown command.

The interrupt lines are interrupt request (INTR), nonmaskable interrupt request (NMI) and system reset (RESET), all of which are active high signals. The INTR line is activated when an external device, such as a hard disk or a serial port, wishes to communicate with the processor. This interrupt is maskable and the processor can ignore the interrupt if it wants. The NMI is a nonmaskable interrupt and is always acted-on, see Section 11.4.2 for different types of NMI. When it becomes active the processor calls the nonmaskable interrupt service routine. The RESET signal causes a hardware reset and is normally made active when the processor is powered-up.

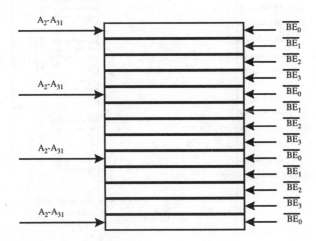

Figure 19.2 Memory addressing.

19.2.1 Direct memory access (DMA)

DMA is a method in which an external device takes over the data and address busses for a short time. A DMA controller controls the transfers and makes the request to the processor take over the transfer.

The DMA interface is controlled by two lines: bus hold acknowledge (HLDA) and bus hold request (HOLD). When the DMA controller wants to take control of the local data and address bus lines it sets the HOLD active, that is, a high level. The processor has completed its current operation it sets the data and address busses into the high impedance state and then sets the HLDA line active high. The DMA controller can then transfer data directly to memory and when complete it sets the HOLD line inactive. When the processor senses this it can then take-over the control of the busses again.

19.3 Programmable Peripheral Interface (8255)

The programming of the 8255 IC was introduced in Chapter 4. It is a 40-pin IC and is used to input and/or output digital signals. Figure 19.3 shows the logic arrangement of the signals and their pin numbers. The connection to the system microprocessor is made through the data bus (D0-D7) and the handshaking and address lines ($\overline{RD}$, $\overline{WR}$, A1, A0, RESET).

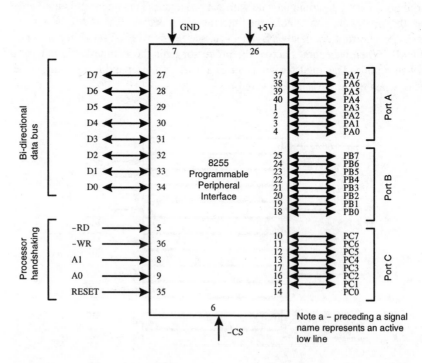

Figure 19.3 8255 pin connections.

There are four registers with the device, these are Port A, Port B, Port C and the Control Registers. The registers Port A, Port B and Port C link to the input/output lines PA0-PA7, PB0-PB7 and PC0-PC7, respectively. They are selected using the two address lines, A0 and A1. If A1 is a 0 and A0 is a 1 then Port A is addressed, if A1A0 is 01 selects Port B, if A1A0 is 10 selects Port C and if A1A0 is 11 selects the Control Register. The timings of the transfers are controlled by the read ($\overline{RD}$) and write ($\overline{WR}$) control signals.

A low input on the RESET input initializes the device and causes the internal registers of the 8255 to be reset. It is normally connected so that at power-up the RESET line is low for a short time. The chip select signal ($\overline{CS}$) must be a low for the device to be activated.

19.4 Programmable Interval Timer (8254)

The 8254 IC was introduced in Chapter 5. It is a 24-pin IC and is used to for counting pulses or in timing applications. Figure 19.4 shows the logic arrangement of the signals and their pin numbers. The connection to the system microprocessor is made through the data bus (D0-D7) and the handshaking and address lines ($\overline{RD}$, $\overline{WR}$, A1 and A0).

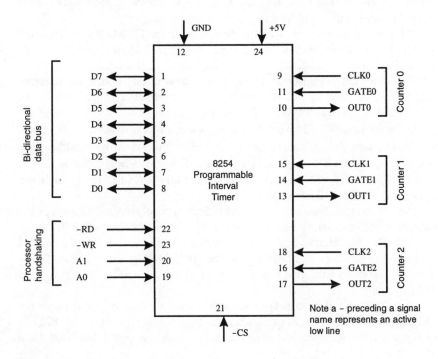

Figure 19.4   8254 pin connections.

There are four registers within the device, these are Counter 0, Counter 1, Counter 2 and the Control Registers. The registers Counter 0, Counter 1 and Counter 2 link to the input/ output lines. They are selected using the two address lines, A_0 and A_1. If A_1 is a 0 and A_0 is a 1 then Counter 0 is addressed, if A_1A_0 is 01 selects Counter 1, if A_1A_0 is 10 selects Counter 2 and if A_1A_0 is 11 selects the Control Register. The timings of the transfers are controlled by the read ($\overline{\text{RD}}$) and write ($\overline{\text{WR}}$) control signals. As with the 8255 the chip select signal ($\overline{\text{CS}}$) must be a low for the device to be activated.

19.5 Universal Asynchronous Receiver Transmitter (8250)

The programming of the 8250 IC was introduced in Chapter 7. It is a 40-pin IC and is used to transmit and receive asynchronous serial communications. Figure 19.5 shows the logic arrangement of the signals and their pin numbers. The connection to the system microprocessor is made through the data bus (D_0-D_7) and the handshaking and address lines ($\overline{\text{DOSTR}}$, $\overline{\text{DISTR}}$, A_2 A_1, A_0, RESET, and so on).

When the processor wishes to write data to the 8250 it sets the DOSTR and $\overline{\text{DOSTR}}$ (Data Output STRobe) lines active, that is, high and low, respectively. When it wants to read data from the 8250 it sets the DISTR and $\overline{\text{DISTR}}$ (Data Input STRobe) lines active, that is, high and low, respectively.

There are seven registers with the device, these are TD/RD Buffer, Interrupt Enable, Interrupt Identify, and so on (refer to Figure 7.25 in Chapter 7). They are selected using the three address lines: A_2, A_1 and A_0. If the address $A_2A_1A_0$ is a 000 then the TD/RD register is address, an address of 001 selects the Interrupt Identify register, and so on. The timings of the transfers are controlled by the write (DOSTR) and read (DISTR) control signals.

The main input RS-232 handshaking lines are: $\overline{\text{RI}}$ (ring indicate), $\overline{\text{DSR}}$ (Data Set Ready) and $\overline{\text{CTS}}$ (Clear To Send), and the main output handshaking lines are: $\overline{\text{RTS}}$ (Ready To Send) and $\overline{\text{DTR}}$ (Data Terminal Ready). Serial data is output from SOUT and inputted from SIN. Refer to Chapter 7 for more information on RS-232 handshaking.

The clock input lines XTAL1 and XTAL2 connect to a crystal to control the internal clock oscillator. Normally on a PC this clock frequency is set at 1.8432 MHz, see Section 7.93. The BAUDOT line is the clock frequency divided by 16 and is equal to the baud rate. As the 1.843 MHz clock is divided by 16 then the maximum baud rate will thus be 1 843 000 divided by 16 which gives 115 200 baud.

The 8255 generates hardware interrupts on the INT line. A low input on the RESET input initializes the device and causes the internal registers of the 8255 to be reset. It is normally connected so that at power-up the RESET line is low for a short time.

The 16450 is the 16-bit equivalent of the 8250.

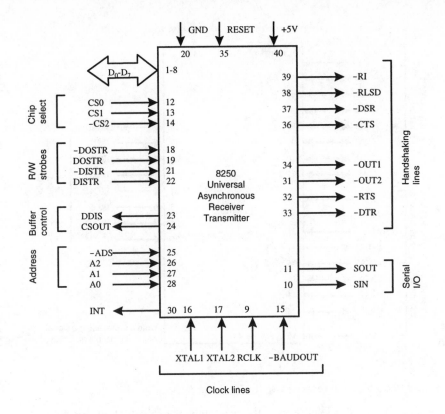

Figure 19.5   8250 pin connections.

19.6 Programmable Interrupt Controller (8259)

Chapter 13 introduced the programming of the 8259 IC. It is a 28-pin IC and is used to generate processor interrupts. Figure 19.6 shows the logic arrangement of the signals and their pin numbers. The connection to the system microprocessor is made through the data bus (D_0-D_7) and the handshaking and address lines ($\overline{RD}$, $\overline{WR}$, A_0, INT, $\overline{INTA}$).

It has two registers, these are Interrupt Control Port (ICP) and the Interrupt Mask Register (IMR), refer to section 13.3. The IMR enables and disables interrupt from interrupting the processor. As there are only two registers there is only one address line, A_0. If A_0 is a 0 then the ICP is addressed, if A_0 is 1 then the IMR is selected. The timing of the transfers is controlled by the read ($\overline{RD}$) and write ($\overline{WR}$) control signals.

When one of the interrupt lines becomes active and if that interrupt has been enabled then the 8259 line generates an interrupt on the processor by setting the interrupt line (INT) high. If the processor accepts the interrupt then it returns back an acknowledgement with the $\overline{INTA}$ line. When the PIC receives this

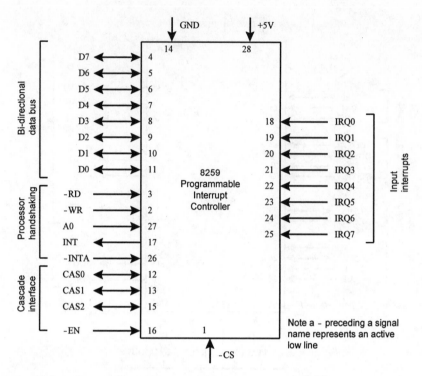

Figure 19.6 8259 pin connections.

acknowledgement then it outputs the type number of the highest-priority active interrupt on the data bus lines D0-D7. This is then read by the processor.

The chip select signal ($\overline{CS}$) must be a low for the device to be activated.

19.7 High-integration peripheral ICs

Many of the ICs discussed in this chapter were used with the original PC. Todays technology allows many functions to be integrated in a single IC. An example of this is the 82341 peripheral combo IC which integrates two serial ports, one parallel port, an IDE controller and a mouse controller on a single IC. The functionality of the devices is exactly the same as the single IC devices.

A typical range of support ICs for modern PCs is the 82340 chip set, these include:

- The 82341 peripheral combo IC which is a 128-pin device;
- The 82344 ISA controller IC which is a 160-pin device that interfaces the processor to the ISA bus.
- The 82346 system controller IC which is a 128-pin IC that decodes the processor signals;
- The 82345 data buffer IC.

The 82341 peripheral combo IC is a 128-pin IC and that integrates several interface devices onto a single IC. The integrated devices are:

- two 16450 serial communications ports;
- parallel printer port;
- real-time clock;
- keyboard and mouse controller;
- an IDE hard disk interface.

Appendix A
Bits and Bytes

A.1 Bits and bytes

A computer operates on binary digits named bits. These can either store a '1' or a '0' (ON/ OFF). A group of 4 bits is a nibble and a group of 8 bits a byte. These 8 bits provide 256 different combinations of ON/OFF, from 00000000 to 11111111. A 16-bit field is known as a word and a 32-bit field as a long word. Binary data is stored in memories which are either permanent or non-permanent. This data is arranged as bytes and each byte has a different memory address, as shown in Figure A.1.

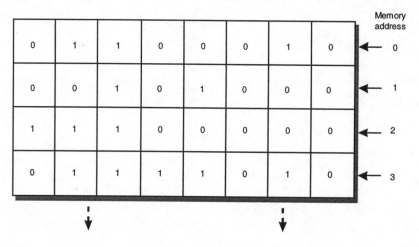

Figure A.1   Memory storage (each address holds eight bits).

A.1.1 Binary numbers

A computer operates on binary digits which uses a base-2 numbering system. To determine the decimal equivalent of a binary number each column is represented by 2 raised to the power of 0, 1, 2, and so on. For example the decimal equivalents of 1000 0001 and 0101 0011 are:

2^7	2^6	2^5	2^4	2^3	2^2	2^1	2^0	
128	64	32	16	8	4	2	1	Decimal
1	0	0	0	0	0	0	1	129
0	1	0	1	0	0	1	1	83

Thus `01001111` gives:

$(0\times128) + (1\times64) + (0\times32) + (0\times16) + (1\times8) + (1\times4) + (1\times2) + (1\times1) = 95$

The number of decimal values that a binary number can represent relates to the number of bits. For example:

- 8 bits gives 0 to 2^8–1 (255) different representations;
- 16 bits gives 0 to 2^{16}–1 (65 535) different representations;
- 32 bits gives 0 to 2^{32}–1 (4 294 967 295) different representations.

The most significant bit (msb) is at the left-hand side of the binary number and the least significant bit (lsb) on the right-hand side. To convert from decimal (base-10) to binary the decimal value is divided by 2 recursively and remainder noted. The first remainder gives the least significant digit (LSD) and the last the most significant digit (MSD). For example:

$$
\begin{array}{r|l}
2 & 54 \\
 & 27 \qquad \text{r 0} <<< \text{LSD} \\
 & 13 \qquad \text{r 1} \\
 & 6 \qquad \text{r 1} \\
 & 3 \qquad \text{r 0} \\
 & 1 \qquad \text{r 1} \\
 & 0 \qquad \text{r 1} <<< \text{MSD}
\end{array}
$$

Thus `110110` in binary is 54 decimal.

A.2 Binary arithmetic

The basic binary addition table is given below.

$$
\begin{aligned}
0 + 0 \;\; &= 0 \\
1 + 0 \;\; &= 1 \\
1 + 1 \;\; &= 10 \\
1 + 1 + 1 &= 11
\end{aligned}
$$

This is used when adding two binary numbers together.

```
 0010001
 0001111
 0100000
  11111
```

A.3 Numbers and representations

A.3.1 Negative numbers

A notation, known as 2s complement, represents negative whole numbers (or integer values). In this representation the binary digits have a '1' in the most significant bit column if the number is negative, else it is a '0'. To convert a decimal value into 2s complement notation, the magnitude of the negative number is represented in binary form. Next, all the bits are inverted and a '1' is added. The following example illustrates the 16-bit 2s complement representation of the decimal value –65.

+65	00000000 01000001
invert	11111111 10111110
add 1	11111111 10111111

Thus, –65 is 11111111 1011111 in 16-bit 2s complement notation. Table A.1 shows that with 16 bits the range of values that can be represented in 2s complement is from –32 767 to 32 768 (that is. 65 536 values).

Table A.1   16-bit 2s complement notation.

Decimal	2s complement
–32 768	10000000 00000000
–32 767	10000000 00000001
::::	::::
–2	11111111 11111110
–1	11111111 11111111
0	00000000 00000000
1	00000000 00000001
2	00000000 00000010
::::	::
32 766	01111111 11111110
32 767	01111111 11111111

To subtract one number from another first the value to be subtracted is converted into 2s complement. This result is then added to the first value to give a result in 2s complement notation. For example to subtract 42 from 65, first 42 is converted into 2s complement (that is, –42) and added to the binary equivalent of 65. The result gives a carry into the sign bit and a carry-out.

```
         65                    0100 0001
        -42                    1101 0110
                      (1)      0001 0111
```

In 16-bit notation values from –32 768 (1000000000000000) to 32 767 (0111 1111 1111 1111) can be represented. A simple C program to convert from a 16-bit signed integer to 2s complement binary is given in Program A.1.

📄 **Program A.1**
```c
/* Program: int2bin.c                                       */
/* Program to convert from a 16-bit signed integer to 2's   */
/* complement binary                                        */
#include <stdio.h>

int   main(void)
{
unsigned  int  bit;
int            val;

   do
   {
      printf("Enter signed int(-32768 to 32767)>>");
      scanf("%d",&val);

      printf("Binary value is ");

      for (bit=0x8000;bit>0;bit>>=1)
      {
         if (bit & val) printf("1");
         else printf("0");
      }
      printf("\n");
   } while (val!=0);
   return(0);
}
```

A sample run is given in Test run A.1.

🖥 Test run A.1
```
Enter signed integer (-32768 to 32767)>>-1
Binary value is 1111111111111111
Enter signed integer (-32768 to 32767)>>-2
Binary value is 1111111111111110
Enter signed integer (-32768 to 32767)>>-3
Binary value is 1111111111111101
Enter signed integer (-32768 to 32767)>>1
Binary value is 0000000000000001
Enter signed integer (-32768 to 32767)>>2
Binary value is 0000000000000010
Enter signed integer (-32768 to 32767)>>100
Binary value is 0000000001100100
Enter signed integer (-32768 to 32767)>>-32767
```

```
Binary value is 1000000000000001
Enter signed integer (-32768 to 32767)>>-32768
Binary value is 1000000000000000
Enter signed integer (-32768 to 32767)>>32767
Binary value is 0111111111111111
Enter signed integer (-32768 to 32767)>>1
Binary value is 0000000000000001
Enter signed integer (-32768 to 32767)>>0
Binary value is 0000000000000000
```

A.3.2 Hexadecimal and octal numbers

In assembly language binary numbers are represented with a proceeding b. For example 010101111010b and 101111101010b are binary numbers. Binary digits can also be represented in hexadecimal (base 16) or octal (base 8) representation. Table A.2 shows the basic conversion between decimal, binary, octal and hexadecimal numbers. In assembly language hexadecimal numbers have a proceeding h and octal number an o. For example 43F1h is a hexadecimal value whereas 4310o is octal.

It is not possible to represent bit patterns in C using a binary format. One solution is to represent the binary digits in hexadecimal (base 16) or octal (base 8) representation. This technique also helps to reduce the number of symbols used to represent the binary value by about one-quarter for hexadecimal and one-third for octal. In this textbook, a binary number is represented by a following b and a hexadecimal with an h.

Table A.2 Decimal, binary, octal and hexadecimal conversions.

Decimal	Binary	Octal	Hex
0	0000	0	0
1	0001	1	1
2	0010	2	2
3	0011	3	3
4	0100	4	4
5	0101	5	5
6	0110	6	6
7	0111	7	7
8	1000	10	8
9	1001	11	9
10	1010	12	A
11	1011	13	B
12	1100	14	C
13	1101	15	D
14	1110	16	E
15	1111	17	F

To represent a binary digit as a hexadecimal value the binary digits are split into groups of four bits (starting from the least significant bit). A hexadecimal equivalent value then replaces each of the binary groups. For example, to represent 0111010111000000b the bits are split into sections of 4 to give

Binary	0111	0101	1100	0000
Hex	7	5	C	0

Thus, 75C0h represents the binary number 0111010111000000b. To convert from decimal to hexadecimal the decimal value is divided by 16 recursively and each remainder noted. The first remainder gives the least significant digit and the final remainder the most significant digit. For example, the following shows the hexadecimal equivalent of the decimal number 1103:

$$
\begin{array}{r|l}
16 & 1103 \\
   & 68 \quad \text{r F} \quad \lll \text{LSD (least significant digit)} \\
   & 4 \quad \text{r 4} \\
   & 0 \quad \text{r 4} \quad \lll \text{MSD (most significant digit)}
\end{array}
$$

Thus the decimal value 1103 is equivalent to 044Fh.

In C hexadecimal constants are preceded by a 0 (zero) and the character 'x' (0x) and an octal number a preceding zero 0 (zero). In Pascal a dollar sign is used to signify a hex number, for example $C4. Examples of various number formats as follows.

Assembly language representation	Pascal representation	C representation	Base of number
F2Ch	$F2C	0xF2C	hexadecimal
432o		0432	octal
321	321	321	decimal
1001001b			binary

Appendix B
Introduction to C

B.1 Compiling, linking and producing an executable program

A microprocessor only understands binary information and operates on a series of binary commands known as machine code. It is extremely difficult to write large programs in machine code, so high-level languages are used instead. A low-level language is one which is similar to machine code and normally involves the usage of keyword macros to replace machine code instructions. A high-level language has a syntax that is almost like written English and thus allows programs which are easy to read and to modify. In most programs the actual operation of the hardware is invisible to the programmer. A compiler then changes the high-level language into machine code. High-level languages include C, BASIC, COBOL, FORTRAN and Pascal; an example of a low-level language is 80386 Assembly Language.

Figure B.1 shows the sequence of events that occurs to generate a machine code program from a C source code program (the filenames used in this example relate to a PC-based system). An editor creates and modifies a C source code file; a compiler then converts this source code into a form which the microprocessor can understand, that is, machine code. The file produced by the compiler is named an object code file. This file cannot be executed as it does not have all the required information to run the program. The final stage of the process is linking; this involves adding extra machine code into the program so that it can use devices such as a keyboard, a monitor, and so on. A linker links the object code file with other object code files and with libraries to produce an executable program. These libraries contain other object code modules that are compiled source code.

If the compilation or linking generates errors or warnings then the source code must be modified to eliminate them. The process of compilation/linking will begin again. Warnings in the compile/ link process do not stop the compiler or linker from producing an output, but errors will. All errors in the compilation or linking stage must be eliminated, whereas it is only advisable to eliminate warnings.

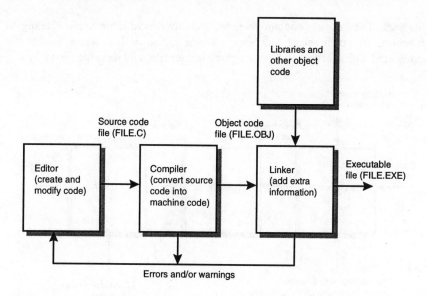

Figure B.1   Edit, compile and link processes.

B.2 Pre-processor

The pre-processor acts on a programs before the compiler. It uses commands that have a number-sign symbol ('#') as the first non-blank character on a line. Figure B.2 shows its main uses. These are: including special files (header files) and defining various macros (or symbolic tokens). The `#include` directive includes a header file and `#define` defines macros. By placing these directives near the top of a source code file all parts of the program have access to the information contained in them.

For example, the pre-processor directive

```
#include "main.h"
```

includes the header file *main.h*. The inverted commas inform the pre-processor that this file will be found in the current working directory, while the directive

```
#include <stdio.h>
```

will include the file *stdio.h* found in the default include directory. This directory is normally set up automatically by the system. For example, Turbo C Version 2.0 stores its header files, by default, in the directory `\TC\INCLUDE` and Borland C uses `\BORLANDC\INCLUDE`. Typically, header files on a UNIX system are stored in the `/usr/include` directory.

Standard header files are used in conjunction with functions contained in libraries. They do not contain program code, but have information relating to functions. A given set of functions, such as maths or I/O, has a header file associated with it. Table B.1 gives typical header files and their functionality.

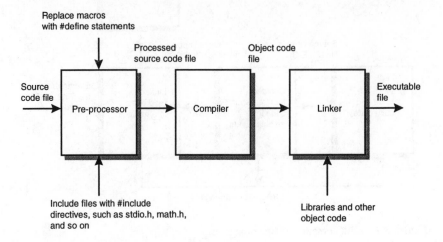

Figure B.2 Operations on the program to produce an file.

Table B.1 Typical header files.

Header file	Comment
ctype.h	character classification and conversion
math.h	maths functions
stddef.h	defines several common data types and macros
stdio.h	Input/output (I/O) routines, such as input from keyboard, output to display and file handling (*stdio* is a contraction of **standard input/output**)
stdlib.h	miscellaneous routines
string.h	string manipulation functions
time.h	time functions

A macro replaces every occurrence of a certain token with another specified token. The following examples show substitutions using the #define directive.

```
#define   PI              3.14
#define   BEGIN           {
#define   END             }
#define   _sqr(X)         ((X)  *  (X))
#define   SPEED_OF_LIGHT  3e8
```

Normally, as a matter of programming style, the definitions of constants, such as π, are given in upper-case characters.

B.3 Structure

Normally programs are split into a number of sub-tasks named functions. These are clearly distinctive pieces of code that perform particular operations. The main function (main()) is the basic routine for controlling the flow of the program and calling other sub-functions. Figure B.3 shows a main function calling other functions.

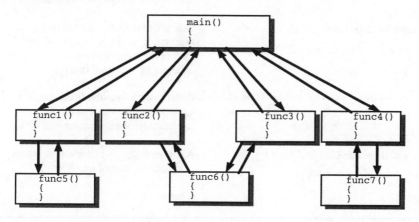

Figure B.3   Modular structure.

Function names are distinguishable with up to 31 characters (names with more than this will depend on the compiler implementation). All function names are followed by an opening set of parentheses and should not be one of C's reserved keywords. The first character of the name must be a letter ('a' – 'z', 'A' – 'Z') followed by either letters, digits, underscores ('_') or dollar signs ('$'). Other characters such as blankspaces or tabspaces are invalid. As a matter of programming style it is typical to use underscores to break up function names into readable form. Table B.2 shows some valid and invalid function names.

Program B.1 is a simple program which uses the puts() function to display the text "Applied PC Interfacing". The puts() function is a standard function used to output text to the display; the header file associated with this is *stdio.h*. This header file is included using the #include directive.

Table B.2   Function names.

Function name	VALID	Notes
calc_impedance_RC()	✓	Well named function as it explains what the function does
get average value()	×	Spaces are used in the name
3_point_rms()	×	Begins with an invalid character

Table B.2 (Cont.).

Function name	VALID	Notes
show_memory	✗	No parentheses at end of function name
$temp1()	✗	Begins with an invalid character
calc1()	✓	Valid name, but it is difficult to determine what this function does
calculateimpedanceofRC()	✓	Difficult to read the name of this function; it would be better to shorten each of the words and insert underscores to delimit them
calc_boolean_eq()	✓	Better than the previous example; it is easier for the user to read this as 'calculate Boolean equation'
CalcImpedanceRC()	✓	A common style is to use capital letters to signify the start of a new word
do()	✗	C keyword

The statement terminator (;) is used to end a line of code (or statement) and braces ({}) show the beginning ({) and end (}) of a block of code. Comments are inserted in the program between a start comment identifier (/*) and an end identifier (*/).

All C programs have a main() function. This defines the entry point into the program and, by means of calling functions, controls general program flow. It can be located anywhere in the source code program but is normally placed near the top of the file in which it is located (making it easier to find). The int keyword preceding main() defines that the program returns a value to the operating system (or calling program). In this case, the return value is 0 (return(0)). Normally, a non-zero return value is used when the program has exited due to an error. The actual value of this gives an indication as to why the program has exited. The void within the parenthesis of main() defines that there is no communication between the operating system and the program when it is first run (that is, no values are passed into the program).

▤ Program B.1

```
/* prog1_1.c                                              */
#include <stdio.h>
int    main(void)
{
        puts("Applied PC Interfacing");
        return(0);

}
```

Figure B.4 shows how the start and end of the program are defined within the main () function.

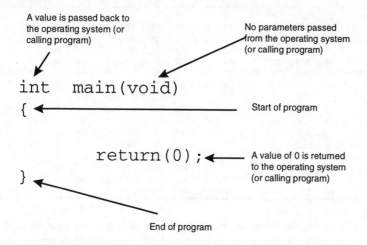

Figure B.4 Start and end points of a program.

B.4 Numbers and representations

B.4.1 Hexadecimal and octal numbers

Relatively large or small numbers can be represented in exponent format. Table B.3 gives some examples of this format.

Table B.3 Exponent format conversions.

Value (or PHYSICAL CONSTANT)	Exponent format
0.000 000 001	1e-9
1 234 320	1.23432e6
1 000 000 000 000	1e12
0.023	2.3e-2
0.943230	9.4323e-1
CHARGE OF ELECTRON	1.602e-19
MASS OF ELECTRON	9.109e-31
PERMITTIVITY OF FREE SPACE	8.854e-12
SPEED OF LIGHT	2.998e8

B.5 Character constants

Typically, characters are stored using either ASCII or EBCDIC codes. ASCII is an acronym for American Standard Code for Information Interchange and EBCDIC for Extended Binary Coded Decimal Interchange Code. Table B.4 gives a full listing of the ASCII character set.

Table B.4   ASCII character set.

Hex	Char	Hex	Char	Hex	Char	Hex	Char	Hex	Char	Hex	Char	Hex	Char	Hex	Char
00	NUL	10	DLE	20	SP	30	0	40	@	50	P	60	'	70	p
01	SOH	11	DC1	21	!	31	1	41	A	51	Q	61	a	71	q
02	STX	12	DC2	22	"	32	2	42	B	52	R	62	b	72	r
03	ETX	13	DC3	23	#	33	3	43	C	53	S	63	c	73	s
04	EOT	14	DC4	24	$	34	4	44	D	54	T	64	d	74	t
05	ENQ	15	NAK	25	%	35	5	45	E	55	U	65	e	75	u
06	ACK	16	SYN	26	&	36	6	46	F	56	V	66	f	76	v
07	BEL	17	ETB	27	'	37	7	47	G	57	W	67	g	77	w
08	BS	18	CAN	28	(	38	8	48	H	58	X	68	h	78	x
09	HT	19	EM	29	)	39	9	49	I	59	Y	69	i	79	y
0A	NL	1A	SUB	2A	*	3A	:	4A	J	5A	Z	6A	j	7A	z
0B	VT	1B	ESC	2B	+	3B	;	4B	K	5B	[	6B	k	7B	{
0C	FF	1C	FS	2C	,	3C	<	4C	L	5C	\	6C	l	7C	|
0D	CR	1D	GS	2D	-	3D	=	4D	M	5D	]	6D	m	7D	}
0E	SO	1E	RS	2E	.	3E	>	4E	N	5E	^	6E	n	7E	~
0F	SI	1F	US	2F	/	3F	?	4F	O	5F	-	6F	o	7F	DEL

ASCII characters from decimal 0 to 32 are non-printing characters that are used either to format the output or to control the hardware. Program B.2 displays an ASCII character for an entered decimal value. The printf() function displays the ASCII character and scanf() gets the decimal value.

📄 **Program B.2**

```
/* prog1_2.c                                                    */
/* Program to display an ASCII character for an entered */
/* decimal value                                                */
#include <stdio.h>

int    main(void)
{
int    value;

    printf("Enter a decimal value >>");
    scanf("%d",&value);
    printf("Equivalent ASCII character is %c\n",value);
    return(0);
}
```

Test run B.1 shows a sample run. In this case the entered decimal value is 65, which gives an ASCII equivalent of 'A'.

💻 **Test run B.1**

```
Enter a decimal value >>65
Equivalent ASCII character is A
```

Characters stored as ASCII codes are stored with the binary digits associated with the character. For example, the ASCII code for the character 'A' is 65 decimal (0x41); the binary storage for this character is thus 0100 0001. A string of characters "Res 1" is stored as the bit pattern given in Figure B.5; the

NULL character terminates the end of a string. Some examples of ASCII codes are given in Table B.5.

01010010	01100101	01110011	0010000	00110001	00000000
'R'	'e'	's'	SPACE	'1'	NULL (end of string)

Figure B.5 ASCII storage for the string "Res 1".

Table B.5 Examples of ASCII characters.

Decimal	Hex	Binary	Character
32	0x20	0010 0000	SPACE
65	0x41	0100 0001	'A'
66	0x42	0100 0010	'B'
90	0x5A	0101 1010	'Z'
97	0x61	0110 0001	'a'
122	0x7A	0111 1010	'z'
7	0x07	0000 0111	Ring the bell
8	0x08	0000 1000	Perform a backspace

Quotes enclose a single character, for example 'a', whereas inverted commas enclose a string of characters, such as "Applied PC Interfacing".

B.6 Data types

Variables within a program can be stored as either numbers or characters. For example, the resistance of a copper wire would be stored as a number (a real value) and the name of a component (such as "R1") would be stored as characters. Table B.6 gives the four basic data types which define the format of variables.

Table B.6 Basic data types.

Type	Usage
char	single character 'a', '1', and so on.
int	signed integer
float	single-precision floating point
double	double-precision floating point

There are three basic extensions for the four types; these are:

- short
- long
- unsigned

An integer is any value without a decimal point. Its range depends on the number of bytes used to store it. A floating-point value is any number and can include a decimal point. This this value is always in a signed format. Again, the range depends on the number of bytes used.

Integers normally take up 2 or 4 bytes in memory, depending on the compiler implementation. This gives ranges of $-32\ 768$ to $32\ 767$ (a 2-byte int) and $-2\ 147\ 483\ 648$ to $2\ 147\ 483\ 647$ (a 4-byte int), respectively. Table B.7 gives some typical ranges for data types.

Table B.7 Typical ranges for data types.

Type	Storage (bytes)	Range
char	1	−128 to 127
unsigned char	1	0 to 255
int	2 or 4	−32 768 to 32 767 or −2 147 483 648 to 2 147 483 647
unsigned int	2 or 4	0 to 65 535 or 0 to 4 294 967 295
short int	2	−32 768 to 32 767
long int	4	−2 147 483 648 to 2 147 483 647
float	4 (typically)	$\pm 3.4 \times 10^{-38}$ to $\pm 3.4 \times 10^{38}$
double	8 (typically)	$\pm 1.7 \times 10^{-308}$ to $\pm 1.7 \times 10^{308}$
long double	10 (typically)	$\pm 3.4 \times 10^{-4932}$ to $\pm 1.1 \times 10^{4932}$

B.7 Declaration of variables

A program uses variables to store data. Before a program can use a variable, its name and its data type must first be declared. A comma groups variables of the same data type. For example, if a program requires integer variables num_steps and bit_mask, floating-point variables resistor1 and resistor2, and two character variables char1 and char2, then the following declarations can be made:

```
int      num_steps,bit_mask;
float    resistor1,resistor2;
char     char1,char2;
```

Program B.3 is a simple program that determines the equivalent parallel resistance of two resistors of 1000 and 500 Ω connected in parallel. It contains three floating-point declarations for the variables `resistor1`, `resistor2` and `eq_resistance`.

📄 **Program B.3**

```
/* Program to determine the parallel equivalent      */
/* resistance of two resistors of 1000 and 500 Ohms  */
#include <stdio.h>

int     main(void)
{
float resistor1, resistor2,equ_resistance;
   resistor1=1000.0;
   resistor2=500.0;

   equ_resistance=1.0/(1.0/resistor1+1.0/resistor2);

   printf("Equivalent resistance is %f\n",equ_resistance);

   return(0);
}
```

It is also possible to assign an initial value to a variable at the point in the program at which it is declared. This is known as variable initialization. Program B.4 gives an example of this with the declared variables `resistor1` and `resistor2` initialized with `1000.0` and `500.0`, respectively.

📄 **Program B.4**

```
/* Program to determine the parallel equivalent      */
/* resistance of two resistors of 1000 and 500 Ohms  */
#include <stdio.h>

int     main(void)
{
float resistor1=1000.0, resistor2=500.0,equ_resistance;

   equ_resistance=1.0/(1.0/resistor1+1.0/resistor2);

   printf("Equivalent resistance is %f \n",equ_resistance);

   return(0);
}
```

B.8 C operators

C has a rich set of operators, of which there are four main types:

- Arithmetic
- Logical
- Bitwise
- Relational

B.8.1 Arithmetic

Arithmetic operators operate on numerical values. The basic arithmetic operations are add (+), subtract (−), multiply (*), divide (/) and modulus division (%). Modulus division gives the remainder of an integer division. The following gives the basic syntax of two operands with an arithmetic operator.

operand *operator* operand

The assignment operator (=) is used when a variable 'takes on the value' of an operation. Other short-handed operators are used with it, including add equals (+=), minus equals (−=), multiplied equals (*=), divide equals (/=) and modulus equals (%=). The following examples illustrate their uses.

Statement	*Equivalent*
x+=3.0;	x=x+3.0;
voltage/=sqrt(2);	voltage=voltage/sqrt(2);
bit_mask *=2;	bit_mask=bit_mask*2;
screen_val%=22+1;	screen_val=screen_val%22+1;

In many applications it is necessary to increment or decrement a variable by 1. For this purpose C has two special operators; ++ for increment and −− for decrement. These can either precede or follow the variable. If they precede, then a pre-increment/decrement is conducted, whereas if they follow it, a post-increment/decrement is conducted. The following examples show their usage.

Statement	*Equivalent*
no_values−−;	no_values=no_values−1;
i−−;	i=i−1;
screen_ptr++;	screen_ptr=screen_ptr+1;

When the following example code is executed the values of i, j, k, y and z will be 10, 12, 13, 10 and 10, respectively. The statement z=−−i decrements i and assigns this value to z (a pre-increment), while y=i++ assigns the value of i to y and then increments i (a post-increment).

```
i=10; j=11; k=12;

y=i++;    /*    assign i to y then increment i       */
z=--i;    /*    decrement i then assign it to z       */
j++;      /*    increment j                           */
++k;      /*    increment k                           */
```

Table B.8 summarizes the arithmetic operators.

Table B.8 Arithmetic operators.

Operator	Operation	Example
-	subtraction or minus	5-4→1
+	addition	4+2→6
*	multiplication	4*3→12
/	division	4/2→2
%	modulus	13%3→1
+=	add equals	x += 2 is equivalent to x=x+2
-=	minus equals	x -= 2 is equivalent to x=x-2
/=	divide equals	x /= y is equivalent to x=x/y
*=	multiplied equals	x *= 32 is equivalent to x=x*32
=	assignment	x = 1
++	increment	Count++ is equivalent to Count=Count+1
--	decrement	Sec-- is equivalent to Sec=Sec-1

B.8.2 Relationship

The relationship operators determine whether the result of a comparison is TRUE or FALSE. These operators are greater than (>), greater than or equal to (>=), less than (<), less than or equal to (<=), equal to (==) and not equal to (!=). Table B.9 lists the relationship operators.

Table B.9 Relationship operators.

Operator	Function	Example	TRUE Condition
>	greater than	(b>a)	when b is greater than a
>=	greater than or equal	(a>=4)	when a is greater than or equal to 4
<	less than	(c<f)	when c is less than f
<=	less than or equal	(x<=4)	when x is less than or equal to 4
==	equal to	(x==2)	when x is equal to 2
!=	not equal to	(y!=x)	when y is not equal to x

B.8.3 Logical (TRUE or FALSE)

A logical operation is one in which a decision is made as to whether the operation performed is TRUE or FALSE. If required, several relationship operations can be grouped together to give the required functionality. C assumes that a numerical value of 0 (zero) is FALSE and that any other value is TRUE. Table B.10 lists the logical operators.

Table B.10 Logical operators.

Operator	Function	Example	TRUE condition
`&&`	AND	`((x==1) && (y<2))`	when x is equal to 1 *and* y is less than 2
`||`	OR	`((a!=b) || (a>0))`	when a is not equal to b *or* a is greater than 0
`!`	NOT	`(!(a>0))`	when a is *not* greater than 0

Logical AND operation will only yield a TRUE only if all the operands are TRUE. Table B.11 gives the result of the AND (`&&`) operator for the operation `Operand1 && Operand2`.

Table B.11 AND logical truth table.

Operand1	Operand2	Result
FALSE	FALSE	FALSE
FALSE	TRUE	FALSE
TRUE	FALSE	FALSE
TRUE	TRUE	TRUE

The logical OR operation yields a TRUE if any one of the operands is TRUE. Table B.12 gives the logical results of the OR (`||`) operator for the statement `Operand1 || Operand2`.

Table B.12 OR logical truth table.

Operand1	Operand2	Result
FALSE	FALSE	FALSE
FALSE	TRUE	TRUE
TRUE	FALSE	TRUE
TRUE	TRUE	TRUE

Table B.13 gives the logical result of the NOT (`!`) operator for the statement `!Operand`.

Table B.13 NOT logical truth table.

Operand	Result
FALSE	TRUE
TRUE	FALSE

For example, if a has the value 1 and b is also 1, then the following relationship statements would apply:

Statement	Result
(a==1) && (b==1)	TRUE
(a>1) && (b==1)	FALSE
(a==10) || (b==1)	TRUE
!(a==12)	TRUE

B.8.4 Bitwise

The bitwise operators are similar to the logical operators but they should not be confused as their operation differs. Bitwise operators operate directly on the individual bits of an operand(s), whereas logical operators determine whether a condition is TRUE or FALSE.

Numerical values are stored as bit patterns in either an unsigned integer format, signed integer (2s complement) or floating-point notation (an exponent and mantissa). Characters are normally stored as ASCII characters.

The basic bitwise operations are AND (&), OR (|), 1s complement or bitwise inversion (~), XOR (^), shift left (<<) and shift right (>>). Table B.14 gives the results of the AND bitwise operation on two bits $Bit1$ and $Bit2$.

Table B.14 Bitwise AND truth table.

Bit1	Bit2	Result
0	0	0
0	1	0
1	0	0
1	1	1

Table B.15 gives the truth table for the bit operation of the OR (|) bitwise operator with two bits $Bit1$ and $Bit2$.

Table B.15 Bitwise OR truth table.

Bit1	Bit2	Result
0	0	0
0	1	1
1	0	1
1	1	1

Table B.16 gives the truth table for the EX-OR (^) bitwise function with two bits *Bit1* and *Bit2*.

Table B.16 Exclusive-OR truth table.

Bit1	Bit2	Result
0	0	0
0	1	1
1	0	1
1	1	0

Table B.17 gives the truth table for the NOT (~) bitwise operator on a single bit.

Table B.17 Bitwise NOT truth table.

Bit	Result
0	1
1	0

The bitwise operators operate on each of the individual bits of the operands. For example, if two decimal integers 58 and 41 (assuming eight-bit unsigned binary values) are operated on using the AND, OR and EX-OR bitwise operators, then the following applies.

	AND	OR	EX-OR
58	00111010b	00111010b	00111010b
41	00101001b	00101001b	00101001b
Result	00101000b	00111011b	00010011b

The results of these bitwise operations are as follows:

```
58 & 41 = 40        (that is, 00101000b)
58 | 41 = 59        (that is, 00111011b)
58 ^ 41 = 19        (that is, 00010011b)
```

The 1s complement operator operates on a single operand. For example, if an operand has the value of 17 (00010001b) then the 1s complement of this, in binary, will be 11101110b.

To perform bit shifts, the << and >> operators are used. These operators shift the bits in the operand by a given number defined by a value given on the right-hand side of the operation. The left shift operator (<<) shifts the bits of the operand to the left and zeros fill the result on the right. The right shift operator (>>) shifts the bits of the operand to the right and zeros fill the result if the integer is positive; otherwise it will fill with 1s. The standard format is:

```
operand >> no_of_bit_shift_positions
operand << no_of_bit_shift_positions
```

For example, if y = 59 (00111011), then y >> 3 will equate to 7 (00000111) and y<<2 to 236 (11101100). Table B.18 gives a summary of the basic bitwise operators.

Table B.18 Bitwise operators.

Operator	Function	Example
&	AND	c = A & B
|	OR	f = Z | y
^	XOR	h = 5 ^ f
~	1s complement	x = ~y
>>	shift right	x = y >> 1
<<	shift left	y = y << 2

The following examples use shortened forms of the bitwise operators:

i<<=2   equivalent to i=i<<2   *shift bits of i 2 positions to the left*

time |= 32   equivalent to time=time | 32   *OR bits of time with 32 decimal*

bitval^=22   equivalent to bitval=bitval^22   *bitval is EX-ORed with 22*

B.9 Precedence

There are several rules for dealing with operators:

• Two operators, apart from the assignment, should never be placed side by side. For example, x * % 3 is invalid.
• Groupings are formed with parentheses; anything within parentheses will be evaluated first. Nested parentheses can also be used to set priorities.
• A priority level or precedence exists for operators. Operators with a higher precedence are evaluated first; if two operators have the same precedence, then the operator on the left-hand side is evaluated first. The priority levels for operators are as follows:

() [] .	primary
! ~ ++ -- -	unary
* / %	multiply
+ -	additive
<< >>	shift
< > <= >=	relation
== !=	equality
&	
^	bitwise
|	
&&	logical
||	
= += -=	assignment

LOWEST PRIORITY

The assignment operator has the lowest precedence. The following example shows how operators are prioritized in a statement (=> shows the steps in determining the result):

```
23 + 5 % 3 / 2 << 1 =>
23 + 2 / 2 << 1      =>
23 + 1 << 1          =>
23 + 2               => 25
```

B.10 Data type conversion

When mixing different data types in an operation with two operands, the following rules determine the data type of the result:

(1) Any character type (such as char, unsigned char, signed char and short int) converts to an integer (int).

(2) Otherwise, if either operand is a long double, the other operand converts to a long double.

(3) Otherwise, if either operand is a double, the other operand converts to a double.

(4) Otherwise, if either operand is a float, the other operand converts to a float.

(5) Otherwise, if either operand is an unsigned long, the other operand converts to an unsigned long.

(6) Otherwise, if either operand is a long int, the other operand converts to a long int.

(7) Otherwise, if either operand is an unsigned int, the other operand converts to unsigned int.

(8) Otherwise, both operands are of type int.

A variable's data type can be changed temporarily using a technique known as casting or coercion. The cast modifier precedes the operand and the data type is defined in parentheses. Typical modifiers are (float), (int), (char) and (double). In Program B.5 two integers b and c are divided and the result is assigned to a. Since b and c are both integers, rule 8 will apply. The result will thus be 1, as an integer division is performed.

📄 Program B.5
```
#include <stdio.h>
int      main(void)
{
float    a;
int      b,c;
   b=6;   c=11;
   a = c / b;
   printf("a = %f",a);
   return(0);
}
```

Program B.6 performs a floating-point division as the variable c has been recast or coerced to a float. Thus rule 4 applies.

📄 Program B.6
```
#include <stdio.h>
int      main(void)
{
float a;
int      b,c;
   b=6;   c=11;
   a = (float)c /b;
   printf("a = %f",a);
   return(0);
}
```

B.11 Keywords

ANSI-C has very few reserved keywords (only 32); these cannot be used as program identifiers and must be in lower-case. Large programs can be built from these simple building blocks. The following gives a list of the keywords.

auto	break	case	char	const	continue
default	do	double	else	enum	extern
float	for	goto	if	int	long
register	return	short	signed	sizeof	static
struct	switch	typedef	union	unsigned	void
volatile	while				

Functions are sections of code that perform a specified operation. They receive some input and produce an output in a way dictated by their functionality. These can be standardized functions which are inserted into libraries or are written by the programmer. ANSI-C defines some standard functions which provide basic input/output to/from the keyboard and display, mathematical functions, character handling, and so on. They are grouped together into library files and are not an intrinsic part of the language. These libraries link into a program to produce an executable program.

B.12 Input/ output

B.12.1 Output functions

There are three basic output functions:

- `printf("format",arg1,arg2...argn)` outputs a formatted text string to the output in a form defined by *"format"* using the arguments *arg1...argn*;

- `puts("string")` outputs a text string to the standard output and appends it with a new line;

- `putchar(ch)` outputs a single character (*ch*) to the standard output.

The `printf()` function sends a formatted string to the standard output (the display). This string can display formatted variables and special control characters, such as new lines (`'\n'`), backspaces (`'\b'`) and tabspaces (`'\t'`); these are listed in Table B.19. The parameters passed into `printf()` are known as arguments; these are separated commas.

The `puts()` function writes a string of text to the standard output and no formatted variables can be used. At the end of the text a new line is automatically appended.

Special control characters use a backslash to inform the program to escape from the way they would be normally be interpreted.

Table B.19 Special control (or escape sequence) characters.

Characters	Function
\"	Double quotes (")
\'	Single quote (')
\\	Backslash (\ )
\nnn	ASCII character in octal code, e.g. \041 gives '!'

Table B.19 (Cont.).

Characters	Function
\0xnn	ASCII character in hexadecimal code, e.g. \0x41 gives an 'A'
\a	Audible bell
\b	Backspace (move back one space)
\f	Form-feed
\n	New line (line-feed)
\r	Carriage return
\t	Horizontal tab spacing

Special control characters

The carriage return ('\r') is used to return the current character pointer on the display back to the start of the line (on many displays this is the leftmost side of the screen). A form-feed control character ('\f') is used to feed line printers on a single sheet and the horizontal tab ('\t') feeds the current character position forward one tab space.

Conversion control characters

Conversion control characters describe the format of how the message string uses the other arguments. If printf() contains more than one argument then the format of the output is defined using a percent (%) character followed by a format description character. A signed integer uses the %d conversion control characters, an unsigned integer %u. A floating point value uses the %f conversion control characters, while scientific notation uses %e. Table B.20 lists the main conversion control characters.

Table B.20 Conversion control characters.

Operator	Format	Operator	Format
%c	single character	%s	string of characters
%d	signed decimal integer	%o	unsigned octal integer
%e	scientific floating point	%%	prints % character
%f	floating point	%x	unsigned hexadecimal integer
%u	unsigned decimal integer	%g	either floating point or scientific notation

Figure B.6 shows an example of the printf() statement with four arguments. The first argument is the message string followed by the parameters to be printed in the message string. In this case the parameters are val1, val2 and ch; val1 is formatted in the message string as a floating point (%f), val2 as an integer (%d) and ch as a character (%c). Finally, a new line character ('\n') is used to force a new line on the output.

A numerical value is output to a given specification using a precision specifier. This specifies the number of characters used to display the value and the number of places after the decimal point. The general format of a floating point value is:

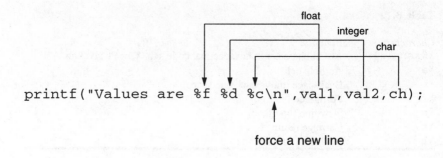

Figure B.6 An example `printf()` statement.

$$\texttt{\%m.nX}$$

where *m* is the width of the value (the number of digits including the decimal point), *n* is the number of digits following the decimal point, and *X* is the format type (f for float).

The general format of a string or integer is:

$$\texttt{\%mX}$$

where *X* is the format type (c for character, s for string or d for integer) and *m* is the width of the output. Table B.21 gives a few examples.

Table B.21 Example of conversion control modifiers.

Format	Function
%.3f	format floating point value with 3 decimal places and a default width
%8.3f	format floating point with 8 reserved spaces and 3 places after the decimal point such as 32.453
%10d	format integer for 10 reserved spaces such as 23
%3o	format octal integer number for 3 hexadecimal characters
%10.6e	format exponent format with 6 decimal places

B.12.2 Input functions

There are three main input functions, these are:

- `scanf` (*"format"*, &*arg1*, &*arg2*..&*argn*)   reads formatted values from the keyboard in a format defined by *format* and loads them into the arguments *arg1*, *arg2*, and so on;

- `gets` (*string*)   reads a string of text from the keyboard into *string* (up to a new line);

- *ch*= `getchar()`   reads a single character from the keyboard into *ch*.

If a numeric or a character variable is used with the `scanf()` function an ampersand (`&`) precedes each parameter in the argument. This prefix causes the memory address of the variable to be used as a parameter and not the value. This allows `scanf()` to change the value of the variable. The general format of the `scanf()` function is:

$$\text{scanf(format, \&arg1, \&arg2...)}$$

The first argument *format* is a string that defines the format of all entered values. For example, `"%f %d"` specifies that *arg1* is entered as a float and *arg2* as an integer. This string should only contain the conversion control characters such as `%d`, `%f`, `%c`, `%s`, and so on., separated by spaces. Figure B.7 shows an example of the `scanf()` function reading a float, an integer and a character into the variables `val1`, `val2` and `ch`.

The `gets(str)` function reads a number of characters into a variable (in this case `str`); these characters are read until the ENTER key is pressed. The `getchar()` function reads a single character from the input. This character is returned via the function header and not through the argument list.

A string is an array of characters which is set-up using the declaration `char strname[SIZE]`, where `SIZE` is the maximum number of characters in the array and `strname` is its name.

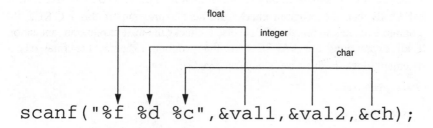

Figure B.7   An example of the `scanf()` statement.

B.13 Selection statements

B.13.1 `if...else`

A decision is made with the `if` statement. It logically determines whether a conditional expression is TRUE or FALSE. For a TRUE, the program executes one block of code; a FALSE causes the execution of another (if any). The keyword `else` identifies the FALSE block. Braces are used to define the start and end of the block.

Relationship operators (`>,<,>=,<=,==,!=`) yield a TRUE or FALSE from their operation. Logical statements (`&&`, `||`, `!`) can then group these together to give the required functionality. If the operation is not a relationship, such as bitwise or an arithmetic operation, then any non-zero value is TRUE and a zero is FALSE.

The following is an example syntax of the `if` statement. If the statement block has only one statement the braces (`{ }`) can be excluded.

```
if (expression)
{
    statement block
}
```

The following is an example format with an `else` extension.

```
if (expression)
{
    statement block1
}
else
{
    statement block2
}
```

It is possible to nest `if...else` statements to give a required functionality. In the next example, *statement block1* is executed if `expression1` is TRUE. If it is FALSE then the program checks the next expression. If this is TRUE the program executes *statement block2*, else it checks the next expression, and so on. If all expressions are FALSE then the program executes the final `else` statement block, in this case, *statement block 4*:

```
if (expression1)
{
    statement block1
}
else if (expression2)
{
    statement block2
}
else if (expression3)
{
    statement block3
}
else
{
    statement block4
}
```

Figure B.8 shows a diagrammatic representation of this example statement.

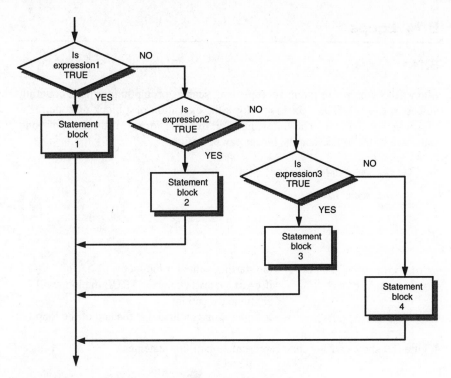

Figure B.8   Structure of the compound if statement.

B.13.2 **switch**

The switch statement is used when there is a multiple decision to be made. It is normally used to replace the if statement when there are many routes of execution the program execution can take. The syntax of switch is as follows.

```
switch (expression)
{
    case const1:    statement(s) : break;
    case const2:    statement(s) ; break;
    :           :
    default:            statement(s) ; break;
}
```

The switch statement checks the expression against each of the constants in sequence (the constant must be an integer or character data type). When a match is found the statement(s) associated with the constant is (are) executed. The execution carries on to all other statements until a break is encountered or to the end of switch, whichever is sooner. If the break is omitted, the execution continues until the end of switch.

If none of the constants matches the switch expression a set of statements associated with the default condition (default:) is executed.

B.14 Loops

B.14.1 `for()`

Many tasks within a program are repetitive, such as prompting for data, counting values, and so on. The `for` loop allows the execution of a block of code for a given control function. The following is an example format; if there is only one statement in the block then the braces can be omitted.

```
for (starting condition; test condition; operation)
{
       statement block
}
```

where :

starting condition - the starting value for the loop;
test condition   - if `test condition` is TRUE the loop will
                     continue execution;
operation   - the operation conducted at the end of the loop.

Figure B.9 shows a flow chart representation of this statement.

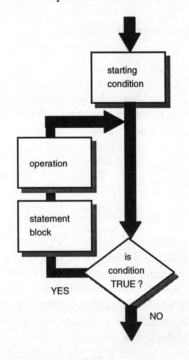

Figure B.9   Flow chart representation of the `for` statement.

B.14.2 `while()`

The `while()` statement allows a block of code to be executed while a specified condition is TRUE. It checks the condition at the start of the block; if this is TRUE the block is executed, else it will exit the loop. The syntax is

```
while (condition)
{
    :           :
    statement block
    :           :
}
```

If the statement block contains a single statement then the braces may be omitted (although it does no harm to keep them).

B.14.3 `do...while()`

The `do...while()` statement is similar in its operation to `while()` except that it tests the condition at the bottom of the loop. This allows *statement block* to be executed at least once. The syntax is

```
do
{
        statement block
} while (condition);
```

As with `for()` and `while()` loops the braces are optional. The `do...while()` loop requires a semicolon at the end of the loop, whereas the `while()` does not.

Figure B.10 shows a flow chart representation of the `do...while()` and the `while()` loops. In both loops a TRUE condition will cause the statement block to be repeated.

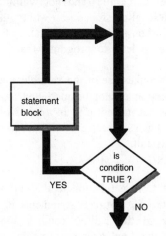 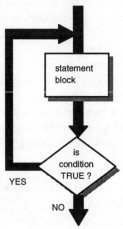

Figure B.10 `do...while()` and `while()` loops.

B.15 Functions

Functions are identifiable pieces of code with a defined interface. They are called from any part of a program and allow large programs to be split into more manageable tasks, each of which can be independently tested.

A function can be thought of as a 'black box' with a set of inputs and outputs. It processes the inputs in a way dictated by its function and provides some output. In most cases the actual operation of the 'black box' is invisible to the rest of the program. A modular program consists of a number of black boxes working independently of all others, of which each uses variables declared within it (local variables) and any parameters sent to it.

B.15.1 Parameter passing

The data types and names of parameters passed into a function are declared in the function header (its interface) and the actual values sent are referred to as arguments. They can be passed either as values (known as 'passing by value') or as pointers (known as 'passing by reference'). Passing by value involves sending a copy of it into the function. It is not possible to change the value of a variable using this method. Variables can only be modified if they are passed by reference.

Figure B.11 shows a program with two functions, main() and function1(). Function main() calls function1() and passes three parameters to it; these are passed as values. A copy of the contents of d goes into g, e into h and f into i.

Variables declared within a function are described as local variables. Figure B.11 shows that d, e and f are local variables within main(); g, h, i, j and k are local within function1(). These will have no links to variables of the same name declared in other functions. Local variables only exist within a function in which they are declared and do not exist once the program leaves the function. Variables declared at the top of the source file (and not within a function) are defined as global variables. These allow functions, within the source file, to access them. Care must be taken when using global variables for many reasons, one of which is that they tend to lead to programs that are unstructured and difficult to maintain.

In Figure B.11 the function function1() makes use of the variable a as this is declared as a global variable. This function cannot be modelled as a 'black box' as it can modify a variable which is not passed to it. In a relatively small program this may not create a problem but as the size of the program increases the control of variables can become difficult.

B.15.2 Return value

The return statement returns a single value from a function to the calling routine, as illustrated in Figure B.12. If there are no return statements in a function the execution returns automatically to the calling routine upon execution of the closing brace (that is, after the final statement within the function).

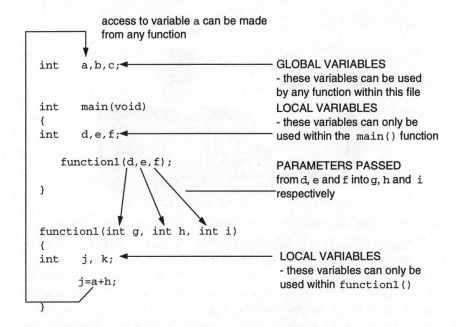

Figure B.11 Local and global variables.

A function can have several return points, although it is normally better to have only one return point. This is normally achieved by restructuring the code. An example of a function with two `returns` is shown next. In this example a decision is made as to whether the value passed into the function is positive or negative. If it is greater than or equal to zero it returns the same value, else it returns a negative value (`return(-value)`).

```
int    magnitude(int value)
{

   if (value >= 0)
      return (value);
   else
      return ( -value);
}
```

B.15.3 Function prototype

It is possible to return any other of C's data types, including `float`, `double` and `char`, by inserting the data type before the function name. If no data type is given then the default return type is `int`. The following gives the general syntax of a function.

```
type_def function_name(parameter list)
{

}
```

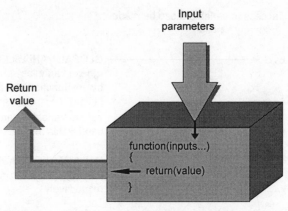

Input
parameters

Return
value

function(inputs...)
{
return(value)

}

Figure B.12 Black-box representation of a function with a return value.

C is a flexible language in its structure. It allows the arrangement of functions in any order and even within different files. If the compiler finds a function that has not been defined (or prototyped) then it assumes the return type will be int. It also assumes that at the linking stage the linker will be able to find the required function either in the current compiled program, the libraries or other object codes. It is thus important that the function return data type is defined when the compiler is compiling the function; otherwise it will assume that the return type is int.

Function declarations (or prototypes) are normally inserted either at the top of each file, locally within a function, or in a header file (the .h files). These declarations allow the compiler to determine the return type and the data types of all parameters passed to the function. It thus allows the compiler to test for illegal data types passed to a function in error. For example, the following are invalid uses of the function printf(), sqrt() and scanf(). The printf() has an incorrect syntax as the first argument should be a format statement (that is, a string), the sqrt() function should be passed a floating-point value and the scanf() function requires a format string as the first argument.

B.16 Pointers

A program uses data which is stored by variables. These are assigned to a unique space in memory; the number of bytes they use depends on their data type. For example, a char uses one byte, an int will typically take two or four bytes, and a float, typically, four or eight bytes. Each memory location contains one byte and has a unique address associated with it (that is, its binary address). This address is normally specified as a hexadecimal value as this can be easily converted to the actual binary address.

Variables sent to a function can have their contents changed by passing a pointer in the argument list. This method involves sending a memory *address* rather than a copy of the variable's value. A preceding ampersand (&) specifies a pointer. This can be thought of as representing *the address of*:

```
&variable_name    {address of variable_name}
```

A pointer to a variable will store the address to the first byte of the area allocated to the variable. An asterisk (*) preceding a pointer is used to access the contents of the location pointed to. The number of bytes accessed will depend on the data type of the pointer. The * operator can be thought of representing *at address*:

```
*ptr    {value stored at address specified by ptr}
```

In order to pass values out of a function through the argument list the address of the variable is passed; that is referred to as *call by reference*. To declare a pointer the data type is specified and the pointer name is preceded by an asterisk. The general format is:

```
type_def *ptr_name;
```

In this case ptr_name is the name of the pointer. The contents of the variable at this address can be accessed using *ptr_name. When a function is to modify a variable then a pointer to its address is sent. For example, if the variable to be modified is value then the argument passed is &value.

Figure B.13 shows an example of a function that swaps the contents of two variables (a and b). It also shows how the compiler checks the parameters passed to the function and the return type. The function prototype, in this case, specifies that the parameters sent are pointers to integer values and the return type is void. The compiler checks that the parameters sent to the function are integer pointers and that nothing is assigned to the return value from the function.

B.17 Arrays

An array stores more than one value, of a common data type, under a collective name. Each value has a unique slot and is referenced using an indexing technique. The declaration of an array specifies the data type, the array name and the number of elements in the array in brackets ([ ]). The standard format for an array declaration is:

```
data_type array_name[size];
```

Figure B.14 shows that the first element of the array is indexed 0 and the last element as size-1. The compiler allocates memory for the first element array_name[0] to the last array element array_name[size-1]. The number of bytes allocated in memory will be the number of elements in the array multiplied by the number of bytes used to store the data type of the array.

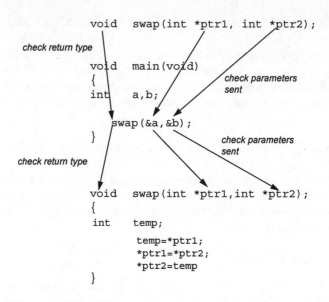

```
void   swap(int *ptr1, int *ptr2);
```
check return type
```
void   main(void)
{
int    a,b;
```
check parameters sent
```
    swap(&a,&b);
}
```
check return type

check parameters sent
```
void   swap(int *ptr1,int *ptr2);
{
int    temp;

    temp=*ptr1;
    *ptr1=*ptr2;
    *ptr2=temp
}
```

Figure B.13   Compiler checking.

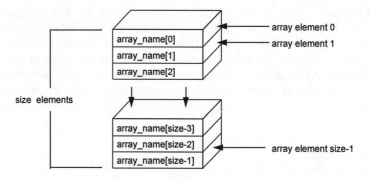

Figure B.14   Array elements.

B.18 Further references

For a more detailed coverage of C refer to the book:

Buchanan W. (1995). *C for Electronic Engineering with Applied Software Engineering*, Prentice Hall International.

Appendix C
Header Files

The following sections document the range of functions available in Turbo/Borland C.

C.1 DOS console I/O

Table C.1   DOS console I/O.

Conversion functions	Header file	Description
`void clrscr(void);`	conio.h	Function: Clear the current text window. Return: None.
`int gettext(int x1, int y1, int x2, int y2, void *ptr);`	conio.h	Function: To get text from the text rectangle from (x1,y1) to (x2,y2) and puts it into memory at a location starting at ptr. Return: A value of 1 if successful, else a 0.
`int gettextinfo (struct text_into *txt);`	conio.h	Function: Determines display text information and puts the result into txt. Return: None.
`void gotoxy(int x, int y);`	conio.h	Function: To move text cursor to position x, y. Return: None.
`int puttext(int x1, int y1, int x2, int y2, void *ptr);`	conio.h	Function: To copy text from memory, starting at the address given by ptr and puts it to a rectangle area on the screen between (x1, y1) and (x2, y2). Return: A non-zero value if successful, else a 0.
`void textattr(int attrib);`	conio.h	Function: To sets the current text attribute. Refer to Table 9.2 for attribute bit definitions. Return: None.

Table C.1 (Cont.).

Conversion functions	Header file	Description
`void` `  textbackground(int col);`	conio.h	Function: To set current text background colour. Return: None.
`void textcolor(int col);`	conio.h	Function: To set current text background colour. Return: None.
`int  textmode(int mode);`	conio.h	Function: To set the display into text mode. Return: None.
`int  wherex(int x);`	conio.h	Function: To return the current horizontal position of the cursor. Return: A value between 1 and 80.
`int  wherey(int y);`	conio.h	Function: To return the current vertical position of the cursor. Return: A value between 1 and 80.

`int  window(`
`  int top, int left,`
`  int bottom, int right);`
	conio.h	Function: Defines a text window for `(top,left)` to `(bottom,right)`.

C.2 Classification routines

Table C.2 Classification functions.

Conversion functions	Header file	Description
`int  isalnum(int ch);`	ctype.h	Function: To determine if character `ch` is a digit ('0'-'9') or a letter ('a'-'z' or 'A'-'Z'). Return: A non-zero value if the character is a digit or letter.
`int  isalpha(int ch);`	ctype.h	Function: To determine if character `ch` is a letter ('a'-'z', 'A'-'Z'). Return: A non-zero value if the character is a letter.

Table C.2   (Cont.).

Conversion functions	Header file	Description
`int iscntrl(int ch);`	ctype.h	Function: To determine if character ch is a control character, i.e. ASCII 0-31 or 127 (DEL). Return: A non-zero value if the character is a control character.
`int isdigit(int ch);`	ctype.h	Function: To determine if character ch is a digit ('0'-'9'). Return: A non-zero value if the character is a digit.
`int isgraph(int ch);`	ctype.h	Function: To determine if character ch is a printing character (the space character is excluded). Return: A non-zero value if the character is printable (excluding the space character).
`int islower(int ch);`	ctype.h	Function: To determine if character ch is a lower-case letter ('a'- 'z'). Return: A non-zero value if the character is a lower-case letter.
`int ispunct(int ch);`	ctype.h	Function: To determine if character ch is a punctuation character. Return: A non-zero value if the character is a punctuation character.
`int isprint(int ch);`	ctype.h	Function: To determine if character ch is a printing character. Return: A non-zero value if the character is printable (including the space character).
`int isspace(int ch);`	ctype.h	Function: To determine if character ch is either a space, horizontal tab, carriage return, new line, vertical tab or form-feed. Return: A non-zero value if the character is either a space, horizontal tab, carriage return, new line, vertical tab or form-feed.
`int isupper(int ch);`	ctype.h	Function: To determine if character ch is an upper-case letter ('A'- 'Z'). Return: A non-zero value if the character is an upper-case letter.
`int isxdigit(int ch);`	ctype.h	Function: To determine if character ch is a hexadecimal digit i.e. '0'-'9', 'a'-'f', 'A'-'F'. Return: A non-zero value if the character is a hexadecimal digit.

A sample program is given in Program C.1.

Program C.1

```c
#include <stdio.h>
#include <ctype.h>
int    main(void)
{
int    ch;

    do
    {
       printf("\nEnter a character >>");
       fflush(stdin);
       ch=getchar();
       puts("This character has the following attributes");

          if (isalnum(ch)) puts("Alphanumeric");
          if (isalpha(ch)) puts("Alphabetic");
          if (iscntrl(ch)) puts("Control character");
          if (isdigit(ch)) puts("Numeric");
          if (islower(ch)) puts("Lower-case");
          if (isupper(ch)) puts("Upper-case");
          if (ispunct(ch)) puts("Punctuation");
          if (isprint(ch)) puts("Printable character");
          if (isspace(ch)) puts("Space character");
          if (isxdigit(ch)) puts("A hex digit");
    } while (ch!=' ');
}
```

Test run C.1 shows a sample run.

Test run C.1

```
Enter a character >>   A
This character has the following attributes
Alphanumeric
Alphabetic
Upper-case
Printable character
A hex digit

Enter a character >>   ^V
This character has the following attributes
Control character

Enter a character >>   0
This character has the following attributes
Alphanumeric
Numeric
Printable character
A hex digit
```

C.3 Conversion routines

Table C.3 Conversion functions.

Conversion functions	Header file	Description
`double atof(char *str);`	stdlib.h	Function: Converts a string `str` into a floating-point number. Return: Converted floating-point value. If value cannot be converted the return value is 0.
`int  atoi(char *str);`	stdlib.h	Function: Converts a string `str` into an integer. Return: Converted integer value. If value cannot be converted the return value is 0.
`long  atol(char *str);`	stdlib.h	Function: Converts a string `str` into a long integer. Return: Converted integer value. If value cannot be converted the return value is 0.
`char *itoa(int val, char *str, int radix);`	stdlib.h	Function: Converts `val` into a string `str`. The number base used is defined by `radix`. Return: A pointer to `str`.
`char *ltoa(long val, char *str, int radix);`	stdlib.h	Function: Converts `val` into a string `str`. The number base used is defined by `radix`. Return: A pointer to `str`.
`int  _tolower(int ch);`	ctype.h	Function: Converts character `ch` to lower-case. Return: Converted value lower-case character. Note, `ch` must be in upper-case when called.
`int  tolower(int ch);`	ctype.h	Function: Converts character `ch` to lower-case. Return: Converted value lower-case character. Return value will be `ch` unless `ch` is in upper-case.
`int  _toupper(int ch);`	ctype.h	Function: Converts character `ch` to upper-case. Return: Converted value lower-case character. Note, `ch` must be in lower-case when called.
`int  toupper(int ch);`	ctype.h	Function: Converts character `ch` to upper-case. Return: Converted value lower-case character. Return value will be `ch` unless `ch` is in lower-case.

C.4 Input/output routines

Table C.4 Input/output functions.

Conversion functions	Header file	Description
`void clearerr(FILE *fptr);`	stdio.h	Function: Resets file error or end-of-file indicator on a file. Return: None.
`int fclose(FILE *fptr);`	stdio.h	Function: Closes a file currently pointed to by file pointer `fptr`. Return: A 0 on success, otherwise, EOF if any errors are encountered.
`int  feof(FILE *fptr);`	stdio.h	Function: Detects the end-of-file. Return: A non-zero if at the end of a file, otherwise a 0.
`int  ferror(FILE *fptr);`	stdio.h	Function: Detects if there has been an error when reading from or writing to a file. Return: A non-zero if an error has occurred, otherwise, a 0 if no error.
`int fflush(FILE *fptr);`	stdio.h	Function: Flushes a currently open file. Return: A 0 on success, otherwise, EOF if any errors are encountered.
`int  fgetc(FILE *fptr);`	stdio.h	Function: Gets a character from a file. Return: The character is read. On an error it returns EOF.
`char *fgets(char *str, int n, FILE *fptr);`	stdio.h	Function: To read a string from the file pointed to by `fptr` into string `str` with n characters or until a new-line character is read (whichever is first). Return: On success, the return value points to string `str`, otherwise a NULL on an error or end-of-file.

Table C.4 (Cont.).

Conversion functions	Header file	Description
`FILE *fopen(char *fname,` `        char *mode);`	stdio.h	Function: Opens a file named `fname` with attributes given by `mode`. Attributes include "r" for read-only access, "w" for read/write access to an existing file, "w+" to create a new file for read/write access, "a" for append, "a+" for append and create file is it does not exist and "b" for binary files. Return: If successful a file pointer, otherwise a `NULL` is returned.
`int fprintf(FILE *fptr,` `     char *fmt,arg1...);`	stdio.h	Function: Writes formatted data to a file. Return: The number of bytes outputted. On an error the return is `EOF`.
`int fputc(int ch,` `      FILE *fptr);`	stdio.h	Function: Writes a character `ch` to a file. Return: The character written, otherwise on an error it returns `EOF`.

`int  fread(void *buff,`
`  size_t size,size_t n,`
`  FILE *fptr);`
	stdio.h	Function: Reads binary data from a file. It reads n items of data, each of length `size` bytes into the block specified by `buff`.
		Return: The number of items read. In the event of an error the return will be less than the specified number (n).

`int fscanf(FILE *fptr,`
`   char *format,`
`   &arg1...);`
	stdio.h	Function: Scans and formats input from a file in a format specified by `format`.
		Return: The number of fields successfully scanned. In the event of a reading from an end-of-file the return is `EOF`.

`int fseek(FILE *fptr,`
`   long offset, int`
`   whence);`
	stdio.h	Function: The file pointer `fptr` is positioned at an offset specified by `offset` beyond the location specified by `whence`. This location can be either to `SEEK_SET` (the start of the file), `SEEK_CUR` (the current file position) or `SEEK_END` (the end-of-file).
		Return: A 0 on success; otherwise, a non-zero value if any errors are encountered.

Table C.4 (Cont.).

Conversion functions	Header file	Description

`int fwrite(void *buff,`
`size_t size, size_t n,`
`FILE *fptr);`
	stdio.h	Function: Writes binary data to a file. It writes n items of data, each of length `size` bytes from the block specified by `buff`.
		Return: The number of items written. On the event of an error the return will be less than the specified number (n).

`int getc(FILE *fptr);`	stdio.h	Function: Gets a character `ch` from a file. Return: The character read, or in the event of an error it returns EOF.
`int getchar(void);`	stdio.h	Function: Gets a character from the standard input (normally the keyboard). Return: The character read, or on an error it returns EOF.
`char *gets(char *str);`	stdio.h	Function: Gets a string `str` from the standard input (normally the keyboard). String input is terminated by a carriage return (and not with spaces or tabs, as with `scanf()`). Return: On success, the return value points to string `str`, otherwise a NULL on an error.
`int printf(char *fmt,` `arg1....);`	stdio.h	Function: Writes formatted data to the standard output (normally the display). Return: The number of bytes output. On an error the return is EOF.
`int putc(int ch,` `FILE *fptr);`	stdio.h	Function: Puts a character `ch` to a file. Return: The character written, else in the event of an error it returns EOF.
`int putchar(int ch);`	stdio.h	Function: Puts a character `ch` to the standard output (normally the display). Return: The character written, else on an error it returns EOF.
`int puts(char *str);`	stdio.h	Function: Puts a string `str` to the standard output (normally the display). The string is appended with a new-line character. Return: The character written, else on an error it returns EOF.

Table C.4 (Cont.).

Conversion functions	Header file	Description
`void rewind(FILE *fptr);`	stdio.h	Function: Repositions a file pointer to the start of a file. Any file errors will be automatically cleared. Return: None.
`int scanf(char *format, &arg1...);`	stdio.h	Function: Scans and formats input from the standard input (normally the keyboard) in a format specified by `format`. Return: The number of fields successfully scanned. In the event of a reading from an end-of-file the return is `EOF`.

C.5 String manipulation routines

Table C.5 String functions.

Conversion functions	Header file	Description
`int strcmp(char *str1,char *str2);`	string.h	Function: Compares two strings str1 and str2. Return: A 0 (zero) is returned if the strings are identical, a negative value if str1 is less than str2, or a positive value if str1 is greater than str2.
`int strlen(char *str);`	string.h	Function: Determines the number of characters in str. Return: Number of characters in str.
`char *strcat(char *str1, char *str2);`	string.h	Function: Appends str2 onto str1. The resultant string str1 will contain str1 and str2. Return: A pointer to the resultant string.
`char *strlwr(char *str1);`	string.h	Function: Converts upper-case letters in a string to lower-case Return: A pointer to the resultant string.
`char *strupr(char *str1);`	string.h	Function: Converts lower-case letters in a string to upper-case. Return: A pointer to the resultant string.

Table C.5 (Cont.).

Conversion functions	Header file	Description
`char *strcpy(char *str1,` `        char *str2);`	string.h	Function: Copies str2 into str1. Return: A pointer to the resultant string.

`int sprintf(char *str,`
`        char *format_str,`
`        arg1,....);`
	stdio.h	Function: Similar to printf() but output goes into string str.
		Return: Number of characters output.

`int sscanf(char *str,`
`        char *format_str,`
`        arg1,...);`
	stdio.h	Function: Similar to scanf() but input is from string str.
		Return: Number of fields successfully scanned.

C.6 Math routines

Table C.6 Math functions.

Conversion functions	Header file	Description
`int abs(int val);`	math.h, stdlib.h	Function: To determine the absolute value of val. Return: Absolute value.
`double acos(double val);`	math.h	Function: To determine the inverse cosine of val. Return: Inverse cosine in radians. If the range of val is invalid then errno is set to EDOM (domain error).
`double asin(double val);`	math.h	Function: To determine the inverse sine of val. Return: Inverse sine in radians. If the range of val is invalid then errno is set to EDOM (domain error).
`double atan(double val);`	math.h	Function: To determine the inverse tangent of val. Return: Inverse tangent in radians.

Table C.6 (Cont.).

Conversion functions	Header file	Description
`double atan2(double val1,` `double val2);`	math.h	Function: To determine the inverse tangent of `val1/val2`. Return: Inverse tangent in radians. If `val1` and `val2` are 0 then `errno` is set to EDOM (domain error).
`double ceil(double val);`	math.h	Function: Rounds `val` up to the nearest whole number. Return: The nearest integer value converted to a `double`.
`double cos(double val);`	math.h	Function: To determine the cosine of `val`. Return: Cosine value.
`double cosh(double val);`	math.h	Function: To determine the hyperbolic cosine of `val`. Return: The hyperbolic cosine. If an overflow occurs the return value is HUGE_VAL and `errno` is set to ERANGE (out of range).
`double exp(double val);`	math.h	Function: To determine the exponential e to the power of `val`. Return: The exponential power. If an overflow occurs the return value is HUGE_VAL and `errno` is set to ERANGE (out of range).
`double fabs(double val);`	math.h	Function: To determine the absolute value of `val`. Return: Absolute value returned as a `double`.
`double floor(double val);`	math.h	Function: Rounds `val` down to the nearest whole number. Return: The nearest integer value converted to a `double`.
`double fmod(double val1,` `double val2);`	math.h	Function: Determines the remainder of a division of `val1` by `val2` and rounds to the nearest whole number. Return: The nearest integer value converted to a `double`.

Table C.6 (Cont.).

Conversion functions	Header file	Description
`double log(double val);`	math.h	Function: Determines the natural logarithm of `val`. Return: The natural logarithm. If the value passed into the function is less than or equal to 0 then `errno` is set to `EDOM` and the value passed back is `HUGE_VAL`.
`double log10(double val);`	math.h	Function: Determines the base-10 logarithm of `val`. Return: The base-10 logarithm. If the value passed into the function is less than or equal to 0 then `errno` is set with `EDOM` and the value passed back is `HUGE_VAL`.
`double pow(double val1,` `double val2);`	math.h	Function: Determines `val1` to the power of `val2`. Return: The raised power. If an overflow occurs or the power is incalculable then the return value is `HUGE_VAL` and `errno` is set to `ERANGE` (out of range) or `EDOM` (domain error). If both arguments passed are 0 then the return is 1.
`int rand(void);`	math.h	Function: Generates a pseudo-random number from 0 to `val-1`. Return: The generated random number.
`double sin(double val);`	math.h	Function: To determine sine of `val`. Return: Sine value.
`double sinh(double val);`	math.h	Function: To determine hyperbolic sine of `val`. Return: The hyperbolic sine. If an overflow occurs the return value is `HUGE_VAL` and `errno` is set to `ERANGE` (out of range).
`double sqrt(double val);`	math.h	Function: Determines the square root of `val`. Return: The square root. If the value passed into the function is less than 0 then `errno` is set with `EDOM` and the value returned is 0.
`void srand(` `unsigned int seed);`	stdlib.h	Function: Initializes the random-generator with seed. Return: None.

Table C.6 (Cont.).

Conversion functions	Header file	Description
`double  tan(double val);`	math.h	Function: To determine the tangent of `val`. Return: The hyperbolic tangent. If an overflow occurs the return value is `HUGE_VAL` and `errno` is set to `ERANGE` (out of range).
`double tanh(double val);`	math.h	Function: To determine the hyperbolic tangent of `val`. Return: The hyperbolic tangent.

C.7 Time and date routines

Table C.7 Time functions.

Conversion functions	Header file	Description
`char *asctime(` `    struct tm *ttt);`	time.h	Function: Converts date and time to string. The time passed as a pointer to a tm structure. Return: A pointer to the date string.
`char *ctime(time_t *ttt);`	time.h	Function: Converts date and time to string. The time passed as a pointer to by ttt. Return: A pointer to the date string.
`double difftime(time_t` `    time2, time_t time1);`	time.h	Function: To determine the number of seconds between time2 and time1. Return: Difference in time returned as a double.
`struct tm *gmtime(` `    time_t *ttt);`	time.h	Function: Converts time into Greenwich Mean Time. The time is passed as a pointer to ttt and the result is put into a tm structure. Return: A pointer to the tm structure.
`int localtime(` `    time_t *ttt);`	time.h	Function: Converts time into local time. The time is passed as a pointer to ttt and the result is put into a tm structure. Return: A pointer to the tm structure.

Table C.7 (Cont.).

Conversion functions	Header file	Description
`time_t time(time *ttt);`	time.h	Function: To determine the time of day. The time is passed as a pointer to ttt and the result gives the number of seconds that have passed since 00:00:00 GMT January 1970. This value is returned through the pointer ttt. Return: The number of seconds that have passed since January 1970.

C.8 Other standard routines

Table C.8 Other standard functions.

Conversion functions	Header file	Description
`void   exit(int status);`	stdlib.h	Function: To terminate the program. The value passed status indicates the termination status. Typically, a 0 indicates a normal exit and any other value indicates an error. Return: None.
`void   free(void *block);`	stdlib.h	Function: To free an area of memory allocated to block. Return: None.
`void   *malloc(` `     size_t size);`	stdlib.h	Function: To allocate an area of memory with size bytes. Return: If there is enough memory a pointer to an area of memory is returned, otherwise a NULL is returned.
`int system(char *cmd);`	stdlib.h	Function: Issues a system command given by cmd. Return: A 0 on success, otherwise a –1.

Appendix D
Memory

D.1 Introduction

Binary information can either be stored, and recalled, electronically in memory circuits, or by using a mechanical device, such as an optical or hard disk. Mechanical storage methods are normally much slower than electronic methods. For example an optical disk can transfer data at a rate of around 300KB/sec whereas an electronic memory can transfer data at more than 100MB/sec. Mechanical storage devices are normally used for mass storage of permanent data. An optical disk can store over 600MB and a hard disk over 1GB.

Electronic memory circuits consist of arrays of transistors. The three main types of memory are:

- Random access Read-Only Memory (ROM);
- Static Random Access Memory (SRAM);
- Dynamic Random Access Memory (DRAM).

A ROM stores data permanently and does not lose its contents when the power is taken away, whereas RAM is a volatile memory. The two main types of RAM are SRAM and DRAM. SRAM is normally faster than DRAM but it uses at least six transistors to store just one bit of information. DRAM, on the other hand, only requires a single transistor to store a single data bit. Thus, for a given amount of transistors, DRAM memory stores at least six times the amount of data than an equivalent SRAM memory. Unfortunately, DRAM suffers two main drawbacks: they require to be refreshed with power several hundred times per second and are slower than equivalent SRAM memories.

Memory circuits have address, data and control lines, as illustrated in Figure D.1. The number of address lines indicates how many addressable locations there are and the number of input/output data lines show how many data bits can be accessed at a time. For example, a 1MB memory has 20 address lines, 2MB has 21 address lines and a 4MB memory has 22 address lines.

When the Select line goes active (that is, LOW) the memory IC is activated. The Read line loads data from the memory, whereas, the Write writes data into the memory. The address location of the memory to be read from, or written to, is defined by the address on the address lines. This address must be placed on the address bus before either activating the Read or Write lines.

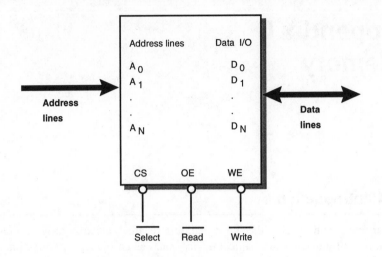

Figure D.1 RAM memory connections.

D.2 ROM

ROM is a permanent memory and is typically used to store programs and system data. A PC uses a ROM to store the BIOS (Basic I/O System) software. BIOS is a set of basic I/O procedures that allows the system to use the keyboard, monitor, hard disk, and so on. The BIOS also contains the software required to start the system (the bootstrap program).

There are four main types of ROM: mask-programmed ROM, erasable programmable ROM (EPROM), programmable ROM (PROM) and EEPROM (electrically erasable programmable ROM). A mask-programmed ROM has a fixed structure and cannot be erased or reprogrammed. It is normally only cost-effective when producing large quantities.

An EPROM is programmed by an EPROM programmer. It can be reprogrammed by first erasing the data by exposing it to a high-intensity ultra-violet light (the EPROM device has a transparent quartz window). A PROM contains fusable links to store data. It is programmed by a PROM programmer but, unlike the EPROM, it cannot be erased. The best solution for flexibility is an EEPROM (or E^2PROM) which is programmed and erased electrically, typically without removing it from the installed system. Most modern PCs use E^2PROMs for their BIOS as they have the advantage of being updated by software. The main types of ROM are thus:

- ROM - permanent memory which cannot be erased. Only economical in large quantities.
- PROM - programmed by a PROM programmer, but cannot be reprogrammed.
- EPROM - programmed using an EPROM programmer and can be unpro-

grammed using UV light.

- EEPROM - programmed and erased electrically.

Some typical EPROMs are:

- 27256 (256 Kb or 262 144 bits);
- 27512 (512 Kb or 524 288 bits);
- 27101 (1024 Kb or 1 048 576 bits).

Typical access times of these devices range from 150 nanoseconds (ns) to 250 ns. Typical EEPROMs are the 2816 (2 KB), the 2864 (8 KB) and the 28256 (32 KB). Access times are similar to EPROMs. All these devices have an 8-bit data bus and normally use low-powered CMOS or NMOS.

An n-bit addressable ROM has up to 2^n address locations, each of which stores a number of data bits. For example, a 9-bit addressable ROM has 512 different addressable locations, as illustrated in Figure D.2. A decoder converts the 9-bit address code into one of 512 different address locations. In this case the ROM stores 8 bits for each address location. The presence, or absence, of a transistor defines a stored bit pattern. These transistors are either fixed (as in a ROM), are sensitive to UV light (as in an EPROM) or can be set up electrically (as in an E^2PROM). When a 0 is stored then the line connecting the output to the address line is connected to ground via a transistor. If a 1 is stored there is no pull-down transistor present to ground the output line. Figure D.3 shows a 9-bit addressable ROM with a 5-bit output. The pull-up transistors give a HIGH when there is no pull-down transistor present. In this case memory location 0 stores the bit pattern 11111, location 1 stores 01110, location 2 stores 10111, and so on to location 511 which stores 10111.

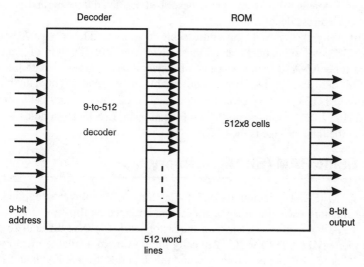

Figure D.2 ROM addressing.

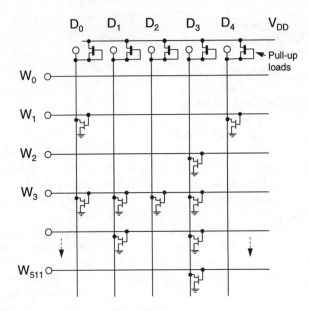

Figure D.3 9-bit addressable NMOS ROM array.

D.3 2D addressing

As the number of address lines increases the larger the address decoder becomes. This is unmanageable for large memories. For example, a 1 MB memory would require over a million addressable memory locations (requiring a 20-to-1 048 576 decoder). An improved memory arrangement is to use a matrix of rows and columns. This technique is described as 2D addressing and is used to reduce the address decoder size.

Figure D.4 shows an 11-bit addressable memory. Address lines A0-A6 accesses 128 rows of data. Each of these rows contains 128 bits of data. The address lines A7-A10 then select one of sixteen lines to give the data lines D0-D7 (128 bits divided by sixteen addressable lines gives eight data bits). It contains 128×128 memory cells giving a total of 65 386 memory cells arranged into 16×128 locations in memory (2 048 locations). Each location holds 8 bits of data and the total storage is thus 2 KB.

D.4 Static RAM (SRAM) memory

Static RAM (SRAM) retains its data for as long as the power is applied. This type of memory uses a number of transistors arranged as flip-flop storage cells. Each stored bit requires at least six transistors and it is thus difficult to get as much memory as a DRAM IC. Typically the maximum available memory on a single IC is 128 kB and is normally found in memories that are less than 512 KB

Figure D.5 shows a typical static RAM cell. Transistors Q_3 and Q_4 are pull-up transistors and are either NMOS depletion-mode or CMOS p-type transistors (depending on whether the technology is NMOS or CMOS). To store a bit the cell is selected with the Cell Select line (that is, it is set active HIGH). If bit is HIGH then Q_2 will be ON and Q_1 OFF as its gate is held LOW by Q_2. A LOW on the Bit line causes Q_1 to be OFF and Q_2 ON. When the Cell Select line is placed inactive the cell stores the state.

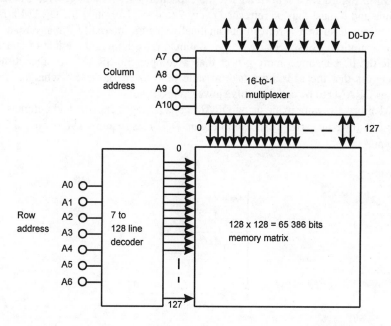

Figure D.4 2D addressing of a 16 Kbit memory (2 KB or 2 048 × 8 bits).

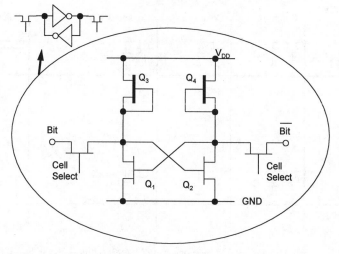

Figure D.5 Static NMOS RAM cell.

D.5 Dynamic RAM (DRAM) memory

A DRAM cell uses fewer transistors than an equivalent SRAM cell and it is thus possible to get a greater amount of DRAM memory on a single IC. This is because DRAM uses small capacitors to store electrical charge, a typical cell is shown in Figure D.6. Unfortunately, the capacitor loses its charge over a period of time and it must thus be refreshed every 2 to 4 ms. Normally the DRAM array is configured so that a refresh automatically occurs internally for any read or write operation. Thus, because of the continual refreshing and the lost of charge a DRAM IC consumes more power than a comparable SRAM. Another disadvantage is that the capacitors take a finite time to charge and discharge. This causes DRAMs to be considerably slower than SRAMs.

Memory array are made using DRAM cells arranged in rows and columns. A 256×256 (64 Kbit) array is shown in Figure D.7. This requires 256 rows and 256 columns.

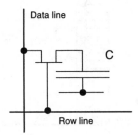

Figure D.6 Basic Dynamic RAM cell.

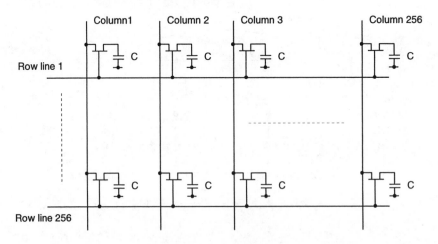

Figure D.7 Basic Dynamic RAM memory array (256×256 bits = 65 536 bits = 64 Kbit).

A DRAM cell is automatically refreshed every time it is read from or written to. It would be difficult to read the contents of every memory cell so DRAM cells are constructed in a way that a single read from memory refreshes a whole row of bits at the same time. The DRAM array in Figure D.8 has 1024 cells in each row. When a single row is selected all 1024 cells within it are automatically refreshed. Thus, in this case, only 256 refreshes are required to update the whole memory. These reads typically occur every 4 ms - one from each internal row.

The array in Figure D.8 is a 256 Kb × 1 DRAM memory. The address lines A0-A7 select one of 1024 rows. These lines are fed into four 1-of-256 multiplexers. The address lines A8-A15 then select one bit from the each of the 1-to-256 multiplexors. One bit is then selected using the address bits A16 and A17. If the single bit is being written to the array then the R/W line is a HIGH and the input on Din is read. A LOW on the R/W line writes the bit to the output line Dout.

To reduce the number of pins on the device the address lines are reduced so that the row and column are latched in two separate operations. The RAS line allows the row address to be latched and CAS the column address. This is shown in Figure D.9. A 256 Kb × 1 DRAM array thus only requires 16 pins (A0-A8, RAS, CAS, DIN, DOUT, R/W, VCC and GND).

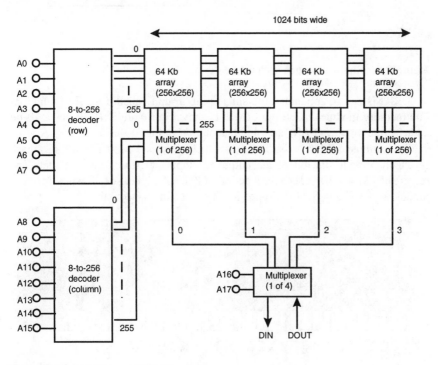

Figure D.8   256 Kbit × 1 DRAM array.

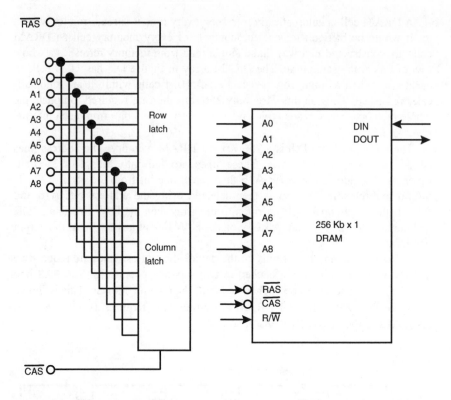

Figure D.9 Row and column latching.

DRAMs can be mounted on a single plug-in unit called a SIMM (single in-line memory module). A 30-pin SIMM is shown in Figure D.10. It has a 10-bit address line input (A0-A9), an 8-bit data output/ input (D0-D7).

An example SIMM is the TMS024 which has 8×1 Mbit DRAM ICs, each of which provide one bit of the output (or input). It stores 1MB of data and requires 512 refresh cycles over a period of 8 ms. A higher specification memory module is the 72-pin SIMM; Appendix I lists its pin connections.

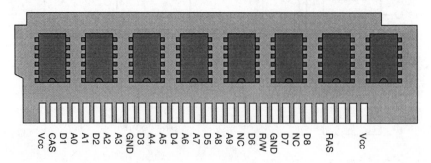

Figure D.10 30-pin DRAM module (SIMM).

D.6 Wait states

If the processor communicates with memory which is relatively slow then the contents of the memory may take longer than a single clock period. For example, DRAM memory can have an access time of 80ns. Whereas, a system operating with a 33MHz system clock has a clock period of 30ns. The processor accesses and reads from memory in two cycles of the clock (that is, 60ns). It must thus wait for another two clock periods (or two wait states) for it to access the memory. This is shown in Figure D.11.

- Put address on address bus   30 ns
- Wait to access   30 ns
- Read memory   30 ns

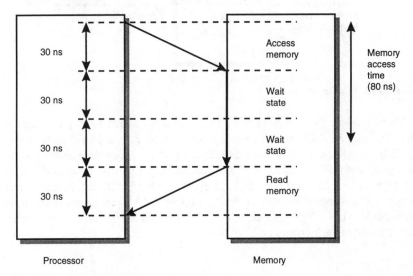

Figure D.11   Example of memory address with two wait states.

D.7 Memory cache

DRAM is a relatively slow type of memory compared with SRAM. A cache memory can be used to overcome this problem (see Figure D.12). This is a bank of fast memory (SRAM) that loads data from main memory (typically DRAM). The cache controller guesses the data the processor requires and loads this into the cache memory. If the controller guesses correctly then it is a cache hit, else if it is wrong it is a cache miss. A miss causes the processor to access the memory in the normal way (that is, there may be wait states). Typical cache memory sizes are 16 KB, 32 KB and 64 KB. This should be compared with the size of the RAM on a typical PC which is typically at least 4 MB.

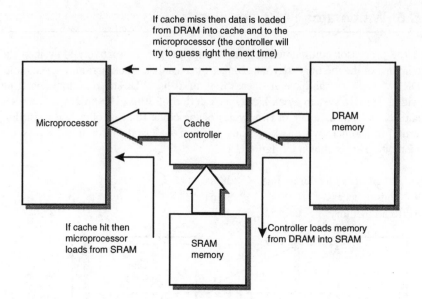

If cache miss then data is loaded
from DRAM into cache and to the
microprocessor (the controller will
try to guess right the next time)

Microprocessor

Cache
controller

DRAM
memory

If cache hit then
microprocessor
loads from SRAM

SRAM
memory

Controller loads memory
from DRAM into SRAM

Figure D.12   Cache operation.

Many modern systems have extra cache memory added to improve the hit
rate. Typically an 8 KB cache memory gives 70% hit rate, a 16 KB cache memory 85%, a 32 K cache 93% and a 64 KB cache 95%. Cache sizes above this do
not significantly effect the hit rate and can actually slow the process down as
they take so long to fill the cache memory. The Intel 80486 and Pentium have
built-in cache controllers and, at least, 8 KB of SRAM cache memory. Intel
claim that this has a 96% hit rate, which is an extremely high hit rate for such a
small amount of cache memory.

D.8 Exercises

The following questions are multiple choice. Please select from a – d.

D.1   Which of the following types of memory can be modified electrically:

(a)   EEPROM   (b)   EPROM
(c)   ROM   (d)   PROM

D.2   Which of the following types of memory cannot be modified once
manufactured:

(a)   EEPROM   (b)   EPROM
(c)   ROM   (d)   PROM

D.3   If a PC has a BIOS IC which can be electrically updated then which of the following types of ROM does it use:

(a)   EEPROM   (b)   EPROM
(c)   ROM   (d)   PROM

D.4   An EPROM is reprogrammed:

(a)   by ultra-violet light   (b)   electrically
(c)   by infra-red light   (d)   by strobe lights

D.5   The two main types of RAM are:

(a)   Static RAM and Detect RAM
(b)   Static RAM and Dynamic RAM
(c)   Simple RAM and Dynamic RAM
(d)   Single RAM and Double RAM

D.6   What is the main advantage of SRAM over DRAM:

(a)   it is faster
(b)   it is possible to create larger memories
(c)   it is easier to purchase
(d)   it less costly for the equivalent memory sizes

D.7   The main reason that DRAM is used over SRAM is that:

(a)   DRAM allows larger memories on ICs
(b)   they are compatiable more systems
(c)   DRAM is faster
(d)   DRAM has lower power dissipation

D.8   How does DRAM store data:

(a)   with diodes arranged as a flip-flop
(b)   by charging capacitors
(c)   with transistors arranged as a flip-flop
(d)   with resistors connected in series

D.9   Wait states are required to allow the:

(a)   memory time to produce addressed data
(b)   processor time to communicate with the memory
(c)   hard disk time to communicate with the processor
(d)   memory time to communicate with the floppy disk

D.10   The main drawbacks of DRAM are that:

    (a)   they are difficult to produce and relatively expensive to purchase
    (b)   they are static sensitive and prone to errors
    (c)   they are difficult to fit onto printed circuit boards and are prone to breakage
    (d)   they are slower than SRAM and require to be refreshed with power

D.11   Memory caches allow:

    (a)   the processor to use a faster clock
    (b)   the memory to be refreshed at a faster rate
    (c)   the processor to communicate with SRAM rather than DRAM
    (d)   more data to be stored

D.12   What size of the memory cache is built into the 80486:

    (a)   8 kB
    (b)   32 kB
    (c)   128 kB
    (d)   1 MB

D.13   A memory cache typically contains which type of memory:

    (a)   DRAM
    (b)   DRAM
    (c)   ROM
    (d)   EEPROM

D.14   The two main types of SIMM memory are:

    (a)   9-pin and 18-pin
    (b)   30-pin and 72-pin
    (c)   36-pin and 72-pin
    (d)   32-pin and 64-pin

Appendix E
Video Displays

E.1 Introduction

Many different types of graphics displays can be connected to a PC. They may differ in the number of displayable colours, the interface technology, the ICs used or in their resolution. The signals that pass between the display and the graphics interface card is either by a digital signal (TTL levels) or an analogue signal (composite video). Originally, PCs used TTL RGB (Red/ Green/ Blue) displays with Colour Graphics Adaptor (CGA) graphics adaptors. Unfortunately, TTL RGB displays can only display a maximum of 16 colours because they use a 4-bit code to transmit colour information. An improved technique is composite video which is used in normal TV transmission and offers higher quality and the possibility of millions of different colours. The main graphics drivers available are:

- CGA (Colour Graphics Adaptor);
- EGA (Enhanced Graphics Adaptor);
- VGA (Variable Graphics Adaptor);
- SVGA (Super VGA).

The graphics driver can be set into a number of modes that effect the resolution of the screen and the number of displayable colours. Also, the number of colours that can be displayed on an SVGA depends on the amount on memory on the interface card. Table E.1 lists some typical parameters for different graphics drivers.

E.2 Graphics interfaces

A graphics display interfaces to a PC either through a graphics adaptor which is integrated into the motherboard of the computer or to a graphics adaptor which is plugged into the I/O bus. A plug-in adaptor allows for future expansion, but many integrated motherboard adaptors now have automatic sensing to allow an upgraded graphics adaptor to be plugged into the I/O bus.

The interface technology used can either be ISA, EISA, VL-Local Bus or PCI local bus, as shown in Figure E.1. Most modern PCs use some form of local bus technology as they much faster when using graphical user interface (GUI) software, such as Microsoft Windows.

Table E.1 Typical video parameters.

Graphics driver	Screen resolution	Colours	Video representation
CGA	320×200	4	TTL RGB
EGA	640×350	16	Composite video
VGA	640×480	16	Composite video
SVGA	1 024×768 or 800×600	256 or 16	Composite video

E.3 Analogue RGB display

Analogue RGB displays use three primary colours: RED, GREEN and BLUE. These colours are sent to the display as analogue voltages in the range of 0 V to +0.7 V. An analogue-to-digital converter (ADC) within the graphics adaptor converts the digital colour code from the PC into the equivalent analogue voltage. Then in the display the analogue voltage converts back into a digital form using a digital-to-analogue converter (DAC).

If the system uses a 6-bit ADC and a 6-bit DAC then each colour has 2^6, or 64, different shades. This means that the total number of colours available is 64×64×64=262144 (256K) colours. A 7-bit system can display over 2 million (2 M) colours. With 8-bit converters 16M colours are displayable. Figure E.2 shows an example of a 6-bit system.

Some monitors have BNC connectors for the direct input of the three primary colours. Most EGA and VGA displays, though, use a 15-pin D-type connection to connect the driver card to the display. The pin connections of these connectors is given in Table E.2.

High-resolution VGA monitors use an 18-bit code to represent each displayable colour (6 bits for each of the primary colours). This gives a total of 16M colours. This code is applied to a high-speed static random access memory (SRAM). The VGA standard only allows 256 colours to be displayed at a time thus the 18-bit code is converted to represent 256 different hues.

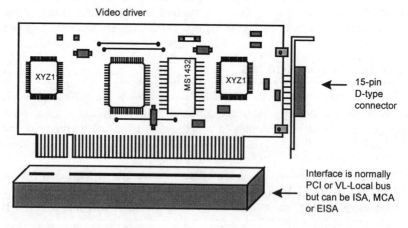

Figure E.1 Video interfacing.

Table E.2   Analogue monitor pin connections.

Pin	Function	Pin	Function
1	Red video	9	Blocked as a key
2	Green video (monochrome video)	10	Ground
3	Blue video	11	Colour detect (ground on a colour monitor)
4	Ground	12	Monochrome detect
5	Ground	13	Horizontal retrace
6	Red ground	14	Vertical retrace
7	Green ground (mono video)	15	Ground
8	Blue ground		

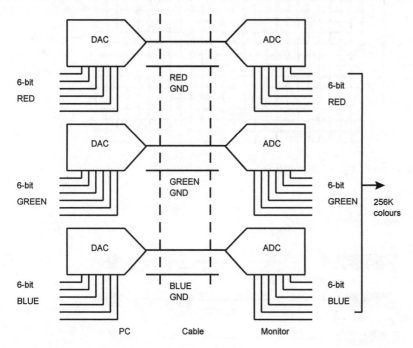

Figure E.2   6-bit video system.

The amount of memory required to store a single screen of video information depends on the resolution of the display and the number of displayable colours. For example, a 640×400 display with 256 displayable colours (8 bits per pixel) requires 640×400 bytes of memory (256000) to store all of the pixels, as illustrated in Figure E.3.

As with a TV system the video is traced in interlacing lines. First the top left-hand corner pixel is sent, followed by each pixel in turn on a single line. After the last pixel on the first line the video trace goes to the start of the next line. This then continues until it reaches the bottom of the screen. After this it returns to the top left-hand pixel and starts again, as shown in Figure E.4. Typical screen refresh rates are 60 Hz, 70 Hz and 75 Hz.

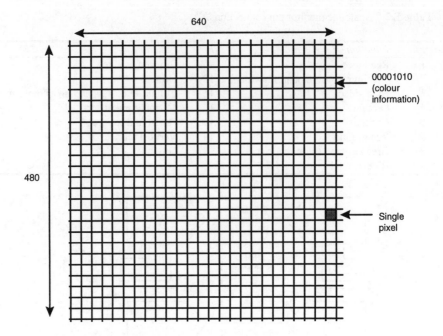

Figure E.3 6-bit video system.

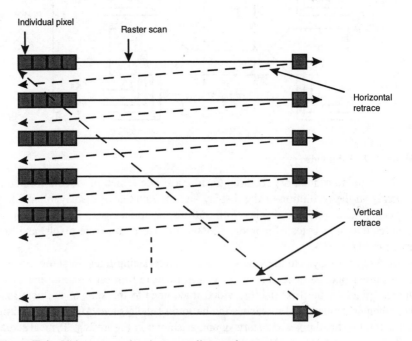

Figure E.4 Video screen showing raster lines and retrace.

A 60 Hz system draws one whole screen every 1/60 of a second (~16.7 ms). This update frequency is also known as the frame rate. A 640×400 display has 640 pixels per lines and 400 video raster lines. The raster line is the smallest subdivision of this horizontal line and its frequency is the frame rate multiplied by the number of raster lines on the screen.

SVGA displays have excellent graphics which have more pixels than a TV system and in 1 024×768 mode they approach the resolution of 35 mm photographic film. Unfortunately, at high resolutions, the required frame rate becomes difficult to achieve. A possible solution is to use an interlaced system which draws half the image for the odd scanning lines, then the other half, using the even scanning lines, as illustrated in Figure E.5. Interlaced systems are more complex than the non-interfaced system but are more efficient as the scanning frequency is reduced by around 50 %. The disadvantage with interlaced screens is that if the update frequency is too low then there is a noticeable flicker. A typical interfaced scanning rate is 43 Hz.

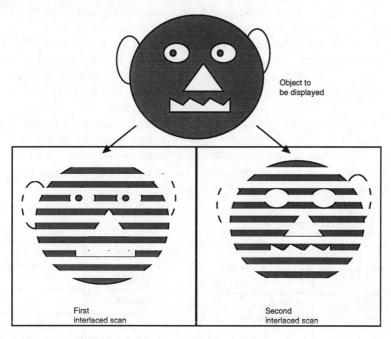

Figure E.5 Video screen showing raster lines and retrace.

E.4 Palettes, pixel planes and VRAMs

The number of displayable colours determines the number of bits used to store each pixel. A monochrome display stores each pixel with a single bit. Colour displays use more than one bit per pixel to represent the red, green and blue data. For example if 4 bits are used to represent each colour then there are 16 different hues of blue, red and green giving a total of 16×16×16 (4096 or 4 K) different colours. A 256 colour display uses 8 bits (1 byte) for each colour and with a resolution of 640×480 requires 640×480×1 byte (or 307 200 bytes) of video memory (known as the frame buffer). To reduce the number of bytes a palette scheme can be used. For example, a palette of 16 colours would only require the storage of 4 bits per pixel.

A limiting factor of high-resolution graphics display is the rate at which pixel data is read from the frame buffer. For example for 1 024×768 screen, 256 colours at 60 frames/sec rate requires 47 185 920 bytes (1 024×768×60×1 byte) to be read each second or 1 byte every 21 ns. Currently available standard Dynamic RAMs (DRAMs) are too slow to be used as frame buffers. The main methods used to reduce data transfer are:

(1) To use a palette scheme to reduce the number of bits per pixel. A typical scheme uses 4 bits per pixel giving 16 colours in the palette. Two pixels are then packed into a single memory location as shown in Figure E.6.
(2) To use special architecture DRAMs called VRAM (or video RAM). The VRAM consists of four arrays, each storing 256 Kbits, which allows it to function as a 256 K × 4 device for read and write operations. Typical data rates for a 800×600 pixel display at 60 frames/sec is 28 800 000 pixels/sec.

The number of colours and pixels in the display is limited by the frame buffer memory. Table E.3 outlines memory requirements; for example, if the display has a frame memory of 1 MB then at 640×480 resolution a total of 16.7 million colours can be displayed. If the resolution is 1 024×768 then only 256 colours can be displayed.

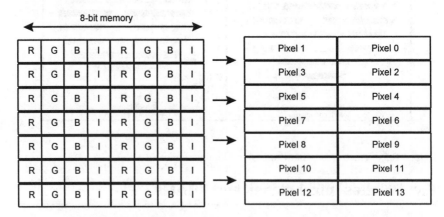

Figure E.6 Frame buffer memory.

Table E.3 Memory requirement for video modes.

Resolution	Colours	Video memory
640×480	16.7 million	1 MB
800×600	64 000	1 MB
800×600	16.7 million	2 MB
1 024×768	256	1 MB
1 024×768	64 000	2 MB
1 024×768	16.7 million	3 MB
1 280×1 024	256	2 MB
1 280×1 024	64 000	3 MB

E.5 Exercises

E.1 What type of video signal does CGA video monitors use:

    (a)   composite video
    (b)   TTL RGB
    (c)   composite digital
    (d)   TLL RYB

E.2 What are the three primary colours used in video monitors:

    (a)   red, yellow, blue
    (b)   red, green, yellow
    (c)   yellow, green, blue
    (d)   red, green, blue

E.3 Which of the following interface technologies offers the best performance for high quality graphics:

    (a)   PCI Bus
    (b)   EISA
    (c)   MCA
    (d)   ISA

E.4 An analogue video signal uses 4-bit analogue-to-digital converters. How many colours can be displayed:

    (a)   4
    (b)   64
    (c)   256
    (d)   4 096

E.5   An analogue video signal uses 8-bit analogue-to-digital converters. How many colours can be displayed:

   (a)   512
   (b)   4 096
   (c)   2 million
   (d)   16 million

E.6   How many pixels does a 640×480 monitor have:

   (a)   1 120
   (b)   307 200
   (c)   640
   (d)   480

E.7   A display has a resolution of 800×600 and a video memory of 1 MB. How many colours can be displayed:

   (a)   16
   (b)   256
   (c)   64 K
   (d)   128 K

E.8   A display has a resolution of 640×480, a frame rate of 60 Hz and can display 256 colours. What is the required data throughput:

   (a)   9 216 000 Bytes/sec
   (b)   18 432 000 Bytes/sec
   (c)   36 864 000 Bytes/sec
   (d)   73 728 000 Bytes/sec

E.9   A display has a resolution of 1 280×1 024, a frame rate of 60 Hz and can display 16 colours. What is the required data throughput:

   (a)   9 830 400 Bytes/sec
   (b)   19 660 800 Bytes/sec
   (c)   39 321 600 Bytes/sec
   (d)   78 643 200 Bytes/sec

Appendix F
Compiler differences

F.1 Input/output statements

Some compilers use the function `inp()` and `outp()` instead of `inportb()` and `outportb()`. If this is the case either replace all occurrence of these functions with their equivalent or insert the following lines after the header files have been included.

```
#define inportb(portid)      inp(portid)
#define outportb(portid,ch)  outp(portid,ch)
```

This replaces all occurances of `inportb()` and `outportb()` with `inp()` and `outp()`, respectively.

F.2 kbhit()

The `kbhit()` function can be replaced with the following lines of code:

```
#include <dos.h>

int    khit(void);

int kbhit(void)
{
union      REGS inregs,outregs;
unsigned int zf;

   inregs.h.ah=1;

   int86(0x16,&inregs,&outregs);

   zf=outregs.x.flags & 0x40;

   if (zf) return(0);
   else return(1);
}
```

F.3 getch()

The getch() function gets a single character from the keyboard. It differs
from getchar() in that there is no need to press the return key after the
character has been entered. The following lines can replace this function.

```
#include <dos.h>

int    getch(void);

int    getch(void)
{
union    REGS inregs,outregs;
int      ch;

    inregs.h.ah=0;

    int86(0x16,&inregs,&outregs);

    ch=outregs.h.al;

    return(ch);
}
```

Appendix G
I/O Interface Connections

G.1 ISA bus

The Industry Standard Architecture (ISA) bus uses a 16-bit data bus (D0-D15) and a 24-bit address bus (A0-A24). The ISA bus pin connections are illustrated in Figure G.1 and are listed in Table G.1.

Table G.1   16-bit ISA bus connections.

Signal name	Description	Bus direction
A0-A23	Address lines A0-A23	Input/output
AEN	Address enable	Output
ALE	Address latch enable	Output
CLK	Clock (ISA: 8.33 MHz or PC: 4.77 MHz)	Output
D0-D15	Data lines D0-D15	Input/output
DACK0-DACK3	DMA acknowledge 0-3	Output
DACK5-DACK7	DMA acknowledge 5-7	Output
DRQ0-DRQ3	DMA request 0-3	Input
DRQ5-DRQ7	DMA request 5-7	Input
I/O CH CK	I/O channel check	Input
I/O CH RDY	I/O channel ready	Input
I/O CS16	I/O 16-bit chip select	Input
IOR	I/O read command	Input/output
IOW	I/O write command	Input/output
IRQ14-IRQ15	Interrupt request 14-15	Input
IRQ3-IRQ7	Interrupt request 3-7	Input
IRQ9-IRQ12	Interrupt request 9-12	Input
MASTER	Master	Input
MEM CS16	Memory 16 chip select	Input
MEMR	Memory read command	Input/output
MEMW	Memory write command	Input/output
OSC	Oscillator (14.3 MHz)	Output
REFRESH	Refresh	Input/output
RESET DRV	Reset drive	Output
SBHE	System high byte enable	Output
SMEMR	System memory read command	Output
SMEMW	System memory write command	Output
T/C	Terminal count	Input

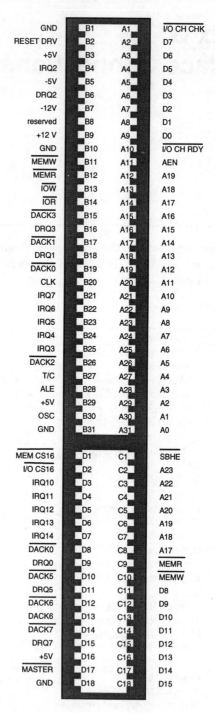

GND	B1 — A1	I/O CH CHK
RESET DRV	B2 — A2	D7
+5V	B3 — A3	D6
IRQ2	B4 — A4	D5
-5V	B5 — A5	D4
DRQ2	B6 — A6	D3
-12V	B7 — A7	D2
reserved	B8 — A8	D1
+12 V	B9 — A9	D0
GND	B10 — A10	I/O CH RDY
MEMW	B11 — A11	AEN
MEMR	B12 — A12	A19
IOW	B13 — A13	A18
IOR	B14 — A14	A17
DACK3	B15 — A15	A16
DRQ3	B16 — A16	A15
DACK1	B17 — A17	A14
DRQ1	B18 — A18	A13
DACK0	B19 — A19	A12
CLK	B20 — A20	A11
IRQ7	B21 — A21	A10
IRQ6	B22 — A22	A9
IRQ5	B23 — A23	A8
IRQ4	B24 — A24	A7
IRQ3	B25 — A25	A6
DACK2	B26 — A26	A5
T/C	B27 — A27	A4
ALE	B28 — A28	A3
+5V	B29 — A29	A2
OSC	B30 — A30	A1
GND	B31 — A31	A0
MEM CS16	D1 — C1	SBHE
I/O CS16	D2 — C2	A23
IRQ10	D3 — C3	A22
IRQ11	D4 — C4	A21
IRQ12	D5 — C5	A20
IRQ13	D6 — C6	A19
IRQ14	D7 — C7	A18
DACK0	D8 — C8	A17
DRQ0	D9 — C9	MEMR
DACK5	D10 — C10	MEMW
DRQ5	D11 — C11	D8
DACK6	D12 — C12	D9
DACK6	D13 — C13	D10
DACK7	D14 — C14	D11
DRQ7	D15 — C15	D12
+5V	D16 — C16	D13
MASTER	D17 — C17	D14
GND	D18 — C18	D15

Figure G.1   ISA bus connections.

G.2 VL-Local bus

The VL-Local bus uses a standard ISA connector and an extra connector to tap into the 32-bit data and address busses. Table G.2 lists the additional 32-bit VESA VL-Local bus connections. It has a 32-bit data bus (D0-D31) and a full 32-bit address bus (A0-A31). The VL-Local bus is an extension to the standard ISA bus and can thus use the interrupt lines on ISA bus connector, that is, IRQ3-IRQ7 and IRQ10-IRQ14. It also has the memory addressing lines ($M/\overline{IO}$ and $R/\overline{W}$).

Table G.2 32-bit VESA VL-Local bus connections.

Pin	Side-A	Side-B	Pin	Side-A	Side-B
1	D0	D1	30	A17	A16
2	D2	D3	31	A15	A14
3	D4	GND	32	VCC	A12
4	D6	D5	33	A13	A10
5	D8	D7	34	A11	A8
6	GND	D9	35	A9	GND
7	D10	D11	36	A7	A6
8	D12	D13	37	A5	A4
9	VCC	D15	38	GND	$\overline{WBACK}$
10	D14	GND	39	A3	$\overline{BE0}$
11	D16	D17	40	A2	VCC
12	D18	VCC	41	NC	$\overline{BE1}$
13	D20	D19	42	$\overline{RESET}$	$\overline{BE2}$
14	GND	D21	43	$D/\overline{C}$	GND
15	D22	D23	44	$M/\overline{IO}$	$\overline{BE3}$
16	D24	D25	45	$W/\overline{R}$	$\overline{ADS}$
17	D26	GND	46	KEY	KEY
18	D28	D27	47	KEY	KEY
19	D30	D29	48	$\overline{RDYRTN}$	$\overline{LRDY}$
20	VCC	D31	49	GND	$\overline{LDEV}$
21	A31	A30	50	IRQ9	$\overline{LREQ}$
22	GND	A28	51	$\overline{BRDY}$	GND
23	A29	A26	52	$\overline{BLAST}$	$\overline{LGNT}$
24	A27	GND	53	IDO	VCC
25	A25	A24	54	ID1	ID2
26	A23	A22	55	GND	ID3
27	A21	VCC	56	LCLK	ID4
28	A19	A20	57	VCC	NC
29	GND	A18	58	$\overline{LBS16}$	$\overline{LEADS}$

G.3 PCI local bus

The PCI local bus is a radical re-design of the PC bus technology and is logically different from the ISA and VL-Local bus. Table G.3 lists the 32-bit, 2×62-pin PCI local bus connections. A 64-bit, 2×94-pin connector version is also available.

Table G.3 32-bit PCI local bus connections.

Pin	Side-A	Side-B	Pin	Side-A	Side-B
1	−12V	$\overline{\text{TRST}}$	32	AD17	AD16
2	TCK	+12V	33	$\overline{\text{C/BE2}}$	+3.3V
3	GND	TMS	34	GND	$\overline{\text{FRAME}}$
4	TDO	TDI	35	$\overline{\text{IRDY}}$	GND
5	+5V	+5V	36	+3.3V	$\overline{\text{TRDY}}$
6	+5V	$\overline{\text{INTA}}$	37	$\overline{\text{DEVSEL}}$	GND
7	$\overline{\text{INTB}}$	$\overline{\text{INTC}}$	38	GND	$\overline{\text{STOP}}$
8	$\overline{\text{INTD}}$	+5V	39	$\overline{\text{LOCK}}$	+3.3V
9	$\overline{\text{PRSNT}}$	Reserved	40	$\overline{\text{PERR}}$	SDONE
10	Reserved	+5V(I/O)	41	+3.3V	$\overline{\text{SBO}}$
11	$\overline{\text{PRSNT2}}$	Reserved	42	$\overline{\text{SERR}}$	GND
12	GND	GND	43	+3.3V	PAR
13	GND	GND	44	$\overline{\text{C/BE1}}$	AD15
14	Reserved	Reserved	45	AD14	+3.3V
15	GND	$\overline{\text{RST}}$	46	GND	AD13
16	CLK	+5V(I/O)	47	AD12	AD11
17	GND	$\overline{\text{GNT}}$	48	AD10	GND
18	$\overline{\text{REQ}}$	GND	49	GND	AD09
19	+5V(I/O)	Reserved	50	KEY	KEY
20	AD31	AD30	51	KEY	KEY
21	AD29	+3.3V	52	AD08	$\overline{\text{C/BE0}}$
22	GND	AD28	53	AD07	+3.3V
23	AD27	AD26	54	+3.3V	AD06
24	AD25	GND	55	AD05	AD04
25	+3.3V	AD24	56	AD03	GND
26	$\overline{\text{C/BE3}}$	IDSEL	57	GND	AD02
27	AD23	+3.3V	58	AD01	AD00
28	GND	$\overline{\text{FRAME}}$	59	+5V(I/O)	+5V(I/O)
29	AD21	AD20	60	$\overline{\text{ACK64}}$	$\overline{\text{REQ64}}$
30	AD19	GND	61	+5V	+5V
31	+3.3V	$\overline{\text{TRDY}}$	62	+5V	+5V

G.4 PCMCIA interface

The Personal Computer Memory Card International Association (PCMCIA) interface allows small thin cards to be plugged into laptop, notebook or palmtop computers. It was originally designed for memory cards but has since been adopted for many other types of adapters, such as fax/modems, sound-cards, local area network cards, CD-ROM controllers, digital I/O cards, and so on. Most PCMCIA cards comply with either PCMCIA Type II or Type III. Type I cards are 3.3 mm thick, Type II cards take cards up to 5 mm thick, Type III allow cards up to 10.5 mm thick. A new standard, Type IV, takes cards which are greater than 10.5 mm. Type II interfaces can accept Type I cards, Type III accept Type I and II and Type IV interfaces accepts Types I, II and III.

The PCMCIA standard uses a 16-bit data bus (D0-D15) and a 26-bit address bus (A0-A25). Table G.4 shows the pin connections.

Table G.4   PCMCIA connections.

Pin	Signal	Pin	Signal
1	GND	35	GND
2	D3	36	$\overline{\text{CARD DETECT 1}}$
3	D4	37	D11
4	D5	38	D12
5	D6	39	D13
6	D7	40	D14
7	$\overline{\text{CARD ENABLE 1}}$	41	D15
8	A10	42	$\overline{\text{CARD DETECT 2}}$
9	$\overline{\text{OUTPUT ENABLE}}$	43	REFRESH
10	A11	44	$\overline{\text{IOR}}$
11	A9	45	$\overline{\text{IOW}}$
12	A8	46	A17
13	A13	47	A18
14	A14	48	A19
15	$\overline{\text{WRITE ENABLE / PROGRAM}}$	49	A20
16	READY / $\overline{\text{PROGRAM}}$	50	A21
17	+5V	51	+5V
18	Vpp1	52	Vpp2
19	A16	53	A22
20	A15	54	A23
21	A12	55	A24
22	A7	56	A25
23	A6	57	RFU
24	A5	58	RESET
25	A4	59	$\overline{\text{WAIT}}$
26	A3	60	$\overline{\text{INPACK}}$
27	A2	61	$\overline{\text{REGISTER SELECT}}$
28	A1	62	$\overline{\text{SPKR}}$
29	A0	63	$\overline{\text{STSCHG}}$
30	D0	64	D8
31	D1	65	D9
32	D2	66	D10
33	$\overline{\text{IOIS16}}$ (Write protect)	67	$\overline{\text{CARD DETECT 2}}$
34	GND	68	GND

G.5 IDE interface

The most popular interface for hard disk drives is the Integrated Drive Electronics (IDE) interface. Its main advantage is that the hard disk controller is built into the disk drive and the interface to the motherboard simply consists of a stripped-down version of the ISA bus. The most common standard is the ANSI-defined ATA-IDE standard. It uses a 40-way ribbon cable to connect to 40-pin header connectors. Table G.5 lists the pin connections. It has a 16-bit data bus (D0-D15) and the only available interrupt line used is IRQ14 (the hard disk uses IRQ14).

The standard allows for the connection of two disk drives in a daisy chain configuration. This can cause problems because both drives have controllers within their drives. The primary drive (Drive 0) is assigned as the master and the secondary driver (Drive 1) as the slave. A drive is set as a master or a slave by setting jumpers on the disk drive. They can also be set by software using the Cable Select (CSEL) pin on the interface.

Table G.5   IDE connections.

Pin	Signal	Pin	Signal
1	$\overline{\text{RESET}}$	2	GND
3	D7	4	D8
5	D6	6	D9
7	D5	8	D10
9	D4	10	D11
11	D3	12	D12
13	D2	14	D13
15	D1	16	D14
17	D0	18	D15
19	GND	20	KEY
21	DRQ3	22	GND
23	$\overline{\text{IOW}}$	24	GND
25	$\overline{\text{IOR}}$	26	GND
27	I/O CH RDY	28	CSEL
29	$\overline{\text{DACK3}}$	30	GND
31	IRQ14	32	$\overline{\text{IOCS16}}$
33	Address bit 1	34	$\overline{\text{PDIAG}}$
35	Address bit 0	36	Address bit 2
37	$\overline{\text{CS1FX}}$	38	$\overline{\text{CS3FX}}$
39	SP / $\overline{\text{DA}}$	40	GND

G.6 SCSI Interface

The Small Computer Systems Interface (SCSI) standard uses a 50-pin header connector and a ribbon cable to connect to up to eight devices. It overcomes the problems of the IDE, where devices have to be assigned as a master and a slave.

One byte at a time is communicated and there is a parity check on each byte. Table G.6 lists the pin connections.

Table G.6 SCSI connections.

Pin	Signal	Pin	Signal
1	GND	2	$\overline{\text{D0}}$
3	GND	4	$\overline{\text{D1}}$
5	GND	6	$\overline{\text{D2}}$
7	GND	8	$\overline{\text{D3}}$
9	GND	10	$\overline{\text{D4}}$
11	GND	12	$\overline{\text{D5}}$
13	GND	14	$\overline{\text{D6}}$
15	GND	16	$\overline{\text{D7}}$
17	GND	18	$\overline{\text{D(PARITY)}}$
19	GND	20	GND
21	GND	22	GND
23	RESERVED	24	RESERVED
25	Open	26	TERMPWR
27	RESERVED	28	RESERVED
29	GND	30	GND
31	GND	32	$\overline{\text{ATN}}$
33	GND	34	GND
35	GND	36	$\overline{\text{BSY}}$
37	GND	38	$\overline{\text{ACK}}$
39	GND	40	$\overline{\text{RST}}$
41	GND	42	$\overline{\text{MSG}}$
43	GND	44	$\overline{\text{SEL}}$
45	GND	46	$\overline{\text{C}}$ / D
47	GND	48	$\overline{\text{REQ}}$
49	GND	50	$\overline{\text{I}}$ / O

Appendix H
Data Communications Standards

H.1 Standards

Table H.1 lists some of the standards relating to data communications. The CCITT (now known as the ITU) and the ISO are the main international standards organizations. The CCITT standards that relate to the transmission of serial data over telephone circuits are defined in the V. series.

Table H.1 Data communications standards

ISO/CCITT standard	Other standard	Description
CCITT V.10	EIA RS-423	Serial transmission up to 300 kbps/ 1200 m
CCITT V.11	EIA RS-422	Serial transmission up to 10 Mbps/ 1200 m
CCITT V.21		Full-duplex modem transmission at 300 bps
CCITT V.22		Half-duplex modem transmission at 600/1200 bps
CCITT V.22bis		Full-duplex modem transmission at 1200/2400 bps
CCITT V.23		Full-duplex modem transmission at 1200 bps and receive at 75 bps
CCITT V.24	EIA RS-232	Serial transmission up to 20 kbps/ 20 m
CCITT V.25bis		Modem command language
CCITT V.27		Full-duplex modem transmission at 2400/ 4800 for leased lines
CCITT V.29		Full-duplex modem transmission at 9600 bps over leased lines
CCITT V.32		Full-duplex modem transmission at 4800/9600 bps
CCITT V.32bis		Full-duplex modem transmission at 7200, 12000 and 14400 bps
CCITT V.35	EIA RS-449	CCITT standard for the RS-449 interface
CCITT V.42		Error control protocol

H.2 International alphabet No. 5

ANSI defined a standard alphabet known as ASCII. This has since been adopted by the CCITT as a standard, known as IA5 (International Alphabet No. 5). The following tables define this alphabet in binary, as a decimal, as a hexadecimal value and as a character.

Binary	Decimal	Hex	Character	Binary	Decimal	Hex	Character
0000000	0	00	NUL	0010000	16	10	DLE
0000001	1	01	SOH	0010001	17	11	DC1
0000010	2	02	STX	0010010	18	12	DC2
0000011	3	03	ETX	0010011	19	13	DC3
0000100	4	04	EOT	0010100	20	14	DC4
0000101	5	05	ENQ	0010101	21	15	NAK
0000110	6	06	ACK	0010110	22	16	SYN
0000111	7	07	BEL	0010111	23	17	ETB
0001000	8	08	BS	0011000	24	18	CAN
0001001	9	09	HT	0011001	25	19	EM
0001010	10	0A	LF	0011010	26	1A	SUB
0001011	11	0B	VT	0011011	27	1B	ESC
001100	12	0C	FF	0011100	28	1C	FS
0001101	13	0D	CR	0011101	29	1D	GS
0001110	14	0E	SO	0011110	30	1E	RS
0001111	15	0F	SI	0011111	31	1F	US

Binary	Decimal	Hex	Character	Binary	Decimal	Hex	Character
0100000	32	20	SPACE	0110000	48	30	0
0100001	33	21	!	0110001	49	31	1
0100010	34	22	"	0110010	50	32	2
0100011	35	23	£/#	0110011	51	33	3
0100100	36	24	$	0110100	52	34	4
0100101	37	25	%	0110101	53	35	5
0100110	38	26	&	0110110	54	36	6
0100111	39	27	/	0110111	55	37	7
0101000	40	28	(	0111000	56	38	8
0101001	41	29	)	0111001	57	39	9
0101010	42	2A	*	0111010	58	3A	:
0101011	43	2B	+	0111011	59	3B	;
0101100	44	2C	,	0111100	60	3C	<
0101101	45	2D	–	0111101	61	3D	=
0101110	46	2E	.	0111110	62	3E	>
0101111	47	2F	/	0111111	63	3F	?

Binary	Decimal	Hex	Character	Binary	Decimal	Hex	Charac
1000000	64	40	@	1010000	80	50	P
1000001	65	41	A	1010001	81	51	Q
1000010	66	42	B	1010010	82	52	R
1000011	67	43	C	1010011	83	53	S
1000100	68	44	D	1010100	84	54	T
1000101	69	45	E	1010101	85	55	U
1000110	70	46	F	1010110	86	56	V
1000111	71	47	G	1010111	87	57	W
1001000	72	48	H	1011000	88	58	X
1001001	73	49	I	1011001	89	59	Y
1001010	74	4A	J	1011010	90	5A	Z
1001011	75	4B	K	1011011	91	5B	[
1001100	76	4C	L	1011100	92	5C	\
1001101	77	4D	M	1011101	93	5D	]
1001110	78	4E	N	1011110	94	5E	`
1001111	79	4F	O	1011111	95	5F	_

Binary	Decimal	Hex	Character	Binary	Decimal	Hex	Charac
1100000	96	60		1110000	112	70	p
1100001	97	61	a	1110001	113	71	q
1100010	98	62	b	1110010	114	72	r
1100011	99	63	c	1110011	115	73	s
1100100	100	64	d	1110100	116	74	t
1100101	101	65	e	1110101	117	75	u
1100110	102	66	f	1110110	118	76	v
1100111	103	67	g	1110111	119	77	w
1101000	104	68	h	1111000	120	78	x
1101001	105	69	i	1111001	121	79	y
1101010	106	6A	j	1111010	122	7A	z
1101011	107	6B	k	1111011	123	7B	{
1101100	108	6C	l	1111100	124	7C	:
1101101	109	6D	m	1111101	125	7D	}
1101110	110	6E	n	1111110	126	7E	~
1101111	111	6F	o	1111111	127	7F	DEL

H.3 RS-232C Interface

Table H.1 RS-232C connections.

9-pin D-type	25-pin D-type	Name	RS-232 name	Description	Signal Direction on DCE
	1		AA	Protective GND	
3	2	TXD	BA	Transmit Data	IN
2	3	RXD	BB	Receive Data	OUT
7	4	RTS	CA	Request to Send	IN
8	5	CTS	CB	Clear to Send	OUT
6	6	DSR	CC	Data Set Ready	OUT
5	7	GND	AB	Signal GND	
1	8	DCD	CF	Received line signal detect	OUT
	9		–	RESERVED	–
	10		–	RESERVED	–
	11			UNASSIGNED	–
	12		SCF	Secondary Received Line Signal Detector	OUT
	13		SCB	Secondary Clear To Send	OUT
	14		SBA	Secondary Transmitted Data	IN
	15		DB	Transmission Signal Element Detector	OUT
	16		SBB	Secondary Received Data	OUT
	17		DD	Receiver Signal Element Time	OUT
	18			UNASSIGNED	–
	19		SCA	Secondary Request To Send	IN
4	20	DTR	CD	Data Terminal Ready	IN
	21		CG	Signal Quality Detector	OUT
9	22	RI	CE	Ring Indicator	OUT
	23		CH/CI	Data Signal Rate Selector	IN/OUT
	24		DA	Transmit Signal Element Timing	IN
	25			UNASSIGNED	–

H.4 RS-449 Interface

RS-449 defines a standard for the function/mechanical interface for DTEs/DCEs for serial communications and is usually used with synchronous transmissions. Table H.2 lists the main connections.

Table H.2 RS-449 connections.

Pin number	Mnemonic	Description
1		Shield
2	SI	Signalling Rate Indicator
3,21		Spare
4,22	SD	Sending Time
5,23	ST	Receive Data
6,24	RD	Receive Data
7,25	RS	Request to Send
8,26	RT	Receive Timing
9,27	CS	Clear To Send
10	LL	Local Loopback
11,29	DM	Data Mode
12,30	TR	Terminal Ready
13,31	RR	Receiver Ready
14	RL	Remote Loopback
15	IC	Incoming Call
16	SF/SR	Select Frequency/ Signalling Rate Select
17,37	TT	Terminal Timing
18	TM	Test Mode
19	SG	Signal Ground
20	RC	Receive Common
28	IS	Terminal in Service
32	SS	Select Standby
33	SQ	Signal Quality
34	NS	New Signal
36	SB	Standby Indicator
37	SC	Send Common

Appendix I
SIMM Modules

I.1 30-pin SIMM

The 30-pin SIMM module has 10 addressing lines (A0-A9) and 8 data lines (D0-D7). The actual address is selected using the Row Address Select (RAS) and the Column Address Select (CAS).

Table I.1 30-pin SIMM connections.

Pin	Signal name	Pin	Signal name
1	+5V	16	D4
2	CAS	17	A8
3	D0	18	A9
4	A0	19	
5	A1	20	D5
6	D1	21	R/W
7	A2	22	GND
8	A3	23	D6
9	GND	24	
10	D2	25	D7
11	A4	26	
12	A5	27	RAS
13	D3	28	
14	A6	29	
15	A7	30	+5V

I.2 72-pin SIMM

The 72-pin SIMM module has 10 addressing lines (A0-A10) and 32 data lines (D0-D31). The actual address using four Row Address Strobe lines (RAS0-RAS3) and four Column Address Strobe lines (CAS0-CAS3). A 72-pin SIMM also has an automatic sensing mechanism using pins 67-70. Table I.3 lists some typical settings.

Table I.2 72-pin SIMM connections.

Pin	Signal name	Pin	Signal name	Pin	Signal name
1	GND	25	BLOCK SEL 0	49	D8
2	D0	26	+5V	50	D24
3	D16	27	A8	51	D9
4	D1	28	A9	52	D25
5	D17	29	RAS3	53	D10
6	D2	30	RAS2	54	D26
7	A18	31		55	D11
8	+5V	32	D6	56	D27
9		33		57	D12
10	A0	34		58	D28
11	A1	35		59	+5V
12	A2	36		60	D29
13	A3	37		61	D13
14	A4	38		62	D30
15	A5	39	GND	63	D14
16	A6	40	CAS0	64	D31
17		41	CAS2	65	D15
18	D4	42	CAS3	66	BLOCK SEL 2
19	D20	43	CAS1	67	PRES DET 0
20	D5	44	RAS0	68	PRES DET 1
21	D21	45	RAS1	69	PRES DET 2
22	D6	46	BLOCK SEL 1	70	PRES DET 3
23	D22	47	R/W	71	BLOCK SEL 3
24	D7	48		72	GND

Table I.3 Presence detect pins.

PRES DET 3	PRES DET 2	PRES DET 1	PRES DET 0	Signal name
NC	NC	NC	NC	NOT VALID
NC	NC	NC	GND	1 MB 120 ns
NC	NC	GND	NC	2 MB 120 ns
NC	NC	GND	GND	2 MB 70 ns
NC	GND	NC	NC	8 MB 70 ns
NC	GND	NC	GND	
NC	GND	GND	NC	2 MB 80 ns
NC	GND	GND	GND	8 MB 80 ns
GND	NC	NC	NC	
GND	NC	NC	GND	1 MB 85 ns
GND	NC	GND	NC	2 MB 85 ns
GND	NC	GND	GND	4 MB 70 ns
GND	GND	NC	NC	4 MB 80 ns
GND	GND	NC	GND	2 MB 100 ns
GND	GND	GND	NC	4 MB 80 ns
GND	GND	GND	GND	2 MB 85 ns

where NC represents not connected.

Index

143, 163, 165, 166
BASIC, 292
Baud rate, 129, 130, 134, 142, 143, 151, 152
BCD, 56, 74
Bell, 121, 122, 160, 161
BGI, 176, 177, 180, 181
Binary, 2, 3, 25, 29, 34, 36, 39, 41, 43, 47, 48, 70, 73, 89, 90, 95, 115, 131, 286-292, 298, 306, 320, 329, 330, 367
    code, 29, 34, 95
    coded decimal, *see* BCD
    commands, 292
Biological stimulus, 79
BIOS
    general, 6, 7, 22, 23, 139, 149, 150, 162, 163, 165, 167-169, 195, 338, 347
    interrupt, *see* Interrupt
    system time, 23, 36, 166, 181
Bit timing, 129
Bitmasking, 41
Bits, 2, 3, 5, 8, 10, 11, 14, 17, 21, 31, 32, 39, 41-44, 47-49, 54-56, 66, 70, 75, 87, 89, 91, 92, 95, 96, 115, 119, 126-129, 135, 139-141, 144, 146, 148, 149, 152, 157, 162, 163, 188, 286-288, 291, 305-307, 337, 339, 340-343, 350, 351, 353, 354
Bits per second, *see* bps
Bitwise, 41, 74, 305, 306-308, 314
Bitwise operator, 305-307
Blink, 170, 171
bps, 116, 129, 132, 366
Braces, 296, 314, 316, 317
Brackets, 321
BS, 119-121, 160, 161, 298, 367
Buffer, 100, 101, 133, 136, 140-149, 354
Bus
    address, 2-12, 14, 20, 21, 157, 337, 345, 359, 361, 363
    control, 2, 3
    controller, 21

data, 2, 3, 5, 6, 11, 12, 14, 16-18, 21, 23, 157, 339, 359, 361, 363, 364
    type, 16, 232
Byte, 2, 5, 6, 8, 20, 25-27, 34, 36, 39, 41, 50, 51, 54, 66, 70-73, 101, 116, 117, 146, 158, 160-162, 164, 166, 167, 286, 300, 320, 321, 354, 359, 365

—C—

Calibration, 81
Call by reference, 321
Capacitive transducer, 83, 85
Carriage Return, *see* CR
CCITT, 119, 366, 367
CGA, 176, 177, 179, 180, 349, 350, 355
char, 34, 36, 44, 50, 52, 123, 145, 146, 148, 149, 151, 158, 160, 161, 164, 165, 169, 171, 172, 180, 185, 186, 299, 300, 308, 309, 313, 319, 320, 327-332, 335, 336
Character array, 313
Character attributes, 171
circle(), 186
cleardevice(), 178
Clear to send, *see* CTS
Clock, 3, 5, 9, 11-14, 16-18, 36, 37, 66, 69-77, 95, 127, 143, 164, 345, 348
Clock doubler, 5
closegraph(), 178, 180-183, 184, 185, 186, 189
COBOL, 292
Code
    machine, 292
    object, 292, 320
    source, 292, 293, 296
Cold junction, 80
COM1, 24, 25, 28, 125, 135, 139, 140, 143-146, 149-153, 163, 166, 195

pulse counting programs, 75, 76
pulse timing programs, 70-74
Pulse dialling, 248, 250
putch(), 229
putchar(), 265
putda(), 109
putimage(), 179, 188, 189
putpixel(), 181
puts(), 265, 295, 310

—Q—

Quantization, 90, 91, 95

—R—

Radar, 61, 95
RAM, 3, 6, 7, 8, 22, 167, 337, 338,
    340, 342, 345, 347, 354
random(), 182, 183
randomize(), 181-183
read_character, 211
read_data(), 269
Ready to send, *see* RTS
Reboot, 195, 209, 218
Receive data, 32, 126, 133, 136,
    139, 202, 252, 254
rectangle(), 183
Reference junction, 80
REGS, 197, 200, 202, 204, 206,
    207, 208, 212, 234, 235, 237-
    239, 242, 246, 277, 357, 358
Relationship operator, 303
reset_vectors(), 223, 229
Resistivity, 82
Resolution, 83, 95, 174, 175, 179,
    183, 236, 349-351, 353, 354, 356
return, 187, 318
RI, 252, 369
Ring indicator, *see* RI
rs_interrupt(), 226, 227
RS-232
    addresses, 139
    baud rate, 143

file transfer, 156
get status, 202
LCR, 141,142
LSR, 140, 141, 143
programs, 144-149
read character, 211
using BIOS, 149-151
RTS, 126, 134, 136-139, 150, 252,
    369

—S—

Sample, 51, 56, 77, 87-89, 90, 94,
    95, 106, 107, 112, 113, 119, 123,
    134, 140, 152, 155, 162, 165-
    167, 168, 169, 172, 173, 176,
    187, 208, 216, 229, 230, 234,
    235, 236, 242, 246, 252, 268,
    270, 271, 272, 289, 298, 326
Samuel Morse, 115
Sawtooth waveform, 111
SC, 92, 96, 98-103, 370
scanf(), 262, 264, 298, 313, 320
Screen resolution, 236
SCSI, 259, 260, 364, 365
Sectors, 206, 256, 257, 258
Security system, 57
Segment, 157, 158, 194
Segment address, 157, 194
Segmented memory, 157
send_character(), 228, 229
Sequence, 3, 45, 46, 47, 49, 51, 53,
    55, 56, 58, 59, 60, 96, 98, 120,
    242, 252, 292, 310, 315
Serial communications, 10, 28,
    115-117, 125, 130, 139, 201,
    202, 212, 221, 282, 285, 369
Serial mouse, 115, 125, 133, 232
Serial port,
    general, 25, 125, 144, 163, 164,
        166, 168, 191, 193, 200, 201-
        203, 214, 216, 218, 225, 232,
        234, 279, 284
    interrupts, *see* IRQ3 and IRQ4
serial.h, 222, 224

set_vectors(), 222, 226, 229
setcolor(), 176
setup_serial(), 145, 148, 152, 222, 229
setvect(), 209
Shift left, 43, 49, 53, 305, 307
Shift register, 117, 128, 150, 202
Shift right, 70, 305, 307
shl, 43, 53, 76
shr, 71
SIMM,
    30-pin, 371
    72-pin, 372, 373
    general, 344, 348, 371, 372
Simplex communications, 117
sizeof(), 266
sleep(), 34
Small Computer Systems Interface, *see* SCSI
Software, 2, 5, 8, 14, 17, 21, 69, 115, 120, 122, 133, 134, 156-168, 174, 192, 194, 195, 197, 216, 221, 233, 256, 278, 338, 364
Software handshaking, 122, 133, 134, 156
Software interrupt, *see* Interrupt
Sound card, 14, 16, 19, 24, 192, 214, 216, 218
Speaker, 23, 28, 119, 122
Special keys, 218, 245
Speed control, 29, 112
Speed controller, 29
speed sensor, 29
sqrt(), 320
SRAM, 6, 7, 337, 340, 342, 345-348, 350
Start bit, 126-129
Start conversion, see SC
Statement block, 316, 317
Statements, 302, 305
Statements
    logical, 314
STB, 101-103
stdlib.h, 182, 183, 294, 327, 332, 336
Stop bit, 127-129, 135, 141, 144,

145, 146, 148, 149, 202, 225, 249
Storage, 3, 6, 87, 89, 261, 286, 298, 299, 337, 340, 354
Strain gauge, 82, 85
string.h, 294, 331, 332
strlen(), 171
Strobe, 33, 69, 100, 117, 347, 371
SUB, 121, 122, 298, 367
Substitute, 121, 122
Superscalar, 6
SVGA, 95, 168, 176, 180, 236, 349, 350, 353
switch(), 315
Synchronous bus, 12
System clock, 3, 5, 12, 13, 16-18, 24, 195, 209, 345
System timer tick, 209

—T—

Temperature, 29, 79, 80, 81, 88, 104-106, 113-115
Temperature sensor IC, 81
Terminal, 66, 118, 125, 130, 251
Terminate and stay resident, *see* TSR
Text attribute, 170, 172, 323
Thermistor, 80, 81
Thermocouple, 80, 81
Threshold, 87, 95, 107
Time, 2, 3, 5, 6, 9, 10, 11, 13, 16, 17, 36, 43, 59, 60, 63, 64, 66, 85, 87, 88, 89, 92, 95, 105, 108, 112, 113, 115, 116, 126, 129, 131, 133, 151, 154, 155, 157, 164, 166, 172, 176, 181, 182, 183, 190, 191, 196, 205, 209-211, 213-215, 218, 221, 231, 233, 246, 247, 251, 253, 259, 260, 261, 274, 279, 280-282, 285, 307, 335-337, 342, 343, 345, 347, 350, 365
time.h, 182, 183, 335, 336
Timer, 37, 63, 64, 65, 70, 77, 78, 166, 181, 194, 195, 209, 210,

214-216, 218, 220
Tracks, 89, 256-258
Traffic lights, 60, 61, 62
Transducer, 79, 80, 83, 85, 87, 115
Transmit data, 89, 126, 136, 147
Triangle, 189
TSR, 195
TTL RGB, 349, 350, 355
Turbine, 86
Turbo Pascal, 26, 27, 37, 40, 42-
  44, 46, 71, 98, 101, 102, 158,
  160, 198, 206

—U—

Unbalanced line, 132
UNIX, 293

—V—

V.21, 249, 366
V.22, 249, 366
V.22bis, 249, 366
V.23, 249, 366
V.24, 249, 251, 366
V.25bis, 366
V.32, 249, 366
V.32bis, 366
V.42, 366
Variable initialization, 301
Variables, 48, 56, 227, 299-301,
  310, 313, 318, 320, 321
Velocity, 85
Vertical Tab, 121, 160, 325
VESA, 13, 15, 361
VGA, 17, 95, 165, 168, 169, 176,
  177, 179-181, 236, 349, 350
VGA BIOS, 168, 169
VL-local bus, 361
Video accelerator, 1
Video display, 164, 198
Video driver, 175
Video driver software, 168
Video graphics memory, 23

video interrupt, 198, 199, 212
Video mode, 163, 165, 169, 198,
  199, 236, 355
Video text memory, 170
Volatile, 2, 250, 310, 337
VRAMs, 353
VT, 121, 160, 161, 298, 367

—W—

Wait states, 345
Walking ones, 54
while(), 317
WIMPs, 232
Window, 57
Wire jumpers, 64
Word, 2, 3, 8, 20, 26, 27, 33, 37,
  122, 144, 158, 162, 163, 167,
  168, 200, 248, 286, 296
WORDREGS, 197

—X—

XOR, 48
XOR_PUT, 188, 189